MAKE THE MOST OF EVERY OCCASION!

From formal affairs to spontaneous soirees, let *Taste of Home Holiday & Celebrations* cookbook help you make every toast-worthy moment as delicious as it is memorable.
In each annual edition, we share never-before-published recipes, new entertaining tips and easy seasonal crafts for Christmas, Thanksgiving, Easter and a selection of special celebrations—from brunches to cocktail parties. With more than 250 recipes from home cooks around the country and 20 inspiring party themes and menus, everything you need to make the most of your special events is at your fingertips.

WOULD YOU LIKE TO SEE ONE OF YOUR FAMILY RECIPES FEATURED IN A *TASTE OF HOME* COLLECTION?

Visit **tasteofhome.com/submit** to share your story and recipes.

ON THE COVER

ON THE FRONT COVER
Honey-Maple Glazed Ham (p. 230).

ON THE BACK COVER Roasted Orange Turkey (p. 95), Gimlet (p. 174), Brandy Old-Fashioned Sweet (p. 175), Amber's Sourdough Stuffing (p. 126), Gingerbread Ice Cream Sandwiches (p. 54).

PAGE 80

PAGE 195   PAGE 47

PAGE 136

PAGE 27   PAGE 208

Taste of Home
Holiday
& CELEBRATIONS

EDITORIAL
Editor-in-Chief **Catherine Cassidy**

Creative Director **Howard Greenberg**
Editorial Operations Director **Kerri Balliet**

Managing Editor/Print and Digital Books **Mark Hagen**
Associate Creative Director **Edwin Robles Jr.**

Editor **Heather Ray**
Art Director **Raeann Sundholm**
Contributing Art Director **Maggie Conners**
Craft Editor **Shalana Frisby**
Layout Designer **Matt Fukuda**
Editorial Production Manager **Dena Ahlers**
Copy Chief **Deb Warlaumont Mulvey**
Copy Editor **Dulcie Shoener**
Contributing Proofreader **Valerie Phillips**

Chief Food Editor **Karen Berner**
Food Editors **James Schend; Peggy Woodward, RD**
Associate Food Editor **Krista Lanphier**
Associate Editor/Food Content **Annie Rundle**
Recipe Editors **Mary King; Jenni Sharp, RD; Irene Yeh**
Content Operations Manager **Colleen King**
Executive Assistant **Marie Brannon**
Editorial Intern **Devin Mulertt**

Test Kitchen and Food Styling Manager **Sarah Thompson**
Test Cooks **Matthew Hass, Lauren Knoelke**
Food Stylists **Kathryn Conrad (Senior), Shannon Roum, Leah Rekau**
Prep Cooks **Megumi Garcia, Nicole Spohrleder, Bethany VanOpdorp**

Photography Director **Stephanie Marchese**
Photographers **Dan Roberts, Jim Wieland**
Photographer/Set Stylist **Grace Natoli Sheldon**
Set Stylists **Stacey Genaw, Melissa Haberman, Dee Dee Jacq**

Business Analyst **Kristy Martin**
Billing Specialist **Mary Ann Koebernik**

BUSINESS
General Manager, Taste of Home Cooking Schools **Erin Puariea**
Vice President, Brand Marketing **Jennifer Smith**
Vice President, Circulation and Continuity Marketing **Dave Fiegel**

READER'S DIGEST NORTH AMERICA
Vice President, Business Development and Marketing **Alain Begun**
President, Books and Home Entertainment **Harold Clarke**
General Manager, Canada **Philippe Cloutier**
Vice President, Operations **Mitch Cooper**
Chief Operating Officer **Howard Halligan**
Vice President, Chief Sales Officer **Mark Josephson**
Vice President, General Manager, Milwaukee **Frank Quigley**
Vice President, Digital Sales **Steve Sottile**
Vice President, Chief Content Officer **Liz Vaccariello**
Vice President, Global Financial Planning and Analysis **Devin White**

THE READER'S DIGEST ASSOCIATION, INC.
President and Chief Executive Officer **Robert E. Guth**

FRONT COVER PHOTOGRAPHY
Photographer **Jim Wieland**
Set Stylist **Stephanie Marchese**
Food Stylist **Kathryn Conrad**

A FEW WEEKS BEFORE

- Prepare two grocery lists: one for nonperishable items to purchase now and one for perishable items to buy a few days before Christmas Day.

- Bake Cloverleaf Rolls. Let cool, place in a heavy-duty resealable plastic bag and freeze.

- Prepare Eggnog Truffle Cups. After piping in the filling and freezing until firm, place cups in a resealable plastic bag and keep frozen.

TWO DAYS BEFORE

- Buy remaining grocery items.

CHRISTMAS EVE

- Set the table.

- Bake the Marbled Cappuccino Fudge Cheesecake and refrigerate.

- Prepare the Stuffed Shrimp Appetizers through Step 1. Cover and refrigerate.

- For the Apple-Gorgonzola Bacon Bundles, complete Steps 1-3, cover and refrigerate.

- For the punch, allow orange juice concentrate to thaw in fridge overnight.

CHRISTMAS DAY

- In the morning, thaw Cloverleaf Rolls to room temperature.

- Take Eggnog Truffle Cups from freezer, remove foil cups, cover and refrigerate.

- In the morning, bake the potatoes for the Twice-Baked Potatoes Supreme.

- While potatoes are baking, prepare the Golden Gouda Mushroom Soup.

- Remove cheesecake from pan, prepare topping, spread on cake and chill until serving.

- When the potatoes are finished, season the Herbed Roast Beef and put it in the oven.

- Finish preparing the Twice-Baked Potatoes Supreme but do not bake yet.

- Cook the Apple-Gorgonzola Bacon Bundles in batches as directed.

- Prepare the Cranberry Endive Appetizers.

- Make the Brussels sprouts but do not broil until beef comes out of the oven.

- While sprouts are simmering, prepare Green Beans with Creamy Pistachio Sauce.

- About 35 minutes before beef is done, bake the stuffed shrimp.

- Combine punch ingredients and mix the Garlic Lemon Butter.

- Place Twice-Baked Potatoes Supreme in the oven 25 minutes before the beef is done.

- When beef and potatoes are done, finish the Brussels sprouts.

- Combine ingredients for the horseradish sauce and reheat soup and rolls.

tis*the*season

Y ou've been counting down the days for weeks, and now it's finally here. You're ready to put your heart and soul into a Christmas celebration that goes above and beyond your dinner guests' expectations. With a handy timeline and plenty of make-ahead options, you can execute a flawless feast that will have everyone inviting themselves back next year.

Set the stage for your formal affair with a wintry color scheme and subtle accents of polished silver. Plated on white or light-colored china, your heartfelt meal becomes the golden star.

Balsamic-Glazed Brussels Sprouts (p. 13)
Twice-Baked Potatoes Supreme (p. 13)
Cloverleaf Rolls (p. 14)
Herbed Roast Beef (p. 12)

tis*the*season

The holidays give us a chance to share favorite traditions and make lasting memories with friends and family. Whether we're baking cookies or trimming the tree, the people we cherish lie at the heart of these special festivities. Here you'll find dozens of scrumptious recipes and easy ideas to make smiles a little bit wider and memories a little bit sweeter for everyone.

TABLE OF **CONTENTS**

Golden Gouda Mushroom Soup

A rich and creamy soup makes a lasting impression as a formal first course.
Sherry and smoked gouda with a hint of holiday spice make every taste better than the last.
—CHARLOTTE ROGERS VIRGINIA BEACH, VA

START TO FINISH: 30 MIN.
MAKES: 6 SERVINGS

- ½ cup butter, cubed
- ½ cup all-purpose flour
- ½ teaspoon pepper
- ½ teaspoon ground allspice
- 1 carton (32 ounces) chicken broth
- ½ cup sherry or additional chicken broth
- ½ cup heavy whipping cream
- ½ pound sliced fresh mushrooms
- 4 garlic cloves, minced
- 2 cups (8 ounces) shredded smoked Gouda cheese
  Chives and smoked paprika

1. In a large saucepan, melt butter. Stir in the flour, pepper and allspice until smooth; gradually add the broth, sherry and cream. Bring to a boil. Add mushrooms and garlic. Reduce heat; cover and simmer for 5-6 minutes or until mushrooms are tender.

2. Add cheese; cook and stir until melted. Garnish servings with chives and paprika.

Stuffed Shrimp Appetizers

Here's a trick I like to do: Make double the filling and use the excess for stuffing button mushrooms. Then bake them alongside the shrimp. Two easy appetizers in one fell swoop!

—SHIRLEY LEASOCK
ROCKWOOD, PA

PREP: 25 MIN. • **BAKE:** 10 MIN.
MAKES: 20 APPETIZERS

- 20 **uncooked large shrimp (about 1 pound)**
- 1 **egg, beaten**
- ½ **cup soft bread crumbs**
- 1 **tablespoon mayonnaise**
- ½ **teaspoon lemon juice**
- ¼ **teaspoon salt-free seasoning blend**
- ¼ **teaspoon pepper**
- ⅛ **teaspoon dried oregano Dash cayenne pepper**
- 1 **can (6 ounces) lump crabmeat, drained**
- 2 **tablespoons grated Parmesan cheese**
- 1 **teaspoon paprika**

1. Peel and devein shrimp, leaving the tails on. Butterfly each shrimp along the outside curve. Open shrimp flat and place butterflied side down in an ungreased 15-in. x 10-in. x 1-in. baking pan.
2. In a small bowl, combine the egg, bread crumbs, mayonnaise, lemon juice and seasonings. Stir in crab. Place 1 tablespoonful of mixture over each shrimp; sprinkle with cheese and paprika. Bake at 350° for 9-11 minutes or until shrimp turn pink. Serve warm.

Champagne Party Punch

Because no holiday party would be complete without the punch, we mixed up a champagne-spiked cocktail that's not too sweet and not too puckery, but just right.

—TASTE OF HOME TEST KITCHEN

PREP: 15 MIN. + CHILLING • **MAKES:** 18 SERVINGS (¾ CUP EACH)

- 1 **cup sugar**
- 1 **cup water**
- 2 **cups unsweetened apple juice**
- 2 **cups unsweetened pineapple juice**
- ½ **cup lemon juice**
- ⅓ **cup thawed orange juice concentrate**
- ¼ **cup lime juice**
- 2 **cups ice cubes**
- 1 **quart ginger ale, chilled**
- 1 **bottle (750 ml) champagne, chilled**

1. In a large pitcher, combine sugar and water; stir until sugar is dissolved. Add the apple juice, pineapple juice, lemon juice, orange juice concentrate and lime juice. Refrigerate until serving.
2. Just before serving, pour into a punch bowl and add ice cubes. Slowly add ginger ale and champagne.

Apple-Gorgonzola Bacon Bundles

Spiced apples and creamy gorgonzola cheese are wrapped in salty bacon, cooked crisp, then drizzled with a pomegranate glaze for a delicious appetizer.
—CHRYSTAL BAKER STUDIO CITY, CA

PREP: 35 MIN. • **COOK:** 5 MIN./BATCH • **MAKES:** 16 APPETIZERS (⅓ CUP GLAZE)

2 **medium apples**
2 **tablespoons butter**
¼ **cup packed brown sugar**
1 **teaspoon ground cinnamon**
½ **teaspoon ground nutmeg**
½ **teaspoon ground ginger**
¼ **teaspoon salt**
1 **cup pomegranate juice**
8 **bacon strips, halved**
⅓ **cup crumbled Gorgonzola cheese**

1. Cut each apple into 8 wedges. In a large skillet, heat butter over medium-high heat. Add apples, brown sugar, spices and salt; cook and stir 5-6 minutes or until apples are tender. Remove from pan; cool slightly.

2. Add pomegranate juice to the same pan; bring to a boil. Cook 7-8 minutes or until the liquid is reduced to about ⅓ cup, stirring frequently. Remove from the heat.

3. Wrap each bacon piece around one apple slice and 1 teaspoon cheese, completely enclosing cheese; secure with a toothpick.

4. In a clean skillet, cook bundles in batches over medium heat 3-5 minutes or until bacon is crisp, turning occasionally. Serve with pomegranate glaze.

Cranberry Endive Appetizers

PICTURED AT FAR LEFT

You can pack a lot of flavor into an elegant appetizer just by using the right combination of ingredients. I created this blue cheese filling for a holiday gathering and everyone loved it.
—MARGEE BERRY WHITE SALMON, WA

START TO FINISH: 20 MIN. • **MAKES:** 2 DOZEN

4 **ounces cream cheese, softened**
2 **tablespoons apple jelly**
⅓ **cup crumbled blue cheese**
¼ **cup dried cranberries, chopped**
24 **leaves Belgian endive**
¼ **cup chopped pecans, toasted**

In a large bowl, beat cream cheese and jelly until smooth. Stir in cheese and cranberries. Spoon heaping teaspoonfuls onto each endive leaf. Sprinkle with pecans.

TOASTY TIPS

Many holiday recipes call for toasted nuts such as pecans, walnuts or almonds. To save time, toast large batches, use what you need, and store extras in an airtight container in the refrigerator for 1 to 2 weeks or freeze them in an airtight container for 1 to 3 months.

Herbed Roast Beef

My mom is a true artist, both on canvas and in the kitchen. So it was no surprise, when she returned from an art workshop in France, that she was all enthused about the meals she had there. That was the year she fashioned a wonderful feast with this herbed roast beef.

—**KERRY SULLIVAN** LONGWOOD, FL

PREP: 10 MIN.
BAKE: 2½ HOURS + STANDING
MAKES: 10-12 SERVINGS

- 2 **teaspoons fennel seed, crushed**
- 2 **teaspoons dried rosemary, crushed**
- 2 **teaspoons each dried basil, marjoram, savory and thyme**
- 2 **teaspoons rubbed sage**
- 1½ **teaspoons salt**
- 2 **bone-in beef rib roasts (4 to 6 pounds each)**
- 2 **medium onions, sliced**
- 6 **fresh rosemary sprigs**

HORSERADISH SAUCE
- 1½ **cups (12 ounces) sour cream**
- ¼ **cup prepared horseradish**
- 3 **tablespoons lemon juice**
- 2 **tablespoons minced chives**

1. In a small bowl, combine the fennel seed, rosemary, basil, marjoram, savory, thyme, sage and salt; rub over roasts. Place roasts fat side up on a rack in a roasting pan. Top with onions and rosemary sprigs.

2. Bake, uncovered, at 350° for 2½ to 3½ hours or until meat reaches desired doneness (for medium-rare, a meat thermometer should read 145°; medium, 160°; well-done, 170°).

3. Discard onions and rosemary. Let roasts stand for 10-15 minutes before slicing. Meanwhile, in a small bowl, combine sauce ingredients. Serve with beef.

Balsamic-Glazed Brussels Sprouts

PICTURED ON PAGE 6 AND AT LEFT

My relatives claim to hate Brussels sprouts, which I took as a challenge one Christmas. This is the recipe I served. I put it on the buffet and by the time I got to it, there wasn't a sprout left in the bowl!

—**CAROLE BESS WHITE** PORTLAND, OR

START TO FINISH: 30 MIN. • **MAKES:** 8 SERVINGS

2 pounds fresh Brussels sprouts
½ pound bacon strips, cut into ½-inch pieces
1 medium onion, sliced
¼ cup white balsamic vinegar
2 tablespoons stone-ground mustard
½ teaspoon garlic powder
⅛ teaspoon salt
½ cup soft bread crumbs

1. Cut an "X" in the core of each Brussels sprout. Place in a large saucepan; add 1 in. of water. Bring to a boil. Reduce heat; cover and simmer for 8-10 minutes or until crisp-tender.

2. Meanwhile, in a large ovenproof skillet, cook bacon over medium heat until crisp. Using a slotted spoon, remove to paper towels; drain, reserving 2 tablespoons drippings.

3. Saute onion in drippings until tender. Stir in the vinegar, mustard, garlic powder, salt, Brussels sprouts and bacon; cook 2-3 minutes longer.

4. Sprinkle with bread crumbs; broil 4-6 in. from the heat for 2-3 minutes or until golden brown.

Twice-Baked Potatoes Supreme

PICTURED ON PAGE 7 AND AT LEFT

On Christmas Day, we invite all our nearby relatives to dinner. One way I make the meal memorable is with my twice-baked potatoes. I add a touch of cayenne and top them with Parmesan.

—**RUTH ANDREWSON** LEAVENWORTH, WA

PREP: 15 MIN. • **BAKE:** 1 HOUR 20 MIN. • **MAKES:** 12 SERVINGS (1 STUFFED POTATO HALF EACH)

8 large baking potatoes
¼ cup butter, softened
½ teaspoon salt
½ teaspoon garlic powder
½ teaspoon dried oregano
¼ teaspoon cayenne pepper
⅛ teaspoon celery salt
⅓ to ½ cup milk
Grated Parmesan cheese
Paprika, optional

1. Pierce potatoes with a fork. Bake at 400° for 60-70 minutes or until tender. Cut potatoes in half lengthwise; scoop out pulp, leaving a thin shell. Set 12 shell halves aside (discard remaining shells or save for another use).

2. In a large bowl, mash pulp; add the butter, salt, garlic powder, oregano, cayenne, celery salt and enough milk to reach desired consistency. Pipe or spoon into shells; place in two greased 13-in. x 9-in. baking pans. Sprinkle with Parmesan cheese and, if desired, paprika. Bake, uncovered, at 350° for 20-25 minutes or until heated through.

Cloverleaf Rolls

PICTURED ON PAGE 7

When I was a girl, it was a rare occasion when Mom made a gourmet meal. Most often, she relied on traditional recipes like this one. My sister and I ate more than our share of these versatile golden rolls.

—**BRENDA DUFRESNE** MIDLAND, MI

PREP: 25 MIN. + RISING • **BAKE:** 15 MIN. • **MAKES:** 2 DOZEN

1 package (¼ ounce) active dry yeast
1¼ cups warm milk (110° to 115°)
¼ cup butter, softened
1 egg
3 tablespoons sugar
1 teaspoon salt
4 to 4½ cups all-purpose flour
Additional butter, melted

1. In a large bowl, dissolve yeast in warm milk. Add butter, egg, sugar, salt and 3 cups flour. Beat until smooth. Stir in enough remaining flour to form a soft dough.

2. Turn onto a floured surface; knead until smooth and elastic, about 6-8 minutes. Place in a greased bowl, turning once to grease the top. Cover with plastic wrap and let rise in a warm place until doubled, about 1 hour.

3. Punch dough down and divide in half. Divide each half into 36 pieces and shape into balls. Place three balls in each greased muffin cup. Cover and let rise until doubled, about 30 minutes. Brush with additional butter.

4. Bake at 375° for 15-18 minutes or until lightly browned. Remove to wire racks. Serve warm.

Green Beans with Creamy Pistachio Sauce

I was asked to bring vegetables to my daughter-in-law's Christmas dinner, and I thought, *How boring*. But then I remembered how Mom used to serve them with butter and evaporated milk. I added the pistachios for crunch, and the beans turned out to be a star at the dinner table!

—**LORETTA OUELLETTE** POMPANO BEACH, FL

START TO FINISH: 30 MIN. • **MAKES:** 10 SERVINGS

2 pounds fresh green beans, trimmed
1 teaspoon salt
½ cup butter, cubed
½ cup pistachios, coarsely chopped
1 cup evaporated milk
Salt and pepper to taste

1. Place green beans and salt in a Dutch oven; add water to cover. Bring to a boil. Cook, uncovered, 5-8 minutes or until tender, stirring occasionally. Drain and remove from pan.

2. In the same pan, melt butter over medium heat. Add pistachios; cook and stir 1-2 minutes or until pistachios begin to brown. Stir in evaporated milk; bring to a boil. Cook 2-4 minutes or until sauce is slightly thickened. Add green beans; heat through, stirring to coat with sauce. Season with salt and pepper to taste.

Marbled Cappuccino Fudge Cheesecake

I came up with this recipe because I love the frozen cappuccino drinks at coffee shops and wanted a cheesecake with the same flavors. If you try it, don't hold the whip. The creamy, mocha-infused topping is the best part!
—**BECKY MCCLAFLIN** BLANCHARD, OK

PREP: 45 MIN.
BAKE: 70 MIN. + CHILLING
MAKES: 12 SERVINGS

1½ cups chocolate graham cracker crumbs (about 8 whole crackers)
3 tablespoons sugar
¼ cup butter, melted

FILLING
4 packages (8 ounces each) cream cheese, softened
1¼ cups sugar
¼ cup heavy whipping cream
3 tablespoons double mocha cappuccino mix
2 tablespoons all-purpose flour
1½ teaspoons vanilla extract
3 eggs, lightly beaten
⅔ cup hot fudge ice cream topping, warmed

CAPPUCCINO CREAM TOPPING
1 cup heavy whipping cream
2 tablespoons double mocha cappuccino mix
1 tablespoon confectioners' sugar
Chocolate curls, optional

1. Place a greased 9-in. springform pan on a double thickness of heavy-duty foil (about 18 in. square). Securely wrap foil around pan.

2. In a small bowl, combine the cracker crumbs, sugar and butter. Press onto the bottom and 2 in. up the sides of prepared pan. Place pan on a baking sheet. Bake at 325° for 7-9 minutes. Cool on a wire rack.

3. In a large bowl, beat cream cheese and sugar until smooth. Beat in the cream, cappuccino mix, flour and vanilla. Add eggs; beat on low speed just until combined. Pour half of batter into the crust. Drizzle with ⅓ cup fudge topping. Repeat layers. Cut through batter with a knife to swirl fudge topping. Place springform pan in a large baking pan; add 1 in. of hot water to larger pan.

4. Bake at 325° for 70-80 minutes or until center is just set and top appears dull. Remove springform pan from water bath. Cool on a wire rack for 10 minutes. Carefully run a knife around edge of pan to loosen; cool 1 hour longer. Refrigerate overnight. Remove sides of pan.

5. For topping, in a small bowl, beat cream until it begins to thicken. Add cappuccino mix and confectioners' sugar; beat until soft peaks form. Spread over cheesecake. Garnish with chocolate curls if desired.

Eggnog Truffle Cups

I can't think of a tastier way to say cheers than with these mini holiday-inspired cups. A little rum extract brings out the flavor in the eggnog we all love so much this time of year.
—**TERRIE MALSOM** VERMILLION, SD

PREP: 30 MIN. + FREEZING • **MAKES:** 3 DOZEN

- 1 **cup (6 ounces) semisweet chocolate chips**
- 2 **teaspoons shortening**
- 6 **tablespoons eggnog**
- 1 **package (10 to 12 ounces) white baking chips**
- ½ **teaspoon rum extract**
- ¼ **to ¾ teaspoon ground nutmeg**

1. In a microwave, melt the semisweet chips and shortening; stir until smooth. Using a narrow pastry brush, brush the inside of 1-in. foil candy liners with ½ teaspoon melted chocolate. Freeze for 45 minutes or until firm.

2. Using ¼ teaspoon chocolate mixture for each cup, brush on another layer of chocolate. Freeze until firm.

3. In a small saucepan, bring eggnog to a boil over low heat. Remove from the heat; stir in white baking chips until melted. Stir in extract. Refrigerate for 30 minutes or until filling begins to set.

4. Spoon or pipe 1½ teaspoons filling into each cup. Freeze until firm. Carefully remove and discard foil cups. Cover and store in an airtight container in the refrigerator. Just before serving, sprinkle with nutmeg.

NOTE *This recipe was tested with commercially prepared eggnog.*

Garlic Lemon Butter

Whenever I serve this alongside corn or fresh bread, I get the same question: "What makes this so good?" It's such a simple way to punch up a side dish.
—**MARGIE WAMPLER** BUTLER, PA

START TO FINISH: 10 MIN. • **MAKES:** ½ CUP

- ½ **cup butter, softened**
- 2 **to 3 teaspoons grated lemon peel**
- 1 **garlic clove, minced**
- 1 **teaspoon minced fresh parsley**
- ¼ **teaspoon salt, optional**
  Pepper to taste

In a small bowl, beat all the ingredients until blended. Store in the refrigerator.

MORE BUTTERS!

Fresh rolls and baked potatoes will never be the same once you discover how easy it is to make flavored butters. In addition to the Garlic Lemon Butter, try Tarragon Butter. Combine 1 cup butter; 2 tablespoons each of minced fresh tarragon, minced chives and minced fresh parsley; 1 garlic clove, minced; and a dash of pepper. For a sweeter spread, try Maple Butter. Combine ¾ cup butter with ½ cup maple syrup.

Please Be Seated

Take your dining room from everyday to formal with a few simple supplies.

WRAPPED FABRIC & BOW CHAIR

- **Choice of fabric (we used a lightweight silk fabric)**
- **Flexible tape measure and quilter's ruler**
- **Rotary cutter and cutting mat**
- **⅝-inch-wide peel-n-stick fabric fuse tape**
- **Standard sewing supplies and sewing machine (optional)**
- **Iron and ironing board**
- **Safety pins**
- **2-inch-wide satin ribbon**
- **Choice of paper flower embellishment**
- **Hot glue and glue sticks**

1. For fabric piece, first measure height of chair back from top edge to seat base. Double measurement and make note for fabric width.

Then, using flexible tape measure, determine length from side to side across chair back, starting at seat base on one side and ending at seat base on the other side. Add 12 in. to this measurement and make note for fabric width. Then add 2 in. to both noted width and length measurements to allow for hem.

2. Using measurements, cut one fabric piece for each chair.

3. Using iron, press a 1-in. hem on all sides of each fabric piece.

4. Use peel-n-stick fabric fuse tape between hem layers to secure the hem in place (or sew with a straight stitch about ½ in. from edge on a sewing machine).

5. To cover each chair, fold a fabric piece in half lengthwise with wrong sides together. Place over chair back with it sandwiched between folded fabric layers. Pull each side of fabric forward, crisscrossing fabric to form a V shape where fabric edges meet. Use a safety pin to secure fabric.

6. Use 2-in.-wide satin ribbon to make a bow. Style the bow and trim tails as desired. Hot glue your choice of paper flower to center of bow. Attach bow with a safety pin where the fabric edges meet in a V shape.

RIBBON & ORNAMENT CHAIR

- **2½-inch-wide wired ribbon**
- **⅛-inch-wide satin ribbon**
- **2½-inch-wide ornament**
- **Several straight pins or safety pins**
- **Flexible tape measure**

1. Wrap flexible tape measure around center of chair back to determine chair's circumference. Add 24 in. to this measurement

(to account for ribbon tails), and cut a length of wired ribbon in this final measurement.

2. Place cut ribbon centered snugly around chair back. Tie a knot to secure in place on back of chair. Trim ribbon ends in inverted V shapes.

3. Cut a 9-in. length of wired ribbon. Wrap loosely around tied knot to cover it. Overlap ribbon ends about 1 in. on back side of knot and secure with pins.

4. Cut an 8-in. length of ⅛-in.-wide satin ribbon. Loop ribbon through metal hoop on ornament and knot end. Use pins to secure knotted end of ribbon centered behind knot on chair ribbon, letting ornament hang down.

Take a vacation from the holiday ham and turkey and escape to Italy for an intimate, family-style feast. Without ever leaving your dining room, you'll relish a taste of the Tuscan countryside as the tree lights twinkle and dance with the candlelight.

Pass the fettuccine, swap inside jokes and revisit favorite holiday memories. Then gather around the fireplace for some Hazelnut Mocha Coffee and Little Italy Pignoli Cookies, along with an indulgent slice of Orange Ricotta Cake Roll. When it comes to this kind of cozy camaraderie, you can kiss your curfew goodbye and kick back for a night of good conversation, laughter and maybe even a carol or two.

SET THE TONE

Illuminate the tablescape with music-inspired decoupage candles. This simple craft can be customized for any theme, and comes in handy for hostess or parting gifts. See p. 27.

Fennel Salad with Orange-Balsamic Vinaigrette (p. 23)
Fettuccine Seafood Alfredo (p. 24)

BUON NATALE!

Portobello Bruschetta with Rosemary Aioli

Caramelized onions, broiled peppers and homemade aioli add dimensions of flavor you won't find in a store-bought bruschetta.
—**STEPHANIE KALINA-METZGER**
CAMP HILL, PA

PREP: 1 HOUR 20 MIN.
BAKE: 15 MIN.
MAKES: 2 DOZEN

AIOLI
- ⅓ **cup mayonnaise**
- 1 **garlic clove, minced**
- 1½ **teaspoons lemon juice**
- 1½ **teaspoons balsamic vinegar**
- 1 **teaspoon minced fresh rosemary**
- 1 **teaspoon Dijon mustard**

MARINADE
- ¼ **cup packed brown sugar**
- ¼ **cup balsamic vinegar**
- ¼ **cup honey**
- 4 **teaspoons minced fresh thyme or 1 teaspoon dried thyme**

BRUSCHETTA
- 6 **large portobello mushrooms, stems and gills removed**
- ½ **cup olive oil, divided**
- 3 **medium red onions, halved and thinly sliced**
- 2 **large sweet red peppers**
- 3 **tablespoons thinly sliced green onions**
- 3 **tablespoons minced fresh basil**
- 1 **garlic clove, minced**
- ¼ **teaspoon salt**
- ⅛ **teaspoon pepper**
- 24 **slices French bread baguette (¼ inch thick)**
- 1 **cup fresh arugula**

1. In a small bowl, mix aioli ingredients. Refrigerate, covered, until serving.

2. Preheat oven to 375°. In a small bowl, whisk marinade ingredients until blended. Place mushrooms in a 13x9-in. baking dish; drizzle with ¼ cup marinade. Bake, covered, 35-40 minutes or until tender. Remove from baking dish; cool slightly. Cut into ½-in. strips.

3. In a large skillet, heat 2 tablespoons oil over medium heat. Add red onions; cook and stir 8-10 minutes or until softened. Reduce heat to medium-low; cook 30-40 minutes or until deep golden brown, stirring occasionally. Add remaining marinade; cook 4-6 minutes or until onions are glazed, stirring occasionally.

4. Place red peppers on a foil-lined baking sheet. Broil 4 in. from heat until skins blister, about 5 minutes. With tongs, rotate peppers a quarter turn. Broil and rotate until all sides are blistered and blackened. Immediately place peppers in a bowl; let stand, covered, 20 minutes.

5. Peel off and discard charred skin from peppers. Remove stems and seeds. Chop peppers; return to bowl. Add green onions, basil, garlic, salt, pepper and 1 tablespoon oil. Toss to combine.

6. Place baguette slices on ungreased baking sheets; brush with remaining oil. Bake at 375° for 4-6 minutes on each side or until golden brown.

7. To serve, top toasts with mushrooms, arugula, onions and pepper mixture. Bake 5-8 minutes longer or until heated through. Drizzle with aioli.

Artichoke & Caper Cream Soup

I adore the flavors of oyster mushrooms, capers and artichokes. So after experimenting with several batches, I came up with this soup. Every year I'm asked to bring it to our office Christmas party.
— **RIOLOBO** TASTE OF HOME ONLINE COMMUNITY

PREP: 20 MIN. • **COOK:** 35 MIN. • **MAKES:** 5 SERVINGS

¼ cup butter, cubed
⅓ pound fresh oyster mushrooms, coarsely chopped
2 cans (14 ounces each) artichoke bottoms, drained and coarsely chopped
2 tablespoons capers, rinsed and drained
1 garlic clove, minced
2 cans (14½ ounces each) chicken broth
2 cups heavy whipping cream
2 tablespoons Cognac or additional chicken broth
⅛ teaspoon pepper

1. In a large skillet, melt butter over medium-high heat. Add mushrooms. Cook and stir 4-5 minutes or until lightly browned. Add artichokes, capers and garlic. Cook and stir 4-5 minutes or until artichokes begin to brown.

2. Meanwhile, in a large saucepan, combine broth, cream, Cognac and pepper; bring to a boil.

3. Reserve 1 cup artichoke mixture. Transfer remaining mixture to a blender; add ¾ cup broth mixture. Cover and process until smooth; add to remaining broth mixture. Bring to a boil. Reduce heat; simmer, uncovered, 30 minutes, stirring frequently. Add reserved artichoke mixture; heat through.

Slow-Cooked Italian Meatballs

What I love about these meatballs is that they can be served as an appetizer right out of the slow cooker or alongside your favorite pasta. They also make a delicious sandwich.
—**JASON ROMANO** DOWNINGTOWN, PA

PREP: 50 MIN. • **COOK:** 3 HOURS • **MAKES:** ABOUT 5 DOZEN

2 tablespoons olive oil
1 small onion, finely chopped
3 garlic cloves, minced
1 cup Italian-style panko (Japanese) bread crumbs
2 eggs, lightly beaten
½ cup grated Parmesan cheese
½ cup minced fresh parsley
¼ cup water
¼ cup minced fresh basil
2 tablespoons Worcestershire sauce
½ teaspoon salt
½ teaspoon pepper
1 pound ground beef
½ pound ground pork
½ pound ground veal
4 cups spaghetti sauce

1. Preheat oven to 400°. In a small skillet, heat oil over medium heat. Add onion and garlic; cook 5-9 minutes or until onion is tender and golden brown. Cool slightly.

2. In a large bowl, combine bread crumbs, eggs, cheese, parsley, water and seasonings. Add ground meats; mix lightly but thoroughly. Shape into 1-in. balls. Place on greased racks in shallow baking pans. Bake 20-25 minutes or until browned.

3. Transfer meatballs to a 4- or 5-qt. slow cooker. Pour spaghetti sauce over top. Cook, covered, on low for 3-4 hours or until meatballs are cooked through.

Marinated Cheese with Peppers and Olives

Cheddar cheese, red peppers and pitted ripe olives make a tasty, rustic appetizer when marinated overnight and served with decorative toothpicks.
—**POLLY BRUNNING** THAXTON, VA

PREP: 10 MIN. + CHILLING
MAKES: 15 SERVINGS

12 **ounces cheddar cheese, cut into ¾-inch cubes**
2 **medium sweet red peppers, cut into ¾-inch pieces**
2 **cans (6 ounces each) pitted ripe olives, drained**
¼ **cup canola oil**
1 **tablespoon white vinegar**
1 **garlic clove, minced**
½ **teaspoon dried basil**
½ **teaspoon dried oregano**

In a large bowl, combine all ingredients. Refrigerate, covered, at least 4 hours or overnight.

WOULD YOU LIKE SOME WINE WITH YOUR CHEESE?

When pairing a wine with a semihard cheese, such as cheddar, a good rule of thumb is to reach for cabernet sauvignon if you prefer red and sauvignon blanc if you prefer white.

Fennel Salad with Orange-Balsamic Vinaigrette

PICTURED ON PAGE 18

A sweet balsamic vinaigrette pulls everything together in this holiday salad. Raspberry is one of my favorite flavors so I'm always looking for unique ways to include it.
—**SUSAN GAUTHIER** FALMOUTH, ME

START TO FINISH: 25 MIN. • **MAKES:** 8 SERVINGS

¼ cup balsamic vinegar
¼ cup maple syrup
2 tablespoons orange marmalade
2 tablespoons seedless raspberry preserves
½ teaspoon ground mustard
¼ teaspoon salt
⅛ teaspoon pepper
½ cup olive oil

SALAD
1 package (5 ounces) spring mix salad greens
2 fennel bulbs, thinly sliced
1 can (15 ounces) mandarin oranges, drained
¼ cup coarsely chopped pistachios, toasted

1. In a small bowl, whisk the first seven ingredients. Gradually whisk in oil until blended.

2. In a large bowl, combine salad greens, fennel and oranges. Divide salad green mixture among eight plates. Sprinkle with pistachios; drizzle with the dressing.

Green Beans with Tomato Sauce

As an alternative to green bean casserole, serve up a saucy Italian side dish sporting festive red and green colors. Also try this sauce with asparagus, broccoli or Brussels sprouts.
—**TASTE OF HOME TEST KITCHEN**

START TO FINISH: 15 MIN. • **MAKES:** 8 SERVINGS

2 pounds fresh green beans, trimmed and cut in half
1 tablespoon olive oil
1 medium onion, chopped
2 garlic cloves, minced
2 cans (15 ounces each) tomato sauce
1 teaspoon sugar
1 teaspoon dried basil
1 teaspoon dried oregano
½ teaspoon salt
½ teaspoon pepper

1. Place green beans in a steamer basket. Place basket in a large saucepan over 1 in. of water; bring to a boil. Steam, covered, 8-10 minutes or until crisp-tender. Transfer to a serving bowl.

2. Meanwhile, in a small saucepan, heat oil over medium-high heat. Add onion and garlic; cook and stir until tender. Stir in the remaining ingredients. Bring to a boil. Reduce heat; simmer, uncovered, 15 minutes. Drizzle over beans.

Fettuccine Seafood Alfredo

PICTURED ON PAGE 19

When I was pregnant with my first daughter, I needed to limit my fat intake because of health problems. I still wanted delicious meals that worked well for entertaining, so I started making this Alfredo for special occasions.

—JACKIE PRICE TRENTON, MO

START TO FINISH: 25 MIN. • **MAKES:** 5 SERVINGS

12 ounces uncooked fettuccine
2 tablespoons olive oil, divided
1 pound uncooked jumbo shrimp, peeled and deveined
6 garlic cloves, minced
1 can (12 ounces) evaporated milk
½ teaspoon salt
¼ cup grated Parmesan cheese
¼ cup sour cream
½ pound lump crabmeat, drained
¼ cup minced fresh basil

1. Cook fettuccine according to package directions.
2. Meanwhile, in a large skillet, heat 1 tablespoon oil over medium-high heat. Add shrimp; cook and stir 4 minutes or until shrimp turn pink. Remove and keep warm.
3. In same pan, heat remaining oil over medium heat. Add garlic; cook and stir 1-2 minutes. Add milk and salt. Bring just to a boil, stirring constantly.
4. Remove from heat; stir in cheese until melted. Whisk in sour cream. Drain fettuccine; add to skillet with shrimp and crab. Heat through. Stir in basil.

Herb-Crusted Beef Tenderloin

We enjoy easy-to-prepare entrees using fresh herbs, so I often serve this tenderloin along with steamed veggies. This one smells amazing in the kitchen and is simple to serve to guests.

—PETER HALFERTY CORPUS CHRISTI, TX

PREP: 20 MIN. • **BAKE:** 30 MIN. + STANDING • **MAKES:** 8 SERVINGS

1 beef tenderloin roast (3 to 3½ pounds)
4 tablespoons olive oil, divided
1 teaspoon pepper
½ teaspoon salt
6 tablespoons Dijon mustard
6 garlic cloves, minced
2 tablespoons plus 1½ teaspoons minced fresh thyme, divided
2 tablespoons plus 1½ teaspoons minced fresh rosemary, divided

1. Rub the tenderloin with 1 tablespoon oil; sprinkle with pepper and salt. In a large skillet, brown beef on all sides. Transfer to a rack in a shallow roasting pan.
2. Combine mustard, garlic, 2 tablespoons thyme, 2 tablespoons rosemary and remaining oil; brush over roast.
3. Bake, uncovered, at 425° for 30-40 minutes or until meat reaches desired doneness (for medium-rare, a thermometer should read 145°; medium, 160°; well-done, 170°). Let stand 10 minutes before slicing. Sprinkle with remaining herbs before serving.

Hazelnut Mocha Coffee

For special celebrations, my chocolaty brew will be the talk of the town. You can make the chocolate mixture a couple of days in advance. When you're ready to serve it, simply brew the coffee and whip the chocolate.
—MARY MARLOWE LEVERETTE
COLUMBIA, SC

PREP: 5 MIN.
COOK: 10 MIN. + CHILLING
MAKES: 6 SERVINGS

- 4 **ounces semisweet chocolate, chopped**
- 1 **cup heavy whipping cream**
- ⅓ **cup sugar**
- ½ **teaspoon ground cinnamon**
- 2 **tablespoons hazelnut liqueur**
- 4½ **cups hot brewed coffee**
  Sweetened whipped cream, optional

1. Place chocolate in a small bowl. In a small saucepan, bring cream just to a boil. Add sugar and cinnamon; cook and stir until sugar is dissolved. Pour over chocolate; stir with a whisk until smooth. Stir in liqueur.

2. Cool to room temperature, stirring occasionally. Refrigerate, covered, until cold. Beat just until soft peaks form, about 15 seconds (do not overbeat). For each serving, spoon ¼ cup into mugs. Top with ¾ cup coffee; stir to dissolve. Top with whipped cream if desired.

Little Italy Pignoli Cookies

Almond paste in these Italian pignoli (meaning "pine nut") cookies gives these morsels an exceptional flavor. They're a real treat served with a hot chocolate or coffee beverage.
—FRAN GREEN TASTE OF HOME ONLINE COMMUNITY

PREP: 5 MIN. • **BAKE:** 15 MIN./BATCH • **MAKES:** 5 DOZEN

- 1 **cup almond paste**
- 1 **egg white**
- 1 **tablespoon honey**
- ¾ **cup confectioners' sugar**
- ¾ **cup pine nuts**

1. Preheat oven to 325°. In a small bowl, beat almond paste, egg white and honey until crumbly. Gradually add confectioners' sugar; mix well.

2. Place pine nuts in a small bowl. Shape teaspoonfuls of dough into balls. Roll in pine nuts. Place 1 in. apart on parchment paper-lined baking sheets. Flatten slightly.

3. Bake 15-18 minutes or until lightly browned. Cool 1 minute before removing from pans to wire racks. Store in an airtight container.

Orange Ricotta Cake Roll

I come from a big Italian family where my mom cooked and baked many delicious meals and desserts from scratch. Now I like to do the same for my family. This cake is my finale to our Italian Christmas Eve dinner.
—**CATHY BANKS** ENCINITAS, CA

PREP: 45 MIN. • **BAKE:** 10 MIN. + CHILLING • **MAKES:** 12 SERVINGS

4 **eggs, separated**
¼ **cup baking cocoa**
2 **tablespoons all-purpose flour**
⅛ **teaspoon salt**
⅔ **cup confectioners' sugar, sifted, divided**
1 **teaspoon vanilla extract**
½ **teaspoon cream of tartar**

FILLING

1 **container (15 ounces) ricotta cheese**
3 **tablespoons Mascarpone cheese**
⅓ **cup sugar**
1 **tablespoon Kahlua (coffee liqueur)**
1 **tablespoon grated orange peel**
½ **teaspoon vanilla extract**
Additional confectioners' sugar
Orange sections, optional

1. Place egg whites in a large bowl; let stand at room temperature 30 minutes.

2. Meanwhile, preheat oven to 325°. Line bottom of a greased 15x10x1-in. baking pan with parchment or waxed paper. Sift cocoa, flour and salt together twice.

3. In another large bowl, beat egg yolks until slightly thickened. Gradually add ⅓ cup confectioners' sugar, beating on high speed until thick and lemon-colored. Beat in vanilla. Fold in flour mixture (batter will be thick).

4. Add cream of tartar to egg whites; with clean beaters, beat on medium until soft peaks form. Gradually add remaining confectioners' sugar, 1 tablespoon at a time, beating on high after each addition until sugar is dissolved. Continue beating until soft glossy peaks form.

5. Fold a fourth of the whites into the batter, then fold in remaining whites. Transfer to prepared pan, spreading evenly.

6. Bake 9-11 minutes or until top springs back when lightly touched. Cool 5 minutes. Invert onto a kitchen towel dusted with confectioners' sugar. Gently peel off paper. Roll up cake in the towel jelly-roll style, starting with a short side. Cool completely on a wire rack.

7. For filling, in a small bowl, beat cheeses and sugar until blended. Stir in Kahlua, orange peel and vanilla.

8. Unroll cake; spread filling over cake to within ½ in. of edges. Roll up again, without towel. Place on a platter, seam side down. Dust with confectioners' sugar. Refrigerate, covered, at least 1 hour before serving. Garnish with orange sections if desired.

YOU'RE ON A ROLL. NOW FREEZE!

Who doesn't love desserts you can make ahead and freeze for an upcoming dinner party? Cake rolls may be frozen for up to 2 months after they have been filled and rolled. Simply place the unfrosted roll on a baking sheet and freeze. Once frozen, wrap in plastic wrap. To serve, frost and garnish as desired.

Set the Tone

Get ready for candlelit carols by making music-inspired stage lighting.

MATERIALS

Choice of candle
Choice of paper or card stock
Flexible tape measure
Decoupage glue
Sponge brush
Ribbon and other
  embellishments (optional)

DIRECTIONS

1. Use the flexible tape measure to measure the circumference and height of the candle. Make note of the measurements. Then cut a piece of paper or card stock to match the exact height and the circumference plus about ½ in. for seam overlap.

2. Use the sponge brush to apply a coat of decoupage glue to the back of the paper or card stock.

3. Wrap glue side of paper or card stock around the candle matching the height and circumference. Slightly overlap the paper or card stock at the seam.

4. To remove air bubbles, either gently roll the covered candle on a flat surface or use your hands to flatten the paper toward the seam. Let the glue dry.

5. If desired, add a coat of decoupage glue to the paper or card stock exterior to seal.

6. Add ribbon or other embellishments as desired, being sure to place them away from the wick and flame area.

NOTE *Although we used real candles, flameless candles can also be used.*

If you've ever baked bread from scratch, then you're in the know—hands down, it's the most amazing aroma that will ever permeate your kitchen. And the rewards only get better from there. Whether it's a basket of soft, hot rolls landing on your holiday dinner table or a freshly baked cheddar scone to start the day, the experience of breaking bread with family and friends will make for a comforting and memorable Christmas meal.

Knead your own dough or use a bread machine—you'll find recipes for both. Either way, your fellow diners will find a place for you in your family's baking hall of fame.

Three-Flour Braid (p. 37)

BREAKING **BREAD**

Sausage and Cheddar Scones

Served with a touch of gourmet mustard, these golden scones could be the stars of your brunch.
I've found they freeze well for up to a month.

—MARY CLAYPOOL GRANADA HILLS, CA

PREP: 35 MIN. • **BAKE:** 15 MIN. • **MAKES:** 16 SCONES

1 pound bulk sage pork sausage
4 cups all-purpose flour
2 tablespoons baking powder
1½ teaspoons ground mustard
½ teaspoon baking soda
½ teaspoon salt
½ teaspoon pepper
6 tablespoons cold butter
4 egg whites
1½ cups buttermilk
2½ cups (10 ounces) shredded
     sharp cheddar cheese, divided
2 egg yolks
2 teaspoons water
   Dijon mustard

1. In a large skillet, cook sausage until no longer pink; drain.

2. In a large bowl, combine the flour, baking powder, ground mustard, baking soda, salt and pepper. Cut in butter until mixture resembles coarse crumbs. Whisk egg whites and buttermilk; stir into crumb mixture just until moistened. Stir in sausage and 2 cups cheese. Turn onto a floured surface; knead 10 times.

3. Divide dough in half; pat each half into an 8-in. circle. Cut each into eight wedges. Separate wedges and place on parchment paper-lined baking sheets. Beat egg yolks and water; brush over tops. Sprinkle with remaining cheese.

4. Bake at 400° for 14-16 minutes or until golden brown. Serve warm with Dijon mustard.

Cheddar-Bacon Swirled Rolls

I let the bread machine do the work to make these homemade rolls. Swirls of onion and bacon
in a rich potato-cheddar dough make for an extra-special bread basket.

—JEANNE HOLT MENDOTA HEIGHTS, MN

PREP: 30 MIN. + RISING • **BAKE:** 30 MIN. • **MAKES:** 9 SERVINGS

⅔ cup warm whole milk
     (70° to 80°)
4½ teaspoons water
4 teaspoons butter, softened
½ teaspoon lemon juice
1 tablespoon sugar
½ teaspoon salt
1¾ cups all-purpose flour
3 tablespoons mashed
     potato flakes
1 package (¼ ounce) active dry
     yeast
½ cup shredded cheddar cheese

FILLING
1 cup finely chopped onion
¼ teaspoon salt
⅛ teaspoon pepper
3 tablespoons butter

8 bacon strips, cooked and
     crumbled (equals ½ cup)

1. In bread machine pan, place the first nine ingredients in order suggested by manufacturer. Select dough setting (check dough after 5 minutes of mixing; add 1-2 tablespoons of water or flour if needed). Just before the final kneading (your machine may audibly signal this), add cheese.

2. While dough is processing, prepare filling. In a large skillet, cook the onion, salt and pepper in butter over medium heat until onion is tender and translucent (do not brown). Stir in bacon bits.

Remove from the heat. Cool.

3. When cycle is completed, turn dough onto a lightly floured surface. Roll into a 12-in. x 8-in. rectangle. Spread onion mixture to within ½ in. of edges. Roll up jelly-roll style, starting with a long side; pinch seam to seal.

4. Cut into 9 rolls. Place cut side up in a greased 9-in.-square baking pan. Cover and let rise in a warm place until doubled, about 30 minutes.

5. Bake at 375° for 30-35 minutes or until golden brown. Remove from pan to a wire rack. Serve warm.

Parmesan-Oat Pull-Aparts

Basil and oregano come through in every bite of these soft and tender pull-apart rolls.
I think they enhance special dinners, but they also make a nice addition to breakfast.
—MARIE RIZZIO INTERLOCHEN, MI

PREP: 40 MIN. + RISING
BAKE: 20 MIN.
MAKES: 2 DOZEN

- 1 cup grated Parmesan cheese
- 1 tablespoon dried basil
- 1 tablespoon dried oregano
- 1 teaspoon garlic powder
- ¼ cup sugar
- 2 packages (¼ ounce each) active dry yeast
- 2 teaspoons salt
- 3 to 3½ cups all-purpose flour
- 1 cup old-fashioned oats
- 1½ cups water
- 3 tablespoons butter
- 1 egg
- ½ cup butter, melted

1. In a small bowl, combine Parmesan cheese, basil, oregano and garlic powder. In a large bowl, mix sugar, yeast, salt and 1½ cups flour. Place oats in another small bowl. In a small saucepan, bring water and butter just to a boil; pour over oats. Let stand until mixture cools to 120°-130°, stirring occasionally.

2. Add to flour mixture; beat on medium speed 2 minutes. Add egg; beat 2 minutes longer. Add ¾ cup of herb mixture; beat until combined. Stir in enough remaining flour to form a stiff dough (dough will be sticky).

3. Punch down dough. Turn onto a floured surface; knead until smooth and elastic, about 6-8 minutes. Place in a greased bowl, turning once to grease the top. Cover with plastic wrap and let rise in a warm place until doubled, about 1 hour.

4. Punch dough down and press evenly into a greased 13x9-in. baking pan. Using a sharp knife, cut diagonal lines 1½ in. apart completely through dough. Repeat in opposite direction, creating a diamond pattern. Cover with a kitchen towel; let rise in a warm place until doubled, about 1 hour.

5. Preheat oven to 375°. Brush dough with 3 tablespoons melted butter. Bake 15 minutes. Brush with remaining butter and sprinkle with remaining herb mixture. Bake 5-10 minutes longer or until golden brown. Serve warm.

Mushroom Corn Muffins with Chive Butter

In this unexpected combination, thyme and mushrooms tucked into a fine-textured corn bread muffin are enhanced with a smear of homemade chive butter.

—LORRAINE CALAND SHUNIAH, ON

PREP: 30 MIN. • **BAKE:** 15 MIN.
MAKES: 1 DOZEN
(½ CUP CHIVE BUTTER)

- 6 tablespoons butter, melted, divided
- 1 cup chopped fresh mushrooms
- 1 cup all-purpose flour
- 1 cup cornmeal
- ¼ cup sugar
- 2 teaspoons baking powder
- ½ teaspoon salt
- 2 eggs
- 1 cup 2% milk
- 1 tablespoon minced fresh thyme

CHIVE BUTTER
- ½ cup butter, softened
- 2 tablespoons minced fresh chives

1. Preheat oven to 400°. In a small skillet, heat 2 tablespoons melted butter over medium-high heat. Add mushrooms; cook and stir until tender.

2. In a large bowl, whisk flour, cornmeal, sugar, baking powder and salt. In another bowl, whisk eggs, milk, thyme and remaining melted butter until blended. Add to flour mixture; stir just until moistened. Fold in mushrooms.

3. Fill greased or foil-lined muffin cups three-fourths full. Bake 12-15 minutes or until a toothpick inserted in center comes out clean. Cool 5 minutes before removing from pans to a wire rack.

4. Meanwhile, in a small bowl, mix softened butter and chives until blended. Serve with warm muffins.

Onion Crescents

I make these crescents for my family on Easter and Christmas. We like the sweetness of the sugar with the onions and the way the aroma of fresh-baked bread fills our home.
—**MARY MAXEINER** LAKEWOOD, CO

PREP: 30 MIN. + RISING • **BAKE:** 10 MIN. • **MAKES:** 2 DOZEN

- ½ **cup butter, softened**
- ½ **cup sugar**
- 2 **eggs**
- 1 **package (¼ ounce) active dry yeast**
- 1 **cup warm milk (110° to 115°)**
- ½ **cup dried minced onion**
- ½ **teaspoon salt**
- 3½ **to 4½ cups all-purpose flour**
- 2 **tablespoons butter, melted**

1. In a large bowl, cream butter and sugar. Add eggs, one at a time, beating well after each addition. Dissolve yeast in warm milk; add to creamed mixture. Add the onion, salt and 2 cups flour. Beat until blended. Stir in enough remaining flour to form a soft dough.

2. Turn onto a floured surface; knead until smooth and elastic, about 6-8 minutes. Place in a greased bowl, turning once to grease top. Cover and let rise in a warm place until doubled, about 1 hour.

3. Punch dough down. Turn onto a lightly floured surface; divide in half. Roll each into a 12-in. circle; cut each circle into 12 wedges. Roll up wedges from the wide end and place point side down 2 in. apart on greased baking sheets. Curve ends to form a crescent shape.

4. Cover and let rise until doubled, about 30 minutes. Bake at 400° for 8-12 minutes or until golden brown. Brush with melted butter; remove to wire racks.

Rosemary Flatbreads

My family loves this as a pizza crust. But with a touch of olive oil and fresh herbs, it makes a classic flatbread appetizer.
—**SUE BROWN** WEST BEND, WI

PREP: 40 MIN. + RISING • **BAKE:** 10 MIN. • **MAKES:** 6 SERVINGS

- 1 **package (¼ ounce) active dry yeast**
- ¼ **cup plus ⅓ cup warm water (110° to 115°), divided**
- ½ **teaspoon honey**
- 2 **cups all-purpose flour, divided**
- 1 **tablespoon olive oil**
- 1 **teaspoon minced fresh rosemary**
- ½ **teaspoon kosher salt**

TOPPING
- 1 **tablespoon olive oil**
- 1 **teaspoon minced fresh rosemary**
- ½ **teaspoon kosher salt**

1. In a small bowl, dissolve yeast in ¼ cup warm water; stir in honey. Add ¼ cup flour; mix until almost smooth. Let stand 30 minutes or until bubbly.

2. Place remaining flour, remaining warm water, oil, rosemary and salt in a food processor; add yeast mixture. Process until dough forms a ball. Process 1 minute more to knead dough, pulsing as needed.

3. Transfer to a greased bowl, turning once to grease the top. Cover with plastic wrap and let rise in a warm place until doubled, about 1 hour.

4. Punch down dough. Turn onto a lightly floured surface; divide and shape dough into six balls. On a greased baking sheet, pat each ball into a 5-in. circle. For topping, brush tops with oil; sprinkle with rosemary and salt. Bake 8-12 minutes or until golden brown. Serve warm.

Seeded Honey Wheat Bread

So full of poppy seed and sunflower seed flavors, this recipe—which I usually have to double—goes quickly in my family. Bread bakers will appreciate its perfect shape and soft texture.
—**RACHEL HEIDENREICH** MARSHALL, MI

PREP: 45 MIN. + RISING • **BAKE:** 25 MIN. + COOLING • **MAKES:** 2 LOAVES (12 SLICES EACH)

- 1 **cup whole wheat flour**
- 2 **packages (¼ ounce each) quick-rise yeast**
- 1 **teaspoon salt**
- 3½ to 4 **cups all-purpose flour**
- 1½ **cups water**
- ¼ **cup butter, cubed**
- ¼ **cup honey**
- ⅓ **cup flaxseed**
- ¼ **cup unsalted sunflower kernels**
- 1 **tablespoon poppy seeds**
- 1 **egg**

1. In a large bowl, combine the whole wheat flour, yeast, salt and 1 cup all-purpose flour; set aside. In a small saucepan, heat the water, butter and honey to 120°-130°. Add to the dry ingredients. Stir in the flax, sunflower kernels, poppy seeds and enough remaining flour to form a stiff dough.

2. Turn onto a floured surface; knead until smooth and elastic, about 6-8 minutes. Cover with plastic wrap and let rest 10 minutes. Punch down dough; divide in half. Shape into loaves. Place in two greased 8-in. x 4-in. loaf pans, seam side down. Cover and let rise in a warm place until doubled, about 15 minutes.

3. In a small bowl, beat egg; brush over loaves. Bake at 350° for 25-30 minutes or until golden brown. Remove from pans to wire racks to cool.

Caraway Rye Dinner Rolls

Caraway seeds give these rye dinner rolls a delicate nutty flavor. Denser than most, the onion-infused buns are ideal for dipping in hearty holiday stews.
—**DEBORAH MAKI** KAMLOOPS, BC

PREP: 35 MIN. + RISING • **BAKE:** 15 MIN. • **MAKES:** 1½ DOZEN

- 1¼ **cups rye flour**
- ½ **cup wheat germ**
- 2 **tablespoons caraway seeds**
- 1 **package (¼ ounce) active dry yeast**
- 1 **teaspoon salt**
- 3 **cups all-purpose flour**
- 1 **cup 2% milk**
- ½ **cup water**
- 3 **tablespoons butter**
- 2 **tablespoons honey**
- ⅓ **cup finely chopped onion**

EGG WASH
- 1 **egg**
- 2 **teaspoons water**

1. In a large bowl, mix the first five ingredients and 1 cup all-purpose flour. In a small saucepan, heat milk, water, butter and honey to 120°-130°. Add to dry ingredients; beat on medium speed 3 minutes. Stir in onion and enough remaining all-purpose flour to form a soft dough (dough will be sticky).

2. Turn dough onto a floured surface; knead until smooth and elastic, about 6-8 minutes. Place in a greased bowl, turning once to grease the top. Cover with plastic wrap and let rise in a warm place until doubled, about 1 hour.

3. Punch down dough. Turn onto a lightly floured surface; divide and shape into 18 balls. Place 2 in. apart on greased baking sheets. Cover with a kitchen towel; let rise in a warm place until almost doubled, about 45 minutes. Preheat oven to 400°.

4. For egg wash, in a small bowl, whisk egg and water; brush over rolls. Bake 11-14 minutes or until lightly browned. Remove to wire racks to cool.

Wild Rice & Cranberry Loaves

This is an incredibly fragrant bread with lots of texture from wild rice and dried cranberries.
It's hearty enough for sandwiches, but with a touch of honey, I could eat it for dessert!

—BARBARA J. MILLER OAKDALE, MN

PREP: 40 MIN. + RISING
BAKE: 40 MIN. + COOLING
MAKES: 2 LOAVES
(16 SLICES EACH)

- 2 **cups whole wheat flour**
- 2 **packages (¼ ounce each)**
  quick-rise yeast
- 1 **tablespoon sugar**
- 1 **tablespoon grated orange peel**
- 2 **teaspoons aniseed**
- 1 **teaspoon salt**
- 1 **teaspoon caraway seeds**
- 4 **to 4½ cups bread flour**
- 2 **cups 2% milk**
- ½ **cup water**
- ¼ **cup molasses**
- 2 **tablespoons butter**
- 1 **cup dried cranberries**
- 1 **cup cooked wild rice, cooled**

1. In a large bowl, mix first seven ingredients and 1½ cups bread flour. In small saucepan, heat milk, water, molasses and butter to 120°-130°. Add to dry ingredients; beat on medium speed 2 minutes. Stir in cranberries, rice and enough bread flour to form a stiff dough (dough will be sticky).

2. Turn dough onto floured surface; knead until smooth and elastic, about 6-8 minutes. Place in greased bowl, turning once to grease top. Cover with plastic wrap and let rest 10 minutes.

3. Punch down dough. Turn onto a lightly floured surface; divide in half. Shape into loaves. Place in two greased 9x5-in. loaf pans, seam side down. Cover with kitchen towels; let rise in a warm place until almost doubled, about 20 minutes. Preheat oven to 350°.

4. Bake 40-45 minutes. Cool in pans 10 minutes. Remove to wire racks to cool.

Bread Machine Dinner Rolls

While looking through my bread recipes one day, I happened upon this one and decided to give it a try. I offered one of the rolls to my dad and ever since then, he's raved about how much he loves them. He even offers samples to friends and family.

— **REBECAH LYTLE** OCALA, FL

PREP: 25 MIN. + RISING
BAKE: 10 MIN.
MAKES: 2 DOZEN

1 **cup water (70° to 80°)**
¼ **cup butter, cubed**
1 **egg**
1¼ **teaspoons salt**
3¾ **cups bread flour**
¼ **cup sugar**
3 **tablespoons nonfat dry milk powder**
1 **package (¼ ounce) quick-rise yeast**

EGG WASH
1 **egg**
4 **teaspoons water**

1. In bread machine pan, place the first eight ingredients in order suggested by manufacturer. Select dough setting. Check dough after 5 minutes of mixing; add 1-2 tablespoons water or flour if needed.

2. When cycle is completed, turn dough onto a lightly floured surface. Divide and shape into 24 balls. Roll each into an 8-in. rope; tie into a loose knot. Tuck ends under.

3. Place 1½ in. apart on greased baking sheets. Cover with a kitchen towel; let rise in a warm place until doubled, about 30 minutes. Preheat oven to 400°.

4. For egg wash, in a small bowl, whisk egg and water; brush over rolls. Bake 8-9 minutes or until golden brown. Remove from pans to wire racks; serve warm.

NOTE *We recommend you do not use a bread machine's time-delay feature for this recipe.*

Three-Flour Braid

PICTURED ON PAGE 28

Wheat, white and rye doughs are beautifully braided into a multicolored loaf. Sliced or whole, this bread freezes well, so you can enjoy it any time of year.

—AUDREY BENSON FLAGLER, CO

PREP: 40 MIN. + RISING • **BAKE:** 25 MIN. + COOLING • **MAKES:** 2 LOAVES (16 SLICES EACH)

- 2 packages (¼ ounce each) active dry yeast
- 2¼ cups warm water (110° to 115°)
- ¼ cup canola oil
- 2 tablespoons sugar
- 1 teaspoon salt
- 3¼ cups all-purpose flour

RYE DOUGH
- 2 tablespoons molasses
- 1 tablespoon baking cocoa
- 1 teaspoon caraway seeds
- 1¼ cups rye flour

WHEAT DOUGH
- 2 tablespoons molasses
- 1 cup whole wheat flour

WHITE DOUGH
- 1¼ cups all-purpose flour
- 1 tablespoon butter, melted

1. In a large bowl, dissolve yeast in water. Add the oil, sugar, salt and 2¼ cups all-purpose flour; beat for 2 minutes. Add remaining all-purpose flour; beat for 2 minutes longer. Divide evenly into three bowls.

2. To the first bowl, add molasses, cocoa and caraway; mix well. Gradually add rye flour. Turn onto a floured surface; knead until smooth and elastic, about 6-8 minutes. Place in a greased bowl, turning once to grease top. Cover and set aside.

3. To the second bowl, add molasses; mix well. Gradually add whole wheat flour. Turn onto a floured surface; knead until smooth and elastic, about 6-8 minutes. Place in a greased bowl, turning once to grease top. Cover and set aside.

4. To the third bowl, gradually add all-purpose flour. Turn onto a floured surface; knead until smooth and elastic, about 6-8 minutes. Place in a greased bowl, turning once to grease top. Cover all three bowls and let rise in a warm place until doubled, about 1 hour.

5. Punch doughs down. Turn onto a lightly floured surface; divide each in half. Shape each half into a 15-in. rope. Place a rope of each dough on a greased baking sheet and braid; pinch ends to seal and tuck under. Repeat with remaining ropes. Cover and let rise until nearly doubled, about 30 minutes.

6. Bake at 350° for 25-30 minutes or until golden brown. Brush with butter. Remove from pan to a wire rack to cool.

NOTE *Use all-purpose flour on kneading surface for all three doughs.*

Parmesan-Sage Beer Bread

I'm asked to bring this savory loaf to nearly every function I attend. It's great as a side dish, but if you're in the mood for an extraordinary sandwich, start with two slices of this beer bread.

—BETSY KING DULUTH, MN

PREP: 10 MIN. • **BAKE:** 45 MIN. + COOLING • **MAKES:** 1 LOAF (12 SLICES)

- 2½ cups all-purpose flour
- 1 cup grated Parmesan cheese
- 2 tablespoons sugar
- 3 teaspoons baking powder
- 1 tablespoon chopped fresh sage
- 1 teaspoon salt
- 1½ cups beer
- ¼ cup melted butter, divided

1. Preheat oven to 375°. In a small bowl, whisk the first six ingredients. Add beer and 3 tablespoons melted butter; stir just until moistened.

2. Transfer to a greased 8x4-in. loaf pan. Drizzle with remaining butter. Bake 45-50 minutes or until a toothpick inserted in center comes out clean. Cool in pan 5 minutes before removing to a wire rack to cool.

A trip to Grandma's for the holidays wouldn't have been complete without the comforts of a home-cooked supper. Let there be saucy sirloin. Let there be candied carrots. Let there be luscious desserts.

But don't let these recipes remain a thing of the past. Take a lesson from Nana and fill the kitchen with aromas of baking biscuits and banana cream pie. With these recipes on hand, no family will be deprived of the joys of a good old-fashioned Christmas.

OLD-FASHIONED **CHRISTMAS**

All-Occasion Punch

To keep the punch cold while adding extra color, I like to make an ice ring out of cherry soda pop. The flavor always brings folks back for more.

—CAROL VAN SICKLE
VERSAILLES, KY

START TO FINISH: 15 MIN.
MAKES: 5½ QUARTS

- 8 **cups cold water**
- 1 **can (12 ounces) frozen lemonade concentrate, thawed, plus ¾ cup thawed lemonade concentrate**
- 2 **liters ginger ale, chilled**
- 1 **liter cherry lemon-lime soda, chilled**
  Ice ring, optional

In a large punch bowl, combine water and lemonade concentrate. Stir in ginger ale and lemon-lime soda. Top with an ice ring if desired. Serve immediately.

NOTE: *To make an ice ring, lightly coat a tube cake pan or gelatin mold with cooking spray; add ½ cup of water or soda. Arrange assorted fruit or herbs as desired. Freeze until solid. Gently add 4½ cups water or soda; arrange more fruit and herbs. Freeze until ready to use. To unmold, wrap bottom of mold in a warm towel until loosened. Float ice ring, fruit side up, in punch bowl.*

Creamy Hot Beef Dip

A neighbor gave me this recipe years ago. Served with crackers, it makes a satisfying snack. I also serve it with raw veggies as an appetizer or on crusty bread with a salad for a light meal. Every time I make this dip, I think of my friend and the fun times our families had together.
—**SUSAN WOLFE** OLATHE, KS

PREP: 10 MIN. • **BAKE:** 30 MIN. • **MAKES:** ABOUT 2 CUPS

1 package (8 ounces) cream cheese, softened
1 cup (8 ounces) sour cream
1 package (2½ ounces) thinly sliced dried beef, finely chopped
2 tablespoons chopped green pepper

4½ teaspoons finely chopped onion
½ teaspoon garlic powder
Pepper to taste
Assorted fresh vegetables or crackers

In a small bowl, combine the first seven ingredients until blended; transfer to a 1-qt. baking dish. Bake, uncovered, at 375° for 30 minutes or until bubbly. Serve with vegetables.

Angel Biscuits

PICTURED ON PAGE 38

I've been making biscuits for more than 25 years. I usually divide the dough into two portions so I can make biscuits for dinner and roll out the other half for cinnamon rolls in the morning. I've also used this dough for pigs in a blanket and pirozhki—buns stuffed with different savory fillings.
—**FAYE HINTZ** SPRINGFIELD, MO

PREP: 20 MIN. + RISING • **BAKE:** 10 MIN. • **MAKES:** 2½ DOZEN

2 packages (¼ ounce each) active dry yeast
¼ cup warm water (110°-115°)
2 cups warm buttermilk (110°-115°)
5 cups all-purpose flour
⅓ cup sugar
2 teaspoons salt
2 teaspoons baking powder
1 teaspoon baking soda
1 cup shortening
Melted butter

1. In a small bowl, dissolve yeast in warm water. Let stand 5 minutes. Stir in warm buttermilk; set aside.

2. In a large bowl, combine the flour, sugar, salt, baking powder and baking soda. Cut in shortening with a pastry blender until mixture resembles coarse crumbs. Stir in yeast mixture.

3. Turn onto a lightly floured surface; knead lightly 3-4 times. Roll out to ½-in. thickness; cut with a 2½-in. biscuit cutter. Place 2 in. apart on lightly greased baking sheets. Cover with kitchen towels and let rise in a warm place until doubled, about 1½ hours.

4. Bake at 450° for 8-10 minutes or until golden brown. Lightly brush tops with melted butter. Serve warm.

Copper Carrot Salad

PICTURED ON PAGE 39

This colorful quick-fix salad has been made by members of my family for many years.
My mom, Jean Hamm, shared the recipe so I could have it in my wedding dinner.
—**DIANNA BADGETT** ST. MARIES, ID

PREP: 10 MIN. + CHILLING • **COOK:** 25 MIN. + COOLING • **MAKES:** 16 SERVINGS

- 5 **pounds carrots, cut into ¼-inch slices**
- 2 **medium green peppers, chopped**
- 1 **large onion, chopped**
- 2 **cans (10¾ ounces each) condensed tomato soup, undiluted**
- 1½ **cups sugar**
- 1½ **cups vinegar**
- 1 **cup vegetable oil**
- 2 **tablespoons Italian seasoning**
- 2 **teaspoons ground mustard**
- 2 **teaspoons curry powder**
- 2 **teaspoons Worcestershire sauce**
- ½ **teaspoon salt**
- ½ **teaspoon pepper**

1. Place carrots in a Dutch oven. Add 1 in. of water. Bring to a boil. Reduce heat; cover and simmer for 15-20 minutes or until carrots are tender. Drain; rinse in cold water.

2. In a large bowl, combine green peppers, onion and carrots; set aside. In a large saucepan, combine the remaining ingredients; cook over medium heat until sugar is dissolved, stirring occasionally. Cool for 10 minutes. Pour over carrot mixture; toss to coat. Cover and refrigerate for 24 hours. Serve with a slotted spoon.

Chicken with Potato Stuffing

My husband and I live out in the country and have two sons. We think this is a wonderful Sunday
meal or holiday dish, as long as you're preparing enough for seconds!
—**CARLA KREIDER** QUARRYVILLE, PA

PREP: 45 MIN. • **BAKE:** 2¼ HOURS • **MAKES:** 8 SERVINGS

- 6 **medium red potatoes, cut into 1-inch cubes**
- 1 **pound Italian sausage links**
- 1 **cup finely chopped onion**
- 1 **tablespoon butter**
- 4 **teaspoons dried parsley flakes, divided**
- 1 **teaspoon salt**
- ¾ **teaspoon dried rosemary, crushed**
- 2¾ **teaspoons dried thyme, divided**
- ½ **teaspoon pepper**
- 1 **roasting chicken (7 to 7½ pounds)**
- 1 **tablespoon canola oil**
- 1 **cup water**

1. Cook the potatoes in boiling salted water until almost tender; drain and set aside. Cook the sausage in boiling water for 10 minutes; drain. Halve each sausage lengthwise, then cut into ½-in. pieces.

2. In a large skillet over medium heat, cook and stir potatoes, sausage and onion in butter until sausage is browned and onion is tender. Add 2 teaspoons parsley, salt, rosemary, ¾ teaspoon thyme and pepper.

3. Stuff the chicken with the potato mixture. Place the remaining stuffing in a greased 1½-qt. baking dish; cover and refrigerate until ready to bake.

4. Place chicken in a roasting pan breast side up; brush with oil and sprinkle with remaining parsley and thyme. Add water to pan. Bake, uncovered, at 350° for 2¼ hours or until a thermometer inserted in stuffing reads 165° and a thermometer inserted in the thigh reads 180°.

5. Bake stuffing in the baking dish for 45 minutes or until heated through and lightly browned. Remove chicken from oven; tent with foil. Let stand 15 minutes before removing stuffing and carving. Skim fat and thicken pan drippings for gravy if desired. Serve with chicken and stuffing.

Parsnips & Turnips Au Gratin

This is a delicious variation on au gratin that features something besides potatoes. I sometimes substitute rutabaga for the turnips. For a long time it's been a well-guarded recipe in my collection.
—PRISCILLA GILBERT INDIAN HARBOUR BEACH, FL

PREP: 20 MIN. • **BAKE:** 15 MIN.
MAKES: 8 SERVINGS

1½ pounds parsnips, peeled and sliced
1¼ pounds turnips, peeled and sliced
1 can (10¾ ounces) reduced-fat reduced-sodium condensed cream of celery soup, undiluted
1 cup fat-free milk
½ teaspoon pepper
1 cup (4 ounces) shredded sharp cheddar cheese
½ cup panko (Japanese) bread crumbs
1 tablespoon butter, melted

1. Place parsnips and turnips in a large saucepan; cover with water. Bring to a boil. Reduce heat; simmer, uncovered, for 5-7 minutes or until crisp-tender.
2. Meanwhile, in a small saucepan, combine the soup, milk and pepper. Bring to a boil; reduce heat to low. Stir in cheese until melted. Drain vegetables; transfer to an 11-in. x 7-in. baking dish coated with cooking spray. Pour sauce over vegetables.
3. Combine bread crumbs and butter; sprinkle over top. Bake, uncovered, at 400° for 15-20 minutes or until vegetables are tender and crumbs are golden brown.

Ambrosia Fruit Salad

One of my most vivid memories as a child growing up in Maine is awakening to the sound of my mother cooking up a storm in the kitchen. She made all her meals from scratch, and her ambrosia fruit salad is one of our family favorites.

—COLLEEN BELBEY WARWICK, RI

START TO FINISH: 20 MIN.
MAKES: 6 SERVINGS

- 2 **cups cubed fresh pineapple**
- 2 **large navel oranges, peeled and sectioned**
- 1½ **cups green grapes**
- 1 **cup miniature marshmallows**
- 1 **large banana, sliced**
- ½ **cup flaked coconut**
- ¼ **cup chopped almonds**
- ¾ **cup (6 ounces) vanilla yogurt**

In a large serving bowl, combine the first seven ingredients. Gently fold in yogurt. Chill until serving.

Nine-Layer Salad

A classic layered salad served in a trifle dish or glass salad bowl is a simple way to add some green to your Christmas tablescape.

—ANNE HALFHILL SUNBURY, OH

PREP: 30 MIN. + CHILLING • **MAKES:** 8 SERVINGS

- 4 cups torn iceberg lettuce
- 4 cups fresh baby spinach
- 1 cup each chopped green pepper, celery and green onions
- 1 package (10 ounces) frozen peas, thawed and patted dry
- 1½ cups mayonnaise
- ½ cup shredded Parmesan cheese
- ½ cup shredded Romano cheese
- 1 cup crumbled cooked bacon

In a large salad bowl, layer the lettuce, spinach, green pepper, celery, green onions and peas. Spread with mayonnaise. Sprinkle cheeses and bacon over mayonnaise. Cover and refrigerate overnight.

Maple Horseradish Beets

Even folks who say they don't like beets will think this simple treatment is a winner. An easy glaze gives the beets a rich flavor with a little zip.

—LESLIE PALMER SWAMPSCOTT, MA

PREP: 50 MIN. • **COOK:** 10 MIN. • **MAKES:** 6 SERVINGS

- 1¾ pounds fresh beets
- 1 tablespoon canola oil
- 2 tablespoons butter
- ¼ cup maple syrup
- 3 tablespoons prepared horseradish
- 2 tablespoons cider vinegar
- ¼ teaspoon salt
- ¼ teaspoon pepper

1. Peel beets and cut into wedges. Place in a 15-in. x 10-in. x 1-in. baking pan; drizzle with oil and toss to coat. Bake at 400° for 40-50 minutes or until beets are tender.

2. In a small saucepan, melt butter. Stir in the syrup, horseradish, vinegar, salt and pepper. Bring to a boil. Carefully stir in beets; cook for 5-6 minutes or until liquid is slightly thickened, gently stirring occasionally.

Sirloin with Bearnaise Sauce
PICTURED ON PAGE 39

A classic bearnaise sauce is typically made with clarified butter, but using regular
cold butter works, too. I've been cooking my whole life, and when I want
a meal to be extra-special, I serve this beef as the centerpiece.
—**WILLA GOVORO** NEVADA, MO

PREP: 10 MIN. • **BAKE:** 2½ HOURS • **MAKES:** 12 SERVINGS

½ teaspoon garlic salt
½ teaspoon pepper
1 beef sirloin tip roast (5 to
   6 pounds)
BEARNAISE SAUCE
¼ cup white wine vinegar
½ cup chopped green onions
1 tablespoon minced fresh
   tarragon or 1 teaspoon dried
   tarragon
¼ teaspoon pepper
4 egg yolks
1 tablespoon cold water
¼ teaspoon salt
⅛ teaspoon cayenne pepper
¾ cup cold butter
1 tablespoon minced fresh
   parsley

1. Combine garlic salt and pepper;
rub over roast. Place on a rack
in a shallow roasting pan. Bake,
uncovered, at 325° for 2½ to
3 hours or until meat reaches
desired doneness (for medium-
rare, a thermometer should read
145°; medium, 160°; well-done,
170°). Let stand for 10-15 minutes
before slicing.
2. Meanwhile, in a saucepan,
combine the vinegar, green onions,
tarragon and pepper; bring to a
boil. Strain, reserving liquid;
discard green onions and tarragon.

3. Place egg yolks in a heavy
saucepan. Gradually whisk in
water, vinegar mixture, salt and
cayenne. Cook and stir until the
mixture begins to thicken. Add
butter, 1 tablespoon at a time, until
the mixture has thickened and
reaches 160°, stirring constantly.
Remove from the heat; stir in
parsley. Cut roast into thin slices;
serve with sauce.

Christmas Special Fruitcake

I've made this quick fruitcake many times for Christmas. I gave one to my doctor
a few years ago and he says it's the best fruitcake he's ever tasted.
—**VIOLET COOPER** PORT ALLEGANY, PA

PREP: 15 MIN. • **BAKE:** 1¾ HOURS + COOLING • **MAKES:** 24 SERVINGS

3 cups coarsely chopped Brazil
   nuts or other nuts (walnuts,
   pecans or hazelnuts)
1 pound pitted dates, coarsely
   chopped
1 cup halved maraschino
   cherries
¾ cup all-purpose flour
¾ cup sugar
½ teaspoon baking powder

½ teaspoon salt
3 eggs
1 teaspoon vanilla extract

1. In a large bowl, combine the
nuts, dates and cherries. Combine
the flour, sugar, baking powder
and salt; add to nut mixture,
stirring until nuts and fruit are
well coated.

2. In a small bowl, beat eggs until
foamy; stir in vanilla. Fold into nut
mixture and mix well. Pour into
a greased and parchment paper-
lined 9-in. x 5-in. loaf pan.
3. Bake at 300° for 1¾ hours or
until a toothpick inserted near the
center comes out clean. Cool for
10 minutes before removing from
pan to a wire rack.

Spiced Pudding Cake

I found this recipe years ago and made a few changes. Now it's a popular comfort food in my family. My mom's church group even serves it for dessert quite regularly.
—**KELLY KIRBY** WESTVILLE, NS

PREP: 25 MIN.
BAKE: 35 MIN. + COOLING
MAKES: 15 SERVINGS

½ cup butter, softened
½ cup sugar
1 egg
1 cup molasses
2½ cups all-purpose flour
1½ teaspoons baking soda
1½ teaspoons ground cinnamon
1¼ teaspoons ground ginger
½ teaspoon ground allspice
¼ teaspoon ground nutmeg
¼ teaspoon salt
2½ cups water, divided
⅔ cup packed brown sugar
¼ cup butter, cubed
   Whipped cream and ground
   cinnamon, optional

1. In a large bowl, cream butter and sugar until light and fluffy. Add egg; beat well. Beat in molasses. Combine the flour, baking soda, spices and salt; add to the creamed mixture alternately with 1 cup water, beating well after each addition.

2. Transfer to an ungreased 13-in. x 9-in. baking pan; sprinkle with brown sugar. In a microwave, heat butter and remaining water until butter is melted; carefully pour over batter.

3. Bake at 350° for 35-40 minutes or until a toothpick inserted near the center comes out clean. Cool on a wire rack. Serve warm. Garnish with whipped cream and cinnamon if desired.

Swedish Rice Ring

This old-fashioned dessert, which originated in Sweden, is famous at our church suppers. A delicious addition at family gatherings and parties, it's so good that I usually make an extra one!

—LORI JEANE SCHLECHT
WIMBLEDON, ND

PREP: 15 MIN.
COOK: 20 MIN. + CHILLING
MAKES: 12 SERVINGS

- 2 **envelopes unflavored gelatin**
- ¼ **cup cold water**
- ½ **cup uncooked long-grain rice**
- 3 **cups milk**
- ½ **cup sugar**
- ½ **teaspoon salt**
- 1 **cup heavy whipping cream**
  Fresh or frozen sweetened strawberries, thawed

1. Soften gelatin in cold water; set aside. In a small heavy saucepan, bring rice, milk, sugar and salt to a boil, stirring occasionally. Reduce heat and cover; cook over low heat until rice is tender, about 15-20 minutes. Remove from the heat; add gelatin mixture, stirring until dissolved. Cover and chill until partially set.

2. In a chilled bowl, whip cream until stiff; fold into chilled rice mixture. Spoon into a 6-cup decorative or ring mold coated with cooking spray. Cover and chill until set, about 3 hours. To unmold, loosen edges with spatula and invert onto a serving platter. Serve with strawberries.

Banana Cream Meringue Pie

I still remember my mom's pies fresh from the oven, waiting for us to enjoy them at suppertime or for special company dinners. Now I love to bake, and I love this pie.

—CAROL MAERTZ SPRUCE GROVE, AB

PREP: 30 MIN. • **BAKE:** 15 MIN. + CHILLING • **MAKES:** 8 SERVINGS

Pastry for single-crust pie (9 inches)
- 1 cup sugar, divided
- ⅓ cup cornstarch
- ½ teaspoon salt
- 1 can (12 ounces) evaporated milk
- 1 cup water
- 3 egg yolks, lightly beaten
- 1 teaspoon vanilla extract
- 3 egg whites
- 1 large firm banana

1. Line a 9-in. pie plate with pastry; trim and flute edges. Line pastry shell with a double thickness of heavy-duty foil. Bake at 450° for 8 minutes. Remove foil; bake 5 minutes longer. Cool on a wire rack.

2. In a large saucepan, combine ⅔ cup sugar, cornstarch and salt. Stir in milk and water until smooth. Cook and stir over medium-high heat until thickened and bubbly. Reduce heat; cook and stir 2 minutes longer. Remove from the heat. Stir a small amount of hot filling into egg yolks; return all to pan, stirring constantly. Bring to a gentle boil; cook and stir 2 minutes longer. Remove from the heat. Gently stir in vanilla. Keep warm.

3. In a large bowl, beat egg whites on medium speed until soft peaks form. Gradually beat in remaining sugar, 1 tablespoon at a time, on high until stiff glossy peaks form and sugar is dissolved. Slice banana into the crust; pour filling over top. Spread meringue evenly over hot filling, sealing edges to the crust.

4. Bake at 350° for 12-15 minutes or until golden brown. Cool on a wire rack for 1 hour. Refrigerate for at least 3 hours before serving.

Pinwheel Mints

My grandmother used to make these pinwheels for Christmas and so did my mom. "How'd you do that?" is what guests always say when they taste them. It's surprising that they're simply cream cheese, extract and confectioners' sugar.

—MARILOU ROTH MILFORD, NE

PREP: 45 MIN. + CHILLING • **MAKES:** ABOUT 3 DOZEN

- 1 package (8 ounces) cream cheese, softened
- ½ to 1 teaspoon mint extract
- 7½ to 8½ cups confectioners' sugar
- Red and green food coloring
- Additional confectioners' sugar

1. In a large bowl, beat cream cheese and extract until smooth. Gradually beat in as much confectioners' sugar as possible.

2. Turn onto a work surface dusted with confectioners' sugar; knead in remaining confectioners' sugar until smooth and sugar is absorbed (mixture will be stiff). Divide mixture in half. Using food coloring, tint one portion pink and the other portion light green, kneading until blended.

3. Divide each portion in half; shape each half into a 10-in. log to make two pink logs and two green logs. Place one log on a 12-in. piece of waxed paper lightly dusted with confectioners' sugar. Flatten log slightly; cover with a second piece of waxed paper. Roll out candy mixture into a 12-in. x 5-in. rectangle. Repeat with remaining logs.

4. Remove top sheet of waxed paper from one pink and one green rectangle. Place one rectangle over the other. Roll up jelly-roll style, starting with a long side. Wrap in waxed paper; twist ends. Repeat with remaining rectangles. Chill overnight.

5. To serve, cut candy into ½-in. slices. Store in an airtight container in the refrigerator for up to 1 week.

True or False: Ginger and spice make everything nice. True! But when it comes to gingerbread, we have a soft spot for cookies. After all, who can resist those cute little cookie canvases, just waiting to be dressed up in candy buttons and bows? We sure can't, especially when they're sandwiching cinnamon-spiked vanilla ice cream.

So thank you, ginger, for being the spice that's so nice to all of our favorite treats. Cheesecake, pie, cake, meringue bars and truffles all warmly embrace your rich, ginger-kissed twist. We know that any one of these goodies will fill our kitchens with a welcome warmth and the inviting aroma of all the nice things to come.

Gingerbread Ice Cream Sandwiches (p. 54)
Gingerbread with Fig-Walnut Sauce (p. 59)

GINGER & SPICE

Gingerbread Kisses

Whether you call them kisses or hugs, these cookies show nothing but love when served fresh from the oven. Little helpers will have a blast pressing the kisses down into each warm cookie.
— **NANCY ZIMMERMAN** CAPE MAY COURT HOUSE, NJ

PREP: 35 MIN. + CHILLING • **BAKE:** 10 MIN./BATCH • **MAKES:** 5 DOZEN

¾ cup butter, softened
¾ cup packed brown sugar
1 egg
½ cup molasses
3 cups all-purpose flour
2 teaspoons ground ginger
1 teaspoon baking soda
1 teaspoon ground cinnamon
¼ teaspoon salt
¼ teaspoon ground nutmeg
¼ cup sugar
60 striped chocolate kisses, unwrapped

1. In a large bowl, cream butter and brown sugar until light and fluffy. Beat in egg and molasses. In another bowl, whisk flour, ginger, baking soda, cinnamon, salt and nutmeg; gradually beat into creamed mixture. Refrigerate, covered, 4 hours or until easy to handle.

2. Preheat oven to 350°. Shape dough into 1-in. balls; roll in sugar. Place 1 in. apart on ungreased baking sheets. Bake 8-10 minutes or until lightly browned. Immediately press a chocolate kiss into the center of each cookie. Remove to wire racks to cool.

Gingerbread Macaroons

The first time we made these ginger macaroons, we felt that they were missing something. Once we adjusted the spices and added a buttery molasses filling, we had ourselves a sandwich cookie we couldn't get enough of!
—**TASTE OF HOME TEST KITCHEN**

PREP: 20 MIN. + STANDING • **BAKE:** 10 MIN./BATCH • **MAKES:** 3 DOZEN

4 egg whites
2 cups confectioners' sugar
1 cup almond flour
1½ teaspoons ground cinnamon
1½ teaspoons ground ginger
½ teaspoon ground allspice
¼ teaspoon ground nutmeg
¾ teaspoon cream of tartar
¼ cup sugar
FILLING
6 tablespoons butter, softened
2 tablespoons molasses
1 cup confectioners' sugar

1. Place egg whites in a large bowl; let stand at room temperature for 30 minutes. Place confectioners' sugar, almond flour and spices in a food processor. Cover and process until well blended.
2. Add cream of tartar to egg whites; beat on medium speed until soft peaks form. Gradually beat in sugar, 1 tablespoon at a time, on high until stiff glossy peaks form and sugar is dissolved. Fold in almond mixture in several additions.

3. Place mixture in a heavy-duty resealable plastic bag; cut a small hole in a corner of bag. Pipe 1-in.-diameter cookies onto parchment paper-lined baking sheets. Let stand at room temperature for 20-30 minutes or until a light crust forms.
4. Bake at 325° for 10-14 minutes or until firm to the touch. Cool completely on pans on wire racks.
5. In a small bowl, beat filling ingredients until fluffy. Spread over bottoms of half of cookies; top with remaining cookies.

Gingerbread Cheesecake

This is my twist on Christmas gingerbread...cheesecake-style! I like to garnish it with small gingerbread men all the way around the sides and a dollop of whipped cream on each slice.

—CINDY ROMBERG MISSISSAUGA, ON

PREP: 40 MIN. • **BAKE:** 55 MIN. + CHILLING • **MAKES:** 12 SERVINGS

1¼ cups crushed gingersnap
　　cookies
¼ cup butter, melted

FILLING

3 packages (8 ounces each)
　　cream cheese, softened
¾ cup sugar
¼ cup molasses
3 teaspoons vanilla extract
1 teaspoon ground cinnamon
1 teaspoon ground ginger
½ teaspoon ground nutmeg
¼ teaspoon ground cloves
3 eggs, lightly beaten

TOPPING

4 ounces semisweet chocolate,
　　coarsely chopped
½ cup heavy whipping cream
　　Melted chocolate, optional

1. Place a greased 9-in. springform pan on a double thickness of heavy-duty foil (about 18 in. square). Securely wrap foil around pan.

2. In a small bowl, combine cookie crumbs and butter. Press onto the bottom of prepared pan. Place pan on a baking sheet. Bake at 325° for 8-12 minutes. Cool on a wire rack.

3. In a large bowl, beat cream cheese and sugar until smooth. Beat in the molasses, vanilla, cinnamon, ginger, nutmeg and cloves. Add eggs; beat on low speed just until combined. Pour into crust.

4. Place springform pan in a large baking pan; add 1 in. of hot water to larger pan. Bake at 325° for 45-55 minutes or until center is just set and top appears dull. Remove springform pan from water bath. Cool on a wire rack for 10 minutes.

Carefully run a knife around edge of pan to loosen; cool 1 hour longer.

5. For topping, place chocolate in a small bowl. In a small saucepan, bring cream just to a boil. Pour over chocolate; whisk until smooth. Cool slightly, stirring occasionally. Pour over the cheesecake. Refrigerate overnight.

6. Remove sides of pan. Drizzle with melted chocolate if desired.

Gingerbread Ice Cream Sandwiches

When it comes to making an ice cream sandwich, not all gingerbread men are created equal. Some are too crispy, others too soft—but these thin yet sturdy boys hold up just right in the freezer.
—TASTE OF HOME TEST KITCHEN

PREP: 30 MIN. + CHILLING
BAKE: 10 MIN./BATCH + FREEZING
MAKES: 1 DOZEN

3 cups vanilla ice cream
¾ teaspoon ground cinnamon
COOKIES
⅓ cup butter, softened
½ cup packed brown sugar
1 egg
⅓ cup molasses
2 cups all-purpose flour
1 teaspoon ground ginger
¾ teaspoon baking soda
¾ teaspoon ground cinnamon
½ teaspoon ground cloves
¼ teaspoon salt

1. In a blender, combine ice cream and cinnamon. Transfer to a freezer container; freeze for at least 2 hours.

2. Meanwhile, in a large bowl, cream butter and brown sugar until light and fluffy. Add egg, then molasses. Combine the flour, ginger, baking soda, cinnamon, cloves and salt; gradually add to creamed mixture and mix well. Cover and refrigerate for 2 hours or until easy to handle.

3. On a lightly floured surface, roll dough to ⅛-in. thickness. Cut with a floured 3½-in. gingerbread-shaped cookie cutter. Place 1 in. apart on ungreased baking sheets. Bake at 350° for 8-10 minutes or until edges are firm. Remove to wire racks to cool.

4. Spread ¼ cup softened ice cream over the bottom of half of the cookies; top with remaining cookies. Wrap individually in plastic wrap. Freeze for at least 1 hour.

Holiday Gingerbread Trifle

My husband and I both enjoy this delicious dessert during the winter holidays, but sometimes we lighten it up by using Splenda Brown Sugar Blend and Lite Cool Whip.

—EILEEN BALLANCE NORFOLK, VA

PREP: 40 MIN. + CHILLING • **BAKE:** 25 MIN. + COOLING • **MAKES:** 18 SERVINGS

1 envelope unflavored gelatin
½ cup cold water
2 cans (15 ounces each) solid-pack pumpkin
⅔ cup packed brown sugar
1 teaspoon ground cinnamon
1 teaspoon ground ginger
1 teaspoon vanilla extract, divided
¾ teaspoon ground nutmeg
¼ teaspoon salt
4 cups heavy whipping cream
¼ cup confectioners' sugar

GINGERBREAD
½ cup unsalted butter, softened
½ cup packed brown sugar
1 egg
½ cup molasses
2 cups all-purpose flour
2 teaspoons ground ginger
1 teaspoon baking soda
½ teaspoon ground cinnamon
½ teaspoon salt
¾ cup buttermilk
½ cup hot water
3 tablespoons crystallized ginger

1. In a small saucepan, sprinkle gelatin over cold water; let stand for 1 minute. Heat over low heat, stirring until gelatin is completely dissolved. Remove from the heat. In a large bowl, combine the pumpkin, brown sugar, cinnamon, ginger, ½ teaspoon vanilla, nutmeg, salt and gelatin mixture.

2. In a large bowl, beat cream until it begins to thicken. Add confectioners' sugar and the remaining vanilla; beat until soft peaks form. Fold 4 cups whipped cream into pumpkin mixture. Cover and refrigerate while preparing cake. Refrigerate remaining whipped cream.

3. For gingerbread, in a large bowl, cream butter and brown sugar until light and fluffy. Beat in egg, then molasses. Combine the flour, ginger, baking soda, cinnamon and salt; add to the creamed mixture alternately with buttermilk, beating well after each addition. Beat in hot water.

4. Transfer to a greased and floured 13-in. x 9-in. baking pan. Bake at 350° for 22-26 minutes or until a toothpick inserted near the center comes out clean. Cool on a wire rack. Cut into cubes.

5. In a 5-qt. trifle bowl or glass serving bowl, layer 4 cups gingerbread cubes, half of the pumpkin mixture and half of the whipped cream. Repeat with remaining gingerbread and pumpkin. Cover and refrigerate for at least 4 hours.

6. Just before serving, spread remaining whipped cream over pumpkin mixture. Carefully arrange remaining gingerbread around edge of bowl; sprinkle with crystallized ginger.

TOUGH COOKIES

Use a light touch when handling gingerbread cookie dough; overhandling it will cause the cookies to be tough. Once the dough is rolled out, position the shapes from the cookie cutters close together to avoid having too many scraps. Reroll the scraps just once to prevent the dough from getting overworked.

Chocolate Gingerbread Toffee Cake with Ginger Whipped Cream

This three-layer cake literally stands above the rest. For me, producing a cake this unique and eye-catching is worth the extra steps involved. With notes of ginger coming though in the frosting and the cake, it can only be described as ginger-licious.

—MARIE RIZZIO INTERLOCHEN, MI

PREP: 45 MIN. + CHILLING • **BAKE:** 30 MIN. + COOLING • **MAKES:** 12 SERVINGS

- 2 **cups heavy whipping cream**
- 5 **slices fresh gingerroot (⅛-inch thick)**

CAKE

- 1½ **cups dark chocolate chips**
- ½ **cup butter, softened**
- 2 **cups packed brown sugar**
- 3 **eggs**
- 2 **teaspoons vanilla extract**
- 2 **cups all-purpose flour**
- ¾ **teaspoon ground ginger**
- ¾ **teaspoon ground cinnamon**
- ½ **teaspoon salt**
- ¼ **teaspoon ground allspice**
- ¼ **teaspoon ground nutmeg**
- 1 **cup (8 ounces) sour cream**
- 1 **cup hot water**
- ½ **cup molasses**
- 1 **teaspoon baking soda**

GANACHE

- 1 **package (12 ounces) dark chocolate chips**
- ¼ **teaspoon salt**
- 1 **can (14 ounces) sweetened condensed milk**
- 2 **tablespoons butter**
- 1 **teaspoon vanilla extract**
- 2 **tablespoons heavy whipping cream**

ASSEMBLY

- 6 **tablespoons confectioners' sugar**
- 1 **cup brickle toffee bits**

1. In a small heavy saucepan, heat cream and ginger until bubbles form around sides of pan. Remove from the heat; let cool slightly. Cover and refrigerate for 8 hours or overnight.

2. In a microwave, melt chocolate; stir until smooth. Set aside. In a large bowl, cream butter and brown sugar until blended. Add eggs, one at a time, beating well after each addition. Beat in melted chocolate and vanilla. Combine the flour, ginger, cinnamon, salt, allspice and nutmeg; add to the creamed mixture alternately with sour cream, beating well after each addition.

3. In a small bowl, combine the hot water, molasses and baking soda (mixture will foam); beat into batter. Transfer to three greased and floured 8-in. round baking pans.

4. Bake at 350° for 30-35 minutes or until a toothpick inserted near the center comes out clean. Cool for 10 minutes before removing from pans to wire racks to cool completely.

5. Meanwhile, for ganache, place chocolate and salt in a double boiler or metal bowl over simmering water; cook and stir for 2-3 minutes or until melted. Stir in condensed milk until smooth. Remove from the heat; stir in butter and vanilla until butter is melted.

6. Cool, stirring occasionally, to room temperature or until ganache reaches a spreading consistency, about 45 minutes. Add cream; beat chocolate mixture until smooth, about 2-3 minutes.

7. Strain ginger-cream mixture, discarding ginger slices. In a large bowl, beat cream until it begins to thicken. Add the confectioners' sugar; beat until stiff peaks form.

8. To assemble, place one cake layer on a serving plate; spread with half the ganache. Sprinkle with half of the toffee bits. Repeat layers once. Top with remaining cake layer; spread ginger whipped cream over top and sides of cake. Refrigerate for at least 2 hours. Store leftovers in the refrigerator.

WHIPPED TIPS

Cream will whip faster if it's chilled. Start by placing the mixing bowl and whisk or beaters in the freezer for a few minutes. You can also use a food processor. (The bowl and blade do not need to be chilled for this method.) Simply place the chilled cream in the bowl and process for about a minute or two until it's thick.

Gingerbread Meringue Bars

To attain the best of both worlds, I combined my grandmother's gingerbread recipe with my aunt's special brown sugar meringue to make these lovable bars.
—EDEN DRANGER LOS ANGELES, CA

PREP: 20 MIN. **BAKE:** 30 MIN. + COOLING **MAKES:** 2 DOZEN

- ¼ cup butter, softened
- 1 cup molasses
- 2 egg yolks
- 1 egg
- ¼ cup canned pumpkin
- 1 teaspoon vanilla extract
- 1½ cups whole wheat flour
- 2½ teaspoons ground cinnamon
- 2 teaspoons ground ginger
- 1 teaspoon baking powder
- 1 teaspoon baking soda
- ¾ teaspoon ground allspice
- ¼ teaspoon salt
- 1 cup miniature marshmallows
- ½ cup chopped pecans
- ½ cup semisweet chocolate chips
- 4 egg whites
- ½ cup packed brown sugar

1. In a large bowl, beat butter and molasses until blended. Add egg yolks and egg, one at a time, beating well after each addition. Beat in pumpkin and vanilla.

2. In small bowl, combine flour, cinnamon, ginger, baking powder, baking soda, allspice and salt. Slowly add to wet mixture. Pour into a greased 13-in. x 9-in. baking pan. Sprinkle with marshmallows, pecans and chocolate chips. Bake at 350° for 20 minutes.

3. Meanwhile, in a small bowl, beat egg whites on medium speed until soft peaks form. Gradually beat in brown sugar, 1 tablespoon at a time, on high until stiff glossy peaks form and sugar is dissolved.

4. Remove gingerbread from oven; spread with meringue. Bake 9-11 minutes longer or until meringue is lightly browned. Cool completely. Cut into bars.

Pear-Cranberry Gingerbread Cake

I love the warm, spicy flavors and festive fall fruits in this upside-down gingerbread cake. It's simple enough to whip up for lunch boxes, but it also has a place at any holiday buffet.

—CHRISTINA METKE CALGARY, AB

PREP: 25 MIN.
BAKE: 35 MIN. + COOLING
MAKES: 24 SERVINGS

- ¾ **cup butter, melted, divided**
- ⅔ **cup packed brown sugar, divided**
- 3 **medium pears, sliced**
- 2 **cups fresh or frozen cranberries, thawed**
- ¾ **cup brewed chai tea**
- ½ **cup sugar**
- ½ **cup molasses**
- 1 **egg**
- 2 **cups all-purpose flour**
- 1 **teaspoon ground ginger**
- 1 **teaspoon ground cinnamon**
- ½ **teaspoon salt**
- ½ **teaspoon baking soda**
- ½ **teaspoon ground cloves**
- ¼ **teaspoon ground nutmeg**

1. Pour ¼ cup melted butter into a 13-in. x 9-in. baking dish; sprinkle with ⅓ cup brown sugar. Arrange pears and cranberries in a single layer over brown sugar.

2. In a small bowl, beat the brewed tea, sugar, molasses, egg and the remaining butter and brown sugar until well blended. Combine the remaining ingredients; gradually beat into tea mixture until blended.

3. Spoon over pears. Bake at 350° for 35-45 minutes or until a toothpick inserted near the center comes out clean. Cool for 10 minutes before inverting onto a serving plate. Serve warm.

Gingerbread with Fig-Walnut Sauce

PICTURED ON PAGE 51

I experimented with aniseed this past holiday season and fell in love with the licorice flavor. It really enhances the gingerbread spices and fig sauce in this extraordinary Bundt cake.
—**SHELLY BEVINGTON-FISHER** HERMISTON, OR

PREP: 30 MIN. • **BAKE:** 40 MIN. + COOLING • **MAKES:** 12 SERVINGS

1 cup unsalted butter, softened
1 cup packed brown sugar
3 eggs
1 cup molasses
2½ cups all-purpose flour
2 teaspoons baking soda
2 teaspoons ground ginger
1½ teaspoons aniseed, crushed
1 teaspoon ground cinnamon
½ teaspoon ground allspice
¼ teaspoon ground cloves
1 teaspoon salt
1 cup buttermilk
1 tablespoon lemon juice
Confectioners' sugar, optional

SAUCE

12 ounces Calimyrna dried figs, cut into eighths
1 cup finely chopped walnuts
2 tablespoons walnut or canola oil

1 tablespoon aniseed, crushed
1 teaspoon ground cinnamon
½ teaspoon ground cloves
1¾ cups water
1 cup sugar
2 tablespoons lemon juice
¼ teaspoon salt

1. In a large bowl, cream butter and brown sugar until light and fluffy. Add eggs, one at a time, beating well after each addition. Beat in molasses (mixture will appear curdled).
2. In a small bowl, combine the flour, baking soda, spices and salt. Add to the creamed mixture alternately with buttermilk and lemon juice, beating well after each addition.

3. Pour batter into a greased and floured 10-in. fluted tube pan. Bake at 350° for 40-50 minutes or until a toothpick inserted near the center comes out clean.
4. Cool for 10 minutes before removing from pan to a wire rack to cool completely. Dust with confectioners' sugar if desired.
5. For sauce, in a large skillet, cook figs and walnuts in oil over medium heat for 4 minutes. Stir in the spices; cook 1-2 minutes longer or until aromatic.
6. Stir in the water, sugar, lemon juice and salt. Bring to a boil. Reduce heat; simmer, uncovered, for 8-12 minutes or until thickened, stirring occasionally. Cool to room temperature. Serve with gingerbread.

Gingerbread Truffles

I never received compliments on my baking until I brought these cinnamon-ginger truffles to a party. Every Christmas, family, friends and even co-workers ask me to make these.
—**ANGELA RANDJELOVIC** INDEPENDENCE, OH

PREP: 50 MIN. • **COOK:** 10 MIN. + CHILLING • **MAKES:** 3 DOZEN

14 ounces white baking chocolate, chopped
½ cup heavy whipping cream
1 teaspoon ground cinnamon
½ teaspoon ground ginger
¼ teaspoon ground cloves
1 package (10 ounces) dark chocolate chips
5 teaspoons shortening
3 tablespoons crystallized ginger

1. Place white chocolate in a small bowl. In a small saucepan, bring whipping cream just to a boil. Pour over white chocolate; whisk until smooth. Stir in the cinnamon, ginger and cloves. Cool to room temperature, stirring occasionally. Cover and refrigerate for 3 hours or until firm.
2. Shape mixture into ¾-in. balls. Place on waxed paper-lined

baking sheets. Refrigerate for at least 1 hour.
3. In a microwave, melt chocolate chips and shortening; stir until smooth. Dip truffles in chocolate; allow excess to drip off. Place on waxed paper. Sprinkle with crystallized ginger. Store in an airtight container in the refrigerator.

Not just for sauces and cosmos, these superfruits do wonders in cakes, candies and dressings. So don't forget to stock your freezer while fresh cranberries are available October through December. You never know when a craving for Cranberry Coconut Cake with Marshmallow Cream Frosting may strike.

Fortunately, dried cranberries are in stores year-round, so there's never an excuse not to make Cinnamon Cranberry Bagels. And if you're looking to turn prepared cranberry sauce into something extraordinary, the marinade used in the Cranberry-Glazed Lamb Skewers will change the way you think about the canned stuff for good.

Cranberry Coconut Cake with Marshmallow Cream Frosting (p. 68)

CRANBERRY **CREATIVITY**

Cinnamon Cranberry Bagels

I love to use this recipe as a starting point to play with new flavor combinations. While there's nothing like this cinnamon-cranberry version, blueberry and cinnamon-raisin are other options.
—**KIMBERLY CLAWSON** YERINGTON, NV

PREP: 30 MIN. + CHILLING • **BAKE:** 15 MIN. + COOLING • **MAKES:** 10 BAGELS

- 2 teaspoons active dry yeast
- 1¼ cups warm water (110° to 115°)
- 2 tablespoons sugar
- 1 tablespoon ground cinnamon
- ½ teaspoon salt
- 3¼ to 3½ cups bread flour
- 1 cup dried cranberries
- 1 egg white
- 1½ teaspoons cinnamon-sugar

1. In a small bowl, dissolve yeast in warm water. In a large bowl, combine the sugar, cinnamon, salt and 1½ cups flour; beat until smooth. Stir in enough remaining flour to form a soft dough; stir in the cranberries.

2. Turn onto a floured surface; knead until smooth and elastic, about 6-8 minutes. Place in a greased bowl, turning once to grease the top. Cover with plastic wrap and let rise in a warm place until doubled, about 1½ hours.

3. Punch dough down; let rest 10 minutes. Shape into 10 balls. Push thumb through centers to form a 1½-in. hole. Stretch and shape dough to form an even ring. Place on a parchment paper-lined baking sheet. Cover and let rest for 30 minutes, then refrigerate overnight.

4. Let stand at room temperature for 30 minutes; flatten bagels slightly. Fill a Dutch oven two-thirds full with water; bring to a boil. Drop bagels, two at a time, into boiling water. Cook for 30 seconds; turn and cook 30 seconds longer. Remove with a slotted spoon; drain well on paper towels.

5. Brush bagels with egg white; sprinkle with cinnamon-sugar. Place 2 in. apart on parchment paper-lined baking sheets. Bake at 425° for 12-16 minutes or until golden brown. Remove to wire racks to cool.

Cranberry Ginger Mojito

A twist on a traditional mojito, this puckery, ginger-infused cocktail is a refreshing summertime drink. But it can also be warmed and served as a cozy wintertime treat.
—**ANDREANN GEISE** MYRTLE BEACH, SC

START TO FINISH: 10 MIN. • **MAKES:** 1 SERVING

- 1 lime wedge
- 1 teaspoon sugar
- 6 fresh mint leaves, thinly sliced
- ¼ cup crushed ice
- 1 tablespoon lime juice
- 1 teaspoon grenadine syrup
- ⅛ teaspoon minced fresh gingerroot
- 3 ice cubes
- ½ cup unsweetened cranberry juice
- 1½ ounces dark rum

GARNISHES
- Lime wedge, crystallized ginger slice and mint sprig

1. Rub lime wedge around the rim of a tall glass. Sprinkle sugar on a plate; dip rim in sugar. Set glass aside.

2. In another glass, muddle the mint leaves, crushed ice, lime juice, grenadine syrup and fresh ginger. Pour into prepared glass. Add ice. Pour in cranberry juice and rum; stir. Serve with garnishes.

Cranberry-Orange Sangria

Letting this sangria sit in the fridge overnight improves its fruitiness, making it the perfect do-ahead drink for a party. It's also nice with a splash of brandy.

—MARIA REGAKIS SOMERVILLE, MA

PREP: 15 MIN. + CHILLING
MAKES: 10 SERVINGS

- 1 **medium orange, halved and thinly sliced**
- 1 **medium apple, quartered and thinly sliced**
- ½ **cup fresh or frozen cranberries**
- 1 **bottle (32 ounces) cranberry juice**
- 1 **bottle (750 ml) zinfandel or other fruity red wine**
- 1 **cup simple syrup**
- ½ **cup orange liqueur
  Ice cubes**

GARNISHES
   Additional thinly sliced oranges and fresh cranberries, optional

In a large pitcher, combine the first seven ingredients; refrigerate overnight. Serve over ice; garnish with oranges and cranberries if desired.

Smoked Gouda and Ham Appetizer Tarts

I call these Star of the Party Tarts because they have that I-want-more appeal. They're so easy to make, too!
—**MARY HAWKES** PRESCOTT, AZ

START TO FINISH: 30 MIN.
MAKES: 2 DOZEN

- 1 **egg, lightly beaten**
- 2 **tablespoons chopped fresh chives**
- 1 **tablespoon minced shallot**
- 1 **tablespoon mayonnaise**
- 2 **teaspoons honey mustard**
- 1 **teaspoon seasoned pepper**
- 1¼ **cups (5 ounces) shredded smoked Gouda cheese**
- ½ **cup finely chopped fully cooked smoked ham**
- 2 **tablespoons chopped dried cranberries**
- 24 **wonton wrappers**
  Cooking spray
  Additional minced fresh chives, optional

1. In a large bowl, combine the first six ingredients. Stir in the cheese, ham and cranberries. Spritz one side of each wonton wrapper with cooking spray. Gently press into miniature muffin cups, coated side up. Spoon 1 tablespoon cheese mixture into each.

2. Bake at 350° for 10-14 minutes or until crusts are golden brown. Sprinkle with fresh chives if desired; serve warm. Refrigerate leftovers.

Cranberry Chevre Lollipops

PICTURED AT TOP LEFT

Get a little creative with cranberries and the fryer. These two-bite pops have a creamy goat cheese filling, an outer crispy crunch and a dipping sauce that will make anyone say "Wow!"

—ELINOR IVES FISKDALE, MA

PREP: 45 MIN. • **COOK:** 5 MIN./BATCH • **MAKES:** 4½ DOZEN (1 CUP SAUCE)

- ⅔ cup whole-berry cranberry sauce
- ⅓ cup stone-ground mustard
- 2½ teaspoons honey
- ¼ teaspoon cayenne pepper
- 2 packages (11 ounces each) fresh goat cheese
- 2 cups dried cranberries, chopped
- 1 teaspoon minced fresh rosemary
- 1 teaspoon minced fresh thyme
- 3 eggs
- ¾ cup panko (Japanese) bread crumbs
- ¾ cup pistachios
- ½ pound thinly sliced prosciutto, cut into 1-inch strips
- Oil for deep-fat frying

1. In a small bowl, combine the cranberry sauce, mustard, honey and cayenne; set aside.
2. In another small bowl, combine the goat cheese, cranberries, rosemary and thyme. Shape into 1-in. balls. Place on baking sheets.
3. Whisk eggs in a shallow bowl. In another shallow bowl, combine bread crumbs and pistachios. Dip cheese balls in eggs, then bread-crumb mixture. Wrap a prosciutto strip around the center of each ball; secure with a wooden appetizer skewer.
4. In an electric skillet or deep fryer, heat oil to 375°. Fry appetizers, a few at a time, for 30-60 seconds or until golden brown. Drain on paper towels. Serve with sauce.

Cranberry-Glazed Lamb Skewers

PICTURED AT BOTTOM LEFT

Lamb marinated with savory cranberry sauce—I love making this for Christmas parties. Guests will appreciate that it's not your average appetizer.

—KIM YUILLE BROOKLYN, NY

PREP: 25 MIN. + MARINATING • **BROIL:** 5 MIN. • **MAKES:** 8 SERVINGS

- 2 cans (14 ounces each) whole-berry cranberry sauce
- 2 tablespoons brown sugar
- 2 tablespoons chili powder
- 1 tablespoon garlic powder
- 1 teaspoon paprika
- ½ teaspoon salt
- 2 pounds boneless leg of lamb, cut into ¼-inch-thick strips

1. In a small bowl, combine the first six ingredients, stirring to dissolve sugar; transfer 1½ cups to a large resealable plastic bag. Add lamb; seal bag and turn to coat. Refrigerate for several hours or overnight. Cover and refrigerate remaining cranberry mixture.
2. Remove lamb from marinade; discard marinade. Thread lamb strips, weaving back and forth, onto 16 metal or soaked wooden skewers. Arrange in foil-lined greased 15-in. x 10-in. x 1-in. baking pans. Broil 4 in. from the heat for 2-3 minutes on each side or until lamb reaches desired doneness.
3. Meanwhile, in a small saucepan, bring reserved cranberry mixture just to a boil over medium heat, stirring frequently. Serve with lamb.

Cranberry-Sesame Vinaigrette
PICTURED AT RIGHT

My husband loves fruity vinaigrettes, and by making our own I can go light on the oil and salt.
I use a sesame or nut oil for added richness; a little goes a long way.
I also use this recipe for marinades or in fruit salads.
—JULIE NEVES SUNBURY, PA

PREP: 20 MIN. + STANDING • **MAKES:** ⅔ CUP

CRANBERRY VINEGAR
- 2 cups fresh or frozen cranberries
- 3 tablespoons tangerine peel strips
- 2 cups rice vinegar
- 2 tablespoons crystallized ginger

VINAIGRETTE
- ½ cup cranberry vinegar
- 2 tablespoons canola oil
- 1 tablespoon sugar
- 1 tablespoon finely chopped crystallized ginger
- 1 tablespoon minced chives

- 1 tablespoon reduced-sodium soy sauce
- 1 tablespoon sesame oil
- 1 teaspoon ground mustard
- ¼ teaspoon salt
- ¼ teaspoon hot pepper sauce
- ⅛ teaspoon pepper

1. Place cranberries and tangerine peel in a food processor; cover and pulse until coarsely chopped. Transfer mixture to a small saucepan. Add vinegar and ginger. Bring to a boil. Reduce heat; simmer, uncovered, for 5 minutes.

2. Transfer to sterilized jars. Cover and let stand in a cool, dark place for at least 2 days. Strain mixture; discard solids. Transfer to a sterilized jar. Seal tightly. Store in a cool, dark place or in the refrigerator for up to 3 months.

3. In a small bowl, whisk the vinaigrette ingredients. Cover and refrigerate until serving. Reserve remaining cranberry vinegar for another use.

Cranberry Cinnamon Applesauce

My grandson Geoff likes warm applesauce, so I've come up with one that looks as good as it tastes. It could also be served in a tall dessert dish, garnished with a cinnamon stick.
—SUE PETERSON NEWVILLE, PA

PREP: 30 MIN. • **COOK:** 15 MIN. • **MAKES:** ABOUT 4 CUPS

- 3 pounds apples, peeled and chopped
- 1 cup fresh or frozen cranberries
- ¾ cup cranberry juice
- 4 teaspoons brown sugar
- 1 teaspoon ground cinnamon
  Additional ground cinnamon, optional

1. In a large saucepan, combine the apples, cranberries, juice, brown sugar and cinnamon. Bring to a boil. Reduce heat; cover and simmer for 15-20 minutes or until tender, stirring occasionally. Remove from the heat.

2. Mash until sauce is desired consistency. Serve warm or cold. Sprinkle with additional cinnamon if desired.

KEEPING CRANBERRIES YEAR-ROUND

Fresh cranberries will keep in the refrigerator for up to 4 weeks. Wash berries only when ready to use. They can be frozen, unwashed, for up to 9 months, stored in a heavy-duty freezer bag or container. When you're ready to use them in recipes, rinse but do not thaw them first.

Beef Tenderloins with Cranberry Sauce

I serve this cranberry sauce with beef tenderloins for occasional family meals, but it also works wonderfully with wild game.
—**STEVEN JONAS** PIERRE, SD

PREP: 15 MIN. • **BAKE:** 20 MIN.
MAKES: 4 SERVINGS

- 4 **beef tenderloin steaks (6 ounces each)**
- ¼ **teaspoon salt**
- ¼ **teaspoon pepper**
- 1 **tablespoon olive oil**

SAUCE
- 1 **pound frozen cranberries, thawed**
- 1½ **cups dry red wine**
- ½ **cup packed brown sugar**
- ½ **cup balsamic vinegar**
- 2 **fresh rosemary sprigs**
- 1 **tablespoon lemon juice**
- 1 **shallot, finely chopped**
- ½ **teaspoon salt**
- ¼ **teaspoon pepper**

1. Sprinkle steaks with salt and pepper. In a large skillet, cook steaks in oil over medium-high heat for 2 minutes on each side. Transfer to a 15-in. x 10-in. x 1-in. baking pan.

2. Bake, uncovered, at 375° for 16-20 minutes or until meat reaches desired doneness (for medium-rare, a thermometer should read 145°; medium, 160°; well-done, 170°). Remove and keep warm.

3. Meanwhile, in the same skillet, combine the cranberries, wine, brown sugar, vinegar, rosemary sprigs, lemon juice, shallot, salt and pepper. Bring to a boil; cook until liquid is reduced by half. Discard rosemary; allow to cool slightly.

4. Transfer to a food processor; cover and process until pureed. Strain sauce, discarding pulp; Serve with steaks.

Cranberry Coconut Cake with Marshmallow Cream Frosting

PICTURED ON PAGE 61

Filled with a homemade cranberry curd and smothered with one of the fluffiest frostings you've ever had, this tall cake will make a memorable impression at any holiday gathering.

—**JULIE MERRIMAN** COLD BROOK, NY

PREP: 1 HOUR + CHILLING • **BAKE:** 35 MIN. + COOLING • **MAKES:** 16 SERVINGS

1½ cups butter, softened
2 cups sugar
5 eggs, separated
1 can (8½ ounces) cream of coconut
¼ cup lime juice
3 teaspoons grated lime peel
3 cups all-purpose flour
1½ teaspoons baking powder
½ teaspoon baking soda
¼ teaspoon salt
1 cup buttermilk
¾ cup flaked coconut

FILLING
5 cups fresh or frozen cranberries, thawed
½ cup cranberry juice
1¼ cups sugar
3 eggs
3 egg yolks
¼ cup butter, cubed
2 tablespoons lime juice
1½ teaspoons grated lime peel

FROSTING
1 package (8 ounces) cream cheese, softened
1 cup marshmallow creme
½ cup butter, softened
3 cups confectioners' sugar
2 cups flaked coconut, toasted
Fresh cranberries, optional

1. Grease and flour two 9-in. round baking pans; set aside.

2. In a large bowl, cream butter and sugar until light and fluffy. Add egg yolks, one at a time, beating well after each addition. Beat in the cream of coconut, lime juice and peel. Combine the flour, baking powder, baking soda and salt; add to the creamed mixture alternately with buttermilk, beating well after each addition. Fold in coconut.

3. In a small bowl, beat egg whites until stiff peaks form; fold into batter. Transfer to prepared pans. Bake at 350° for 35-40 minutes or until a toothpick inserted near the center comes out clean.

4. Cool for 10 minutes before removing from pans to wire racks to cool completely.

5. For the filling, in a large saucepan, combine cranberries and cranberry juice. Cook over medium heat until berries pop, about 12 minutes. Press cranberries through a food mill into a small bowl; discard seeds and pulp.

6. In a small heavy saucepan over medium heat, combine cranberry mixture and sugar. Bring to a boil; cook and stir for 1 minute or until thickened. Remove from the heat.

7. Stir a small amount of hot mixture into eggs and egg yolks; return all to the pan, stirring constantly. Bring to a gentle boil; cook and stir 2 minutes longer. Remove from the heat. Stir in butter. Gently stir in lime juice and peel. Cool to room temperature without stirring. Cover and refrigerate until chilled.

8. In a large bowl, beat the cream cheese, marshmallow cream and butter until light and fluffy. Add confectioners' sugar; beat until smooth.

9. Cut each cake horizontally into two layers. Place bottom layer on a serving plate; top with a third of the filling. Repeat layers twice. Top with remaining cake layer. Frost cake. Press toasted coconut over top and sides of cake. Garnish with cranberries if desired.

TO MAKE AHEAD *Cake layers can be baked the day before serving. Store each layer in a resealable plastic bag at room temperature.*

COCONUT MILK OR CREAM? THE DIFFERENCE COULD DRIVE YOU COCONUTS!

Coconut milk is made by simmering 1 part shredded coconut in 1 part water. Coconut cream, however, is much thicker and is made by simmering 4 parts shredded coconut in 1 part water. Cream of coconut is essentially coconut cream that has been sweetened for use in baked goods.

Cranberry-Lime Semifreddo with Pound Cake

Everyone has a favorite way to serve—or eat—pound cake, but no one will expect this. It's also a terrific way to use up leftover cranberry sauce.
—CHRISTINE WENDLAND BROWNS MILLS, NJ

PREP: 1¼ HOURS + FREEZING
MAKES: 2 SEMIFREDDOS (8 SLICES EACH)

- 2 **cups fresh or frozen cranberries, coarsely chopped**
- 2 **cups sugar**
- 1 **cup apple cider or juice**
- ¼ **cup lime juice, divided**
- 2 **tablespoons cold water**
- 1 **envelope unflavored gelatin**
- 6 **egg yolks**
- ½ **cup agave nectar**
- 1½ **teaspoons grated lime peel**
- 1½ **cups heavy whipping cream**

CAKE LAYER
- 5 **ounces cream cheese, softened**
- 4 **teaspoons agave nectar**
- 4 **teaspoons plus ¼ cup dark rum, divided**
- 3 **tablespoons minced fresh mint**
- 1 **loaf (10¾ ounces) frozen pound cake, thawed and cut into 16 slices**

1. Line two 8-in. x 4-in. loaf pans with plastic wrap, letting edges hang over sides. In a small saucepan, combine the cranberries, sugar and cider. Cook over medium heat until slightly thickened, about 25 minutes. Remove from the heat. Stir in half of the lime juice. Cool to room temperature; cover and refrigerate until chilled.

2. Place cold water and remaining lime juice in a small bowl; sprinkle with gelatin. In a double boiler or metal bowl over simmering water, constantly whisk egg yolks and agave nectar until mixture coats the back of a spoon.

3. Remove from the heat and whisk in gelatin mixture and lime peel until blended. Refrigerate until slightly chilled, about 15 minutes. In a large bowl, combine cranberry and egg mixtures; beat until well blended. In a small bowl, beat cream until stiff peaks form. Fold whipped cream into cranberry mixture.

4. For cake layer, in a small bowl, beat cream cheese, agave nectar and 4 teaspoons dark rum until light and fluffy. Fold in mint. Brush pound cake slices with remaining

dark rum. Spread cream cheese mixture over eight cake slices; top with remaining slices.

5. In the prepared pans, layer half of the cranberry mixture, filled cake layers and the remaining cranberry mixture. Smooth the top; cover with overhanging plastic wrap. Freeze overnight or until firm.

6. To serve, unmold dessert, using ends of plastic wrap to lift from pan. Remove plastic. Cut into slices.

Friends and family love them. Co-workers adore them. Kids beg for them. Santa expects them. But when it comes to making them, not all cookies are created equal.

Some cookies call for fridge or freezer time before baking, while others require no baking at all. Here you'll find an assortment of Christmas favorites grouped by level of difficulty, from easy to advanced.

Running out of time before the holiday bake sale? Turn to the four-ingredient Lemon Snowflakes on p. 75. Ready to wow cookie lovers with colorful layers or cranberry and orange squares? Cran-Orange Icebox Cookies on p. 73 should do the trick. Don't be afraid to test your skills and try one from each group—everyone will thank you.

CANDY STRIPES

Learn the trick to making festive candy cane stripes on p. 78.

COOKIES
EASY TO ADVANCED

EASY ▶ Macaroon Kisses

PICTURED ON PAGE 70

These tempting cookies are sure to delight fans of coconut and chocolate.
The sweet combination is simply irresistible.

—**LEE ROBERTS** RACINE, WI

PREP: 45 MIN. + CHILLING • **BAKE:** 10 MIN./BATCH + COOLING • **MAKES:** 4 DOZEN

⅓ cup butter, softened
1 package (3 ounces) cream cheese, softened
¾ cup sugar
1 egg yolk
2 teaspoons almond extract
1½ cups all-purpose flour
2 teaspoons baking powder
½ teaspoon salt
5 cups flaked coconut, divided
48 milk chocolate kisses
Coarse sugar

1. In a large bowl, cream the butter, cream cheese and sugar until light and fluffy. Beat in egg yolk and extract. Combine the flour, baking powder and salt; gradually add to creamed mixture and mix well. Stir in 3 cups coconut. Cover and refrigerate for 1 hour or until dough is easy to handle.

2. Preheat oven to 350°. Shape dough into 1-in. balls and roll in the remaining coconut. Place 2 in. apart on ungreased baking sheets.

3. Bake 10-12 minutes or until lightly browned. Immediately press a chocolate kiss into the center of each cookie; sprinkle with coarse sugar. Cool on pan 2-3 minutes or until chocolate is softened. Remove to wire racks to cool completely.

INTERMEDIATE ▶ Linzer Cookies

This specialty cookie takes a little extra effort, but the results are sweet!
They really help to make the holidays feel special.

—**JANE PEARCY** VERONA, WI

PREP: 30 MIN. + CHILLING • **BAKE:** 10 MIN./BATCH + COOLING • **MAKES:** 3 DOZEN

1¼ cups butter, softened
1 cup sugar
2 eggs
3 cups all-purpose flour
1 tablespoon baking cocoa
½ teaspoon salt
¼ teaspoon ground cinnamon
¼ teaspoon ground nutmeg
⅛ teaspoon ground cloves
2 cups ground almonds
6 tablespoons seedless raspberry jam
3 tablespoons confectioners' sugar

1. In a large bowl, cream butter and sugar until light and fluffy. Add eggs, one at a time, beating well after each addition. Combine the flour, cocoa, salt and spices; gradually add to creamed mixture and mix well. Stir in almonds. Refrigerate for 1 hour or until easy to handle.

2. On a lightly floured surface, roll out dough to ⅛-in. thickness. Cut with a floured 2½-in. round cookie cutter. From the center of half of the cookies, cut out a 1½-in. shape.

3. Place on ungreased baking sheets. Bake at 350° for 10-12 minutes or until edges are golden brown. Remove to wire racks to cool.

4. Spread the bottom of each solid cookie with ½ teaspoon jam. Sprinkle cutout cookies with confectioners' sugar; carefully place over jam.

Cran-Orange Icebox Cookies

Cranberry-orange is a favorite Christmastime combo in our home. Chilling the dough in a loaf pan is the trick to giving them a distinct square shape for showing off those layers.
—**NANCY ROLLAG** KEWASKUM, WI

PREP: 30 MIN. + CHILLING
BAKE: 10 MIN./BATCH
MAKES: 4 DOZEN

- 1 cup butter, softened
- 1 cup sugar
- 1 egg
- 2 tablespoons 2% milk
- 1 teaspoon vanilla extract
- 3 cups all-purpose flour
- 1½ teaspoons baking powder
- 2 teaspoons grated orange peel
- ⅔ cup chopped dried cranberries
- ¼ cup chopped pecans
- 8 to 10 drops red food coloring, optional

1. In a large bowl, cream butter and sugar until light and fluffy. Beat in the egg, milk and vanilla. Combine flour and baking powder; gradually add to creamed mixture and mix well.

2. Transfer 1 cup dough to a small bowl; stir in orange peel and set aside. Add the cranberries, pecans and, if desired, food coloring to remaining dough; divide in half.

3. Line an 8-in. x 4-in. loaf pan with waxed paper. Press one portion of cranberry dough evenly into pan; top with orange dough, then remaining cranberry dough. Cover and refrigerate for 2 hours or until firm.

4. Remove dough from pan; cut in half lengthwise. Cut each portion into ¼-in. slices. Place 1 in. apart on lightly greased baking sheets.

5. Bake at 375° for 8-10 minutes or until edges begin to brown. Remove to wire racks. Store in an airtight container.

ADVANCED ▶

Good Fortune & Cheer Cookies

May your future be full of scrumptious cookies and kind words.
Coming up with custom fortunes is half the fun in making these cripsy treats.
—BEVERLY PRESTON FOND DU LAC, WI

PREP: 30 MIN. • **BAKE:** 5 MIN./BATCH + STANDING • **MAKES:** 1½ DOZEN

- **6 tablespoons butter, softened**
- **⅓ cup sugar**
- **2 egg whites**
- **½ teaspoon vanilla extract**
- **½ teaspoon rum extract**
- **⅔ cup all-purpose flour**
- **3 ounces white baking chocolate, chopped**
  Crushed peppermint candies
  Red, white and green nonpareils

1. Write fortunes on small strips of paper (3 in. x ½ in.); set aside. Using a pencil, draw two 3-in. circles on a sheet of parchment paper. Place paper, pencil mark down, on a baking sheet; set aside.

2. In a large bowl, beat the butter, sugar, egg whites and extracts until well blended. Add flour; mix well (batter will be thick). Spread a scant tablespoonful of batter over each circle. Bake at 400° for 4-5 minutes or until edges are lightly browned.

3. Slide parchment paper onto a work surface. Cover one cookie with a kitchen towel to keep warm. Place a fortune in the center of the other cookie; loosen cookie from parchment paper with a thin spatula. Fold cookie in half over fortune so the edges meet; hold edges together for 3 seconds.

4. Place center of cookie over the rim of a glass; gently press ends down to bend cookie. Cool for 1 minute before removing to a wire rack. Repeat with second cookie. If cookies become too cool to fold, return to oven to soften for 1 minute. Repeat with remaining batter and fortunes.

5. In a microwave, melt chocolate; stir until smooth. Partially dip cookies or drizzle as desired; place on waxed paper. Sprinkle with crushed candies and nonpareils. Let stand until set. Store in an airtight container.

INTERMEDIATE ▶ Vanilla Walnut Crescents

PICTURED ON PAGE 70

I know it's going to be a happy day when I'm in the kitchen baking. These are my favorite cookies to make and the ones my friends and family look forward to receiving during the holidays.
—**BETTY LAWTON** PENNINGTON, NJ

PREP: 30 MIN. + CHILLING • **BAKE:** 20 MIN./BATCH • **MAKES:** 3 DOZEN

2 **cups all-purpose flour**
⅛ **teaspoon salt**
1 **cup cold butter, cubed**
1 **egg, separated**
⅔ **cup sour cream**
½ **teaspoon vanilla extract**
⅔ **cup finely chopped walnuts**
⅔ **cup sugar**
1 **teaspoon ground cinnamon**

1. In a large bowl, combine flour and salt; cut in butter until mixture resembles coarse crumbs. In a small bowl, whisk the egg yolk, sour cream and vanilla; add to crumb mixture and mix well. Cover and refrigerate for 4 hours or overnight.

2. Divide dough into thirds. On a lightly floured surface, roll each portion into a 10-in. circle. Combine the walnuts, sugar and cinnamon; sprinkle ¼ cup over each circle. Cut each circle into 12 wedges.

3. Roll up each wedge from the wide end and place point side down 1 in. apart on greased baking sheets. Curve ends to form crescents. Whisk egg white until foamy; brush over crescents. Sprinkle with remaining nut mixture.

4. Bake at 350° for 18-20 minutes or until lightly browned. Remove to wire racks to cool. Store in an airtight container.

EASY ▶ Lemon Snowflakes

Confectioners' sugar highlights the cracked tops, so they resemble snowflakes.
—**LINDA BARRY** DIANNA, TX

PREP: 30 MIN.
BAKE: 10 MIN./BATCH
MAKES: 5½ DOZEN

1 **package lemon cake mix (regular size)**
2¼ **cups whipped topping**
1 **egg**
   Confectioners' sugar

1. In large bowl, combine cake mix, whipped topping and egg until blended. Batter will be sticky.

2. Drop by teaspoonfuls into confectioners' sugar; roll lightly to coat. Place on ungreased baking sheets. Bake at 350° for 10-12 minutes or until lightly browned and tops are cracked. Remove to wire racks to cool.

HOST A BAKE SALE

Using money earned from a bake sale to donate to your favorite charity is a sweet reward for the entire community. Here are a few tips on how to host a successful event.

- Ask family and friends to join in and help you prepare, bake for and participate in your sale.
- Talk to schools and community centers to borrow tables and chairs.
- Organize a team and assign responsibilities and roles. Decide who is baking, who is packaging and who will help run the sale.
- Decorate your tables and consider creating a theme.
- Promote your bake sale by putting up fliers around the community, adding the event to your organization's website, sending email to friends, and mentioning it on Facebook, on Twitter and/or in a newsletter.
- Have some gluten-free and nut-free options available.
- Let your customers know where you are going to donate the money.

ADVANCED ▸ Browned-Butter Sandwich Spritz

Browning butter gives it a deep, intense flavor that enhances the maple in these spritz cookies. If you don't have a cookie press, this recipe alone would make it worth the investment. You won't be disappointed.
—**DEIRDRE COX** KANSAS CITY, KS

PREP: 50 MIN. + CHILLING • **BAKE:** 10 MIN./BATCH + COOLING • **MAKES:** ABOUT 3 DOZEN

1 cup plus 2 tablespoons butter, cubed
1¼ cups confectioners' sugar, divided
1 egg
1 egg yolk
2 teaspoons vanilla extract
2¼ cups all-purpose flour
½ teaspoon salt
½ cup maple syrup

1. In a small heavy saucepan, cook and stir butter over medium heat for 8-10 minutes or until golden brown. Transfer to a small bowl; refrigerate until firm, about 1 hour.

2. Set aside 2 tablespoons browned butter for filling. In a large bowl, beat ½ cup confectioners' sugar and the remaining browned butter until smooth. Beat in the egg, yolk and vanilla. Combine flour and salt; gradually add to creamed mixture and mix well.

3. Using a cookie press fitted with the disk of your choice, press dough 2 in. apart onto parchment paper-lined baking sheets. Bake at 375° for 8-9 minutes or until set (do not brown). Remove to wire racks to cool.

4. In a small heavy saucepan, bring syrup to a boil. Cool slightly. Whisk in remaining confectioners' sugar until smooth. Beat reserved browned butter until light and fluffy. Beat in syrup mixture until smooth.

5. Spread 1 teaspoon filling over the bottom of half of the cookies. Top with remaining cookies.

INTERMEDIATE ▸ Coconut Almond Bombs

I make these beautiful cookies for holiday parties and weddings. For a very special occasion, I use a new small paintbrush to add a light coating of pearl dust on the sliced almonds.
—**DEB HOLBROOK** ABINGTON, MA

PREP: 50 MIN. + CHILLING • **BAKE:** 15 MIN./BATCH • **MAKES:** 3½ DOZEN

1 package (7 ounces) almond paste
2 cups confectioners' sugar
1 package (14 ounces) flaked coconut
3 egg whites
1 teaspoon vanilla extract
1 carton (8 ounces) Mascarpone cheese
2 pounds white candy coating, chopped
⅔ cup sliced almonds
Gold pearl dust

1. Place almond paste in a food processor; cover and process until finely chopped. Transfer to a large bowl; add confectioners' sugar and coconut. Beat until mixture resembles coarse crumbs. In a small bowl, beat egg whites and vanilla until stiff peaks form; fold into coconut mixture.

2. Drop by tablespoonfuls 2 in. apart onto parchment paper-lined baking sheets. Bake at 325° for 14-18 minutes or until lightly browned. Remove to wire racks to cool.

3. Spread about 1 teaspoon cheese over each cookie; refrigerate for 20 minutes or until cheese is firm.

4. In a microwave, melt candy coating; stir until smooth. Dip cookies in coating; allow excess to drip off. Place on waxed paper; sprinkle with almonds. Let stand until set. Brush pearl dust over almonds. Store in an airtight container in the refrigerator.

NOTE *Pearl dust is available from Wilton Industries* (wilton.com).

Roly-Poly Santas

I tuck one of these fanciful Santas into every gift cookie tray I make.
They're a guaranteed hit with the kids.
—MRS. ANDREW SYER OAK RIDGE, MO

PREP: 1 HOUR
BAKE: 15 MIN. + COOLING
MAKES: 1 DOZEN

1 **cup butter, softened**
½ **cup sugar**
1 **tablespoon milk**
1 **teaspoon vanilla extract**
2¼ **cups all-purpose flour**
   Red paste food coloring
   Miniature chocolate chips

ICING
½ **cup shortening**
½ **teaspoon vanilla extract**
2⅓ **cups confectioners' sugar,**
   divided
2 **tablespoons milk, divided**

ASSEMBLY
   White nonpareils, sugar pearls
   and red-hot candies
   Additional miniature
   semisweet chocolate chips,
   melted

1. In a large bowl, cream butter and sugar until light and fluffy. Add milk and vanilla; mix well. Add flour and mix well. Remove 1¾ cups dough; tint red. Shape white dough into 12 balls, ¾ in. each, and 60 balls, ¼ in. each. Shape red dough into 12 balls, 1 in. each, and 60 balls, ½ in. each.

2. Place the 1-in. red balls on two ungreased baking sheets for the body of 12 Santas; flatten to ½-in. thickness. Attach ¾-in. white balls for heads; flatten to ½-in. thickness. Attach four ½-in. red balls to each Santa for arms and legs. Attach ¼-in. white balls to ends of arms and legs for hands and feet.

3. Shape remaining ½-in. red balls into hats. Attach remaining ¼-in. white balls to tips of hats.

Place inverted chocolate chips for eyes and buttons.

4. Bake at 325° for 12-15 minutes or until set. Cool for 10 minutes; carefully remove from pans to wire racks (cookies will be fragile).

5. For icing, combine shortening and vanilla in a small bowl; mix well. Gradually add 1⅓ cups confectioners' sugar; add 1 tablespoon milk. Gradually add remaining sugar and milk.

6. Pipe a band of icing on hat, cuffs at hands and feet, and down the front and at bottom of jacket. Pipe swirls of icing on tip of hat and for beard. Sprinkle nonpareils and sugar pearls over icing on hat and beard. Place a red-hot candy for mouth. Spread melted chocolate for boots. Let stand until set.

EASY ▸ No-Bake Cookie Balls

These quick bites are wonderful when you're short on time or don't want to turn on the oven.
I make them a day or two ahead to let the flavors blend.
—CARMELETTA DAILEY WINFIELD, TX

PREP: 25 MIN. • **MAKES:** 5 DOZEN

1 cup (6 ounces) semisweet
   chocolate chips
3 cups confectioners' sugar
1¾ cups crushed vanilla wafers
   (about 55 wafers)
1 cup chopped walnuts, toasted

⅓ cup orange juice
3 tablespoons light corn syrup
   Additional confectioners' sugar

1. In a large microwave-safe bowl, melt chocolate chips; stir until smooth. Stir in the confectioners' sugar, vanilla wafers, walnuts, orange juice and corn syrup.

2. Shape into 1-in. balls; roll in additional confectioners' sugar. Store in an airtight container.

ADVANCED ▸ Meringue Candy Canes

PICTURED ON PAGE 70

Stripes are all the rage this holiday season.
Show off your stylish new trick on a melt-in-your-mouth meringue cookie.
—ANNE LINDWAY INDIANAPOLIS, IN

PREP: 20 MIN. • **BAKE:** 50 MIN. + STANDING • **MAKES:** 4 DOZEN

3 egg whites
½ teaspoon cream of tartar
¾ cup sugar
¼ teaspoon peppermint extract
   Red paste food coloring

1. In a large bowl, beat egg whites until foamy. Add cream of tartar; beat on medium speed until soft peaks form. Gradually add sugar, 1 tablespoon at a time, beating on high until stiff peaks form and the sugar is dissolved, about 6 minutes. Beat in extract.

2. Cut a small hole in the corner of a pastry bag; insert star tip #21. With a new paintbrush, brush three evenly spaced ¼-in. strips of red food coloring on the inside of the bag from the tip to three-fourths of the way to the top of the bag, as shown below.

Carefully fill bag with meringue.

3. Pipe 3-in. candy canes onto parchment-lined baking sheets. Bake at 225° for 25 minutes; rotate baking sheets to a different oven rack. Bake 25 minutes longer or until firm to the touch. Turn oven off; leave cookies in oven with door ajar for at least 1 hour or until cool.

Holiday Shortbread Cookies

EASY

Using holiday cookie cutters as stencils for confectioners' sugar makes decorating these shortbreads simple and fun.
—**ERMA HILTPOLD** KERRVILLE, TX

PREP: 10 MIN.
BAKE: 35 MIN. + COOLING
MAKES: 5 DOZEN

- 5 **cups all-purpose flour**
- 1 **cup sugar**
- ½ **teaspoon salt**
- 2 **cups cold butter, cubed**

1. In a large bowl, combine flour, sugar and salt. Cut in butter until mixture resembles fine crumbs. Pat into an ungreased 15-in. x 10-in. x 1-in. baking pan. Prick all over with a fork.

2. Bake at 325° for 35 minutes or until center is set. Cool for 10-15 minutes. Cut into small squares. Continue to cool to room temperature.

The countdown to Christmas has come and gone and the whirlwind of the holiday frenzy is beginning to taper. Instead of having a mini meltdown, invite the friends you didn't get a chance to see, and wrap up the season with a new kind of meltdown—fondue!

Where there's cheese, *queso*, chocolate and more chocolate, smiles and laughter are sure to follow. It's the perfect occasion for swapping holiday highlights and sharing silly stories. Kids, too, will love dipping French bread into Pizza Fondue while dessert seekers skewer up bananas and berries for the Raspberry Fondue Dip.

SNOWFLAKE RUNNER

The chocolate may be melting, but that doesn't mean the snow is. Mimic the beauty of winter indoors—where it's warm—with a homemade snowflake table runner. See p. 88.

Kiwi Tiki Torches (p. 89)
Chocolate Almond Fondue (p. 86)

POST-HOLIDAY **MELTDOWN**

German Chocolate Fondue

We especially like this with banana dippers, but strawberries and marshmallows are equally delicious.
—**HELEN PHILLIPS** HORSEHEADS, NY

START TO FINISH: 15 MIN. • **MAKES:** 2 CUPS

⅔ cup light corn syrup
½ cup heavy whipping cream
8 ounces German sweet chocolate, chopped
    Shortbread cookies and/or assorted fruit

In a microwave-safe bowl, combine corn syrup and cream. Cover and microwave on high for 2 to 2½ minutes or until mixture just comes to a boil, stirring twice. Stir in chocolate until melted. Transfer to a fondue pot and keep warm. Serve with cookies and/or fruit.
NOTE *This recipe was tested in a 1,100-watt microwave.*

Super Sausage Dip

Although I love spicy food, I married a man who grew up in Tennessee and did not share my taste for Mexican-type food. When we moved to the Southwest, he decided to give it a chance. Now he likes foods hotter than I can handle!
—**KAYE CHRISTIANSEN** FREISTATT, MO

PREP: 15 MIN. • **COOK:** 35 MIN. • **MAKES:** 5 CUPS

1 pound bulk pork sausage
1 small onion, chopped
½ cup chopped green pepper
3 medium tomatoes, chopped
1 can (4 ounces) chopped green chilies
1 package (8 ounces) cream cheese, cubed
2 cups (16 ounces) sour cream
    Tortilla chips

1. In a large skillet, cook the sausage, onion and green pepper over medium heat until meat is no longer pink; drain.
2. Stir in tomatoes and chilies. Bring to a boil. Reduce heat; simmer, uncovered, for 30 minutes, stirring occasionally.
3. Add cream cheese; stir until melted. Stir in sour cream; heat through. (Do not boil.) Transfer to a fondue pot and keep warm. Serve with chips.

Tomato Cheddar Fondue

I serve this cheesy fondue with French bread cubes and shrimp. Every bite tastes like a little gourmet grilled cheese sandwich.
—ROBERTA ROTELLE
HONEY BROOK, PA

START TO FINISH: 30 MIN.
MAKES: 3½ CUPS

- 1 garlic clove, halved
- 6 medium tomatoes, seeded and diced
- ⅔ cup dry white wine
- 6 tablespoons butter, cubed
- 1½ teaspoons dried basil
  Dash cayenne pepper
- 2 cups (8 ounces) shredded cheddar cheese
- 1 tablespoon all-purpose flour
  Cubed French bread and cooked shrimp

1. Rub garlic clove over the bottom and sides of a fondue pot; discard garlic and set pot aside.
2. In a large saucepan, combine the tomatoes, wine, butter, basil and cayenne; bring to a simmer over medium-low heat. Reduce heat to low. Toss cheese with flour; gradually add to tomato mixture, stirring after each addition until cheese is melted.
3. Transfer to prepared fondue pot and keep warm. Serve with bread cubes and shrimp.

Pizza Fondue

It's time to rethink the way your family does pizza night. I heard about this recipe on a talk show and then personalized it by using home-canned sauce.
—**SUSAN CARLSON** PERRY, NY

START TO FINISH: 25 MIN.
MAKES: 12 SERVINGS

- ½ **pound ground beef**
- 1 **medium onion, chopped**
- 3 **cans (8 ounces each) pizza sauce, divided**
- 1½ **teaspoons fennel seed**
- 1½ **teaspoons dried oregano**
- ¼ **teaspoon garlic powder**
- 1 **tablespoon cornstarch**
- 1 **cup (4 ounces) shredded cheddar cheese**
- 1 **cup (4 ounces) shredded part-skim mozzarella cheese**
- 1 **loaf French bread, cubed**

1. In a large saucepan, cook beef and onion over medium heat until meat is no longer pink; drain. Stir in 2 cans pizza sauce and the seasonings. In a small bowl, combine cornstarch and remaining pizza sauce until blended; stir into beef mixture. Add cheddar cheese, ½ cup at a time, stirring after each addition until cheese is completely melted.
2. Transfer to a fondue pot. Stir in mozzarella cheese until melted. Serve with bread cubes.

Marinated Beef Fondue

My guests find it fun to cook their own meat and then dip it into one of two sauces—zippy horseradish or tangy barbecue.
—DEETTA RASMUSSEN FORT MADISON, IA

PREP: 20 MIN. + MARINATING • **COOK:** 5 MIN./BATCH • **MAKES:** 16 SERVINGS

¾ cup reduced-sodium soy sauce
¼ cup Worcestershire sauce
2 garlic cloves, minced
2½ pounds beef tenderloin, cut into 1-inch cubes
2½ pounds pork tenderloin, cut into 1-inch cubes

HORSERADISH SAUCE
1 cup (8 ounces) sour cream
3 tablespoons prepared horseradish
1 tablespoon chopped onion
1 teaspoon white vinegar
½ teaspoon salt
¼ teaspoon pepper

BARBECUE SAUCE
1 can (8 ounces) tomato sauce
⅓ cup steak sauce
2 tablespoons brown sugar
6 to 9 cups peanut or canola oil (for cooking)

1. In a 1-cup measure, combine soy sauce, Worcestershire sauce and garlic. Divide mixture between two large resealable plastic bags. Add beef to one bag; add pork to the second bag. Seal bags and turn to coat; refrigerate for 4 hours, turning occasionally.

2. Meanwhile, in a small bowl, combine the horseradish sauce ingredients. In another bowl, combine the tomato sauce, steak sauce and brown sugar. Cover and refrigerate sauces until serving.

3. Drain meat and discard marinade. Pat meat dry with paper towels. Using one fondue pot for every six people, heat 2-3 cups oil in each pot to 375°. With fondue forks, cook meat in oil until it reaches desired doneness. Serve with sauces.

Chili con Queso Dip

I can always count on a room full of smiles whenever I make this quick and easy dip.
—TAMMY LEIBER NAVASOTA, TX

START TO FINISH: 25 MIN. • **MAKES:** 4 CUPS

1 pound ground beef
1 medium onion, chopped
1 pound process cheese (Velveeta), cubed
2 cans (8 ounces each) tomato sauce
1 can (4 ounces) chopped green chilies
1 tablespoon Worcestershire sauce
1 to 2 teaspoons chili powder, optional
¼ to ½ teaspoon garlic powder
Tortilla or corn chips

In a large skillet, cook beef and onion over medium heat until meat is no longer pink; drain. Add the cheese, tomato sauce, green chilies, Worcestershire sauce, chili powder if desired and garlic powder; cook and stir over medium heat until cheese is melted. Transfer to a fondue pot and keep warm. Serve with chips.

UTENSIL SUBS

Most fondue pots hold up to six fondue forks. If you don't have fondue forks, use regular forks or wooden skewers. Electric fondue pots are better for oil cooking since they allow you to maintain a higher temperature. For recipes where the fondue simply needs to be warmed, you could use a small slow cooker instead.

Raspberry Fondue Dip

I delight guests with this fun, nontraditional fondue. Creamy apple butter and cinnamon red hots are the secrets to giving it a party twist. I call it my apple-merry fondue.

—EDNA HOFFMAN HEBRON, IN

START TO FINISH: 25 MIN. • **MAKES:** ABOUT 1 CUP

- 1 package (10 ounces) frozen sweetened raspberries
- 1 cup apple butter
- 1 tablespoon red-hot candies
- 2 teaspoons cornstarch
  Assorted fresh fruit

1. Thaw and drain raspberries, reserving 1 tablespoon juice. Mash raspberries. Press through a fine-mesh strainer into a small saucepan; discard seeds.

2. Add apple butter and red hots to strained raspberries; cook over medium heat until candies are dissolved, stirring occasionally.

Combine cornstarch and reserved juice until smooth; stir into berry mixture. Bring to a boil; cook and stir over medium heat for 1-2 minutes or until thickened.

3. To serve warm, transfer to a small fondue pot and keep warm. Or, to serve cold, refrigerate until chilled. Serve with fruit.

Chocolate Almond Fondue

PICTURED ON PAGE 81

Since fondue has become popular again, I've had fun searching for recipes like this, which is always requested at my get-togethers. I like to serve it with fruit and cubes of pound cake.

—ANGELA HUTTON KAPOLEI, HI

START TO FINISH: 20 MIN. • **MAKES:** ABOUT 4 CUPS

- ¾ cup heavy whipping cream
- 2 milk chocolate candy bars (4.4 ounces each), broken into small pieces
- 1 jar (7 ounces) marshmallow creme
- 3 ounces white baking chocolate, chopped
- ¼ cup chopped almonds, toasted
- 3 tablespoons amaretto or ½ teaspoon almond extract
  Assorted fresh fruit and cubed pound cake

In a heavy saucepan, heat cream over low heat until warmed. Add the chocolate, marshmallow creme and white chocolate; cook and stir until melted. Remove from the heat; stir in almonds and amaretto. Transfer to a fondue pot and keep warm. Serve with fruit and cake cubes.

NOTE *To toast nuts, spread in a 15x10x1-in. baking pan. Bake at 350° for 5-10 minutes or until lightly browned, stirring occasionally. Or, spread in a dry nonstick skillet and heat over low heat until lightly browned, stirring occasionally.*

PARTY PREP

The day before your fondue party, cut up meats and fruits (except fruit that may brown). Store in airtight containers and refrigerate perishable items. Set out fondue pots, forks and dishes. Also have salad plates, knives and forks available. A few hours before the party, cube bread and store in a resealable plastic bag. Place meats and fruits in serving containers, cover with plastic wrap and refrigerate. As guests arrive, heat fondue ingredients and set out the items to be dipped.

Three-Cheese Fondue

My youngest daughter lives in France and gave me this recipe. I love to make it for my family.
—**BETTY MANGAS** TOLEDO, OH

START TO FINISH: 30 MIN.
MAKES: 4 CUPS

½ pound each Emmenthaler, Gruyere and Jarlsberg cheeses, shredded
2 tablespoons cornstarch, divided
4 teaspoons cherry brandy
2 cups dry white wine
⅛ teaspoon ground nutmeg
⅛ teaspoon paprika
Dash cayenne pepper
Cubed French bread baguette, boiled red potatoes and/or tiny whole pickles

1. In a large bowl, combine cheeses and 1 tablespoon cornstarch. In a small bowl, combine remaining cornstarch and brandy; set aside. In a large saucepan, heat wine over medium heat until bubbles form around sides of pan.

2. Reduce heat to medium-low; add a handful of cheese mixture. Stir constantly, using a figure-eight motion, until cheese is almost completely melted. Continue adding cheese, one handful at a time, allowing cheese to almost completely melt between additions.

3. Stir brandy mixture; gradually stir into cheese mixture. Add spices; cook and stir until mixture is thickened and smooth.

4. Transfer to a fondue pot and keep warm. Serve with bread cubes, potatoes and/or pickles.

Paper Snowflake Runner

MATERIALS

Square sheets of white paper in several sizes
Sharp scissors
Hot glue gun and glue sticks or permanent glue dots

DIRECTIONS

1. Referring to the paper-folding diagram, fold each square piece of paper as directed.

2. Using sharp scissors, cut out segments on all or some sides of the triangle to form the pattern on each snowflake. You can cut out curved or angular segments. Experiment to see what shapes you like best for your snowflakes.

3. Follow Steps 1-2 to make each snowflake. For an 18-in. x 36-in. table runner, we recommend cutting about 40 snowflakes, each 3-5 in. across.

4. Once you have cut out several snowflakes, lay them on a flat surface, overlapping edges in a random pattern. Use hot glue or glue dots to adhere small overlapping areas together to form a connected runner.

NOTE *This is an excellent craft for children of appropriate ages. Be sure to assist young children with the scissors and glue. You can also substitute safety scissors and tacky glue for small children participating in the fun.*

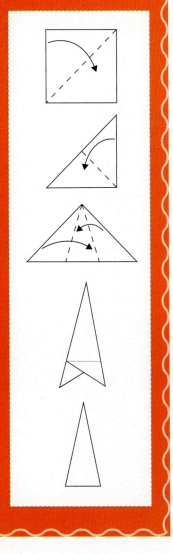

Chocolate Caramel Fondue

I need only three ingredients and 10 minutes to whip up this instant party favorite. I serve it in punch cups, so guests can carry it on a dessert plate with their choice of dippers.
—**CHERYL ARNOLD** LAKE ZURICH, IL

START TO FINISH: 10 MIN. • **MAKES:** 2½ CUPS

1 can (14 ounces) sweetened condensed milk
1 jar (12 ounces) caramel ice cream topping
3 ounces unsweetened chocolate, chopped
    Assorted fresh fruit and/or pretzels

In a small saucepan, combine the milk, caramel topping and chocolate. Cook and stir over low heat until chocolate is melted. Transfer to a fondue pot and keep warm. Serve with fruit and/or pretzels.

Kiwi Tiki Torches

PICTURED ON PAGE 80
Aloha from Texas!
This is my simple dessert recipe to dress up a meal. Toasted coconut and macadamia nuts give it a Hawaiian flair that partygoers will love.
—**ELAINE SWEET** DALLAS, TX

PREP: 30 MIN. • **COOK:** 10 MIN. • **MAKES:** 12 SERVINGS

1 fresh pineapple, peeled and cut into 1-inch chunks
4 medium kiwifruit, peeled and cut into ¾-inch chunks
2 cups fresh strawberries, halved
WHITE CHOCOLATE DIPPING SAUCE
1 cup heavy whipping cream
6 white chocolate Toblerone candy bars (3.52 ounces each), broken into pieces
¼ cup finely chopped macadamia nuts
1 to 2 teaspoons rum extract
⅓ cup flaked coconut, toasted

1. Alternately thread the pineapple, kiwi and strawberries onto 12 metal or wooden skewers; set aside. In a large saucepan over medium heat, bring cream just to a boil. Reduce heat to low; stir in Toblerone until melted. Remove from the heat; stir in nuts and extract.
2. Transfer to a fondue pot and keep warm. Sprinkle with coconut. Serve with fruit kabobs.
NOTE *To toast coconut, spread in a 15x10x1-in. baking pan. Bake at 350° for 5-10 minutes or until golden brown, stirring frequently.*

giving*thanks*

Thanksgiving offers families many special reasons to gather for a heartwarming meal. As your loved ones flock to the dinner table, treat them to the flavors of home-style cooking with these comforting recipes. And for couples celebrating a romantic feast for two, we have a festive menu custom-fit just for you.

W hen it comes to food-focused holidays and traditions, Thanksgiving trumps all. Markets enthusiastically take orders for turkeys and stock the produce aisles with sweet potatoes and parsnips. Bags of cranberries are piled into shopping carts along with pumpkin, garlic and green beans as families prepare for a day of cooking, feasting and giving thanks.

It's the meal you've been waiting for since the first chilly breeze of fall, and while millions of Americans will be dining on turkey, potatoes and pie, no two menus are created equal.

So how will you dress your menu this year? With dozens of down-home picks to choose from, customizing your menu is half the fun. But whatever you decide, we've got a game plan to keep you on schedule. See p. 94.

Make-Ahead Corn Bread Dressing (p. 104)
Roasted Orange Turkey (p. 95)
Potato Pumpkin Mash (p. 107)
Pear & Blue Cheese Salad (p. 110)

MIX & MATCH
THANKSGIVING

givingthanks | MIX & MATCH MENU

A FEW WEEKS BEFORE

- Ask your guests if they have allergies or dietary restrictions. Create a menu and find out if anyone is bringing a dish. Prepare two grocery lists: one for nonperishable items to purchase now and one for perishables to buy a few days before.

- Order a fresh turkey, or buy and freeze a frozen turkey.

- Plan your centerpiece.

FOUR TO FIVE DAYS BEFORE

- Thaw frozen turkey in a pan in refrigerator. (Allow 24 hours thawing for every 5 pounds.)

TWO TO THREE DAYS BEFORE

- Buy remaining groceries, including the fresh turkey, if ordered.

THE DAY BEFORE

- Sharpen knives, set dinner table and arrange centerpiece.

- Pull out utensils and serving dishes. (Put a note in each dish saying what food it will hold, to aid guests who want to help.)

- If making the Cider-Brined Turkey, follow the method for brining overnight.

- If making the Pumpkin Pie Cannoli, prepare the filling and store in fridge.

- Dishes such as the Make-Ahead Corn Bread Dressing can be prepped and stored in the fridge overnight.

- If you're preparing a recipe with fresh pumpkin puree or cooked squash, cook the pumpkin or squash and store it in an airtight container in the fridge.

- Toast or caramelize nuts or seeds for salads such as Roasted Butternut Squash Salad with Caramelized Pumpkin Seeds. Once cool, store in an airtight container.

THANKSGIVING DAY

- Put turkey in the oven or smoker or on grill at appropriate time.

- Prepare the trimmings of your choice.

- If making the Pumpkin Pie Cannoli, fry the shells and assemble just before serving.

- Twenty minutes before you're ready to serve, toss the salad together.

- Some desserts, such as the Thanksgiving Baked Apples, can be prepped while the turkey is baking and baked while you're eating dinner.

- Count your blessings, give thanks and eat up!

Roasted Orange Turkey

I like to bake my turkey a little differently every year, so I came up with an orange mixture to rub under the skin. It gives the meat a delicate orange flavor that tastes even better the next day.
—**BRENDA BROOKS** BOWIE, MD

PREP: 20 MIN.
BAKE: 3 HOURS + STANDING
MAKES: 12 SERVINGS

- 1 **turkey (12 to 14 pounds)**
- ½ **cup butter, softened**
- ½ **cup packed brown sugar**
- ¼ **cup grated orange peel**
- ½ **teaspoon ground ginger**
- 1 **large navel orange, quartered**
- 1 **large apple, quartered**
- 1 **small onion, quartered**
- 1 **cup unsweetened apple juice**
- ½ **cup orange juice**

1. Place turkey on a rack in a shallow roasting pan, breast side up. In a small bowl, combine the butter, brown sugar, orange peel and ginger. With fingers, carefully loosen skin from the turkey breast; rub some of the butter mixture under the skin. Secure skin to underside of breast with toothpicks.

2. Rub remaining butter mixture inside turkey cavity; fill with orange, apple and onion. Tuck wings under turkey; tie drumsticks together. Carefully pour juices over turkey.

3. Bake, uncovered, at 325° for 3 to 3¾ hours or until a thermometer inserted into thigh reads 180°, basting occasionally with pan drippings. Cover loosely with foil if turkey browns too quickly.

4. Discard toothpicks. Cover and let stand for 20 minutes before carving. Discard fruit and onion from cavity. Skim fat and thicken pan juices if desired.

Roasted Turkey with Maple Cranberry Glaze

I prepare turkey with a taste of Canada in mind. The sweet maple flavor comes through even in the breast meat. You may start to notice its caramelized color after about two hours. That's when I cover it loosely with foil while it finishes cooking. The meat will stay tender and juicy.
—**SUZANNE ANCTIL** WEST VANCOUVER, BC

PREP: 10 MIN.
BAKE: 3 HOURS + STANDING
MAKES: 12 SERVINGS

- 1 **turkey (12 to 14 pounds)**
- 1 **cup maple syrup**
- ¾ **cup whole-berry cranberry sauce**
- ¼ **cup finely chopped walnuts**

1. Place turkey on a rack in a shallow roasting pan, breast side up. Tuck wings under turkey; tie drumsticks together. In a small bowl, combine the maple syrup, cranberry sauce and walnuts. Pour over turkey.

2. Bake, uncovered, at 325° for 3 to 3¾ hours or until a thermometer inserted into thigh reads 180°, basting occasionally with pan drippings. Cover loosely with foil if turkey browns too quickly. Cover and let stand for 20 minutes before carving.

Lemon Garlic Turkey

Lemon and garlic are all you need to turn out a juicy bird for Thanksgiving. While your turkey is cooking, your kitchen will be filled with the most aromatic scent.
—**TERRY LORENZ** CRETE, IL

PREP: 10 MIN. • **BAKE:** 3 HOURS + STANDING • **MAKES:** 12 SERVINGS

1 **turkey (12 to 14 pounds)**
3 **whole garlic bulbs**
2 **medium lemons, halved**

1. Place turkey on a rack in a shallow roasting pan, breast side up. Remove papery outer skin from garlic bulbs, but do not peel or separate the cloves. Cut off top of garlic bulbs, exposing individual cloves. Place garlic and lemons inside the cavity. Tuck wings under turkey; tie drumsticks together.

2. Bake, uncovered, at 325° for 3 to 3¾ hours or until a thermometer inserted into thigh reads 180°, basting occasionally with pan drippings. Cover loosely with foil if turkey browns too quickly.

3. Remove garlic and lemons from cavity (save roasted garlic for another use). Cover and let stand for 20 minutes before carving. When lemons are cool enough to handle, squeeze juice over turkey if desired.

Thyme Roasted Turkey

It's easy for flavors to get lost when using too many seasonings together. When in doubt, a simple combination of butter and fresh thyme captures the essence of Thanksgiving for a classic turkey dinner.
—**ALMA WINBERRY** GREAT FALLS, MT

PREP: 15 MIN. • **BAKE:** 3 HOURS + STANDING • **MAKES:** 12 SERVINGS

⅓ **cup unsalted butter, softened**
3 **tablespoons minced fresh thyme**
1 **teaspoon salt**
¼ **teaspoon pepper**
1 **turkey (12 to 14 pounds)**

1. In a small bowl, mix the butter, thyme, salt and pepper. Place turkey on a rack in a shallow roasting pan, breast side up. With fingers, carefully loosen skin from turkey breast; rub half of the butter mixture under the skin. Secure skin to underside of breast with toothpicks. Rub outside of turkey with remaining butter mixture. Tuck wings under turkey; tie drumsticks together.

2. Bake, uncovered, at 325° for 3 to 3¾ hours or until a thermometer inserted into thigh reads 180°, basting occasionally with pan drippings. Cover loosely with foil if turkey browns too quickly.

3. Discard toothpicks. Cover and let stand for 20 minutes before carving.

PROS & CONS OF FRESH VS. FROZEN TURKEY

FRESH
Pros: Don't need to thaw; rarely self-basting; more options to choose from, including heritage breeds and locally raised; many people prefer a fresh bird's natural taste and texture.
Cons: Higher cost; must use quickly; most need to be ordered ahead.

FROZEN
Pros: Lower cost; can buy in advance to take advantage of sales and coupons.
Cons: Needs to thaw for several days; almost all are self-basting; limited breed choice.

TIP Self-basting turkeys should not be used for brining or deep-frying. Self-basting turkeys are injected with a solution that includes some combination of broth, water, salt, seasoning and fat. This produces a juicier bird, but can also cause a mushy texture.

Cider-Brined Turkey

My family had been going through some rough times, and when we were finally able to get together for Thanksgiving one year, I made this turkey. It brings back such good memories of joyful family gatherings.
—**NICOLE KELLER** WATERFORD, PA

PREP: 50 MIN. + MARINATING
BAKE: 3½ HOURS + STANDING
MAKES: 18 SERVINGS

- 1 **gallon apple cider or juice**
- 1¾ **cups kosher salt**
- 1 **cup sugar**
- 1 **tablespoon dried minced onion**
- 1 **tablespoon whole peppercorns**
- 2 **garlic cloves, minced**
- 1 **teaspoon crushed juniper berries**
- 1 **teaspoon dried marjoram**
- 1 **teaspoon dried sage leaves**
- 1 **teaspoon dried thyme**
- 3 **bottles (12 ounces each) dark beer, chilled**
- 6 **cans (14½ ounces each) chicken broth, chilled**
- 2 **turkey-size oven roasting bags**
- 1 **turkey (18 to 20 pounds)**
- ½ **cup butter, melted**
- ½ **teaspoon salt**
- ½ **teaspoon pepper**

1. In a stockpot, combine the first 10 ingredients. Bring to a boil; cook and stir until salt and sugar are dissolved. Remove from the heat. Add cold beer and broth to cool the brine to room temperature.

2. Place one turkey-size oven roasting bag inside the other. Place turkey inside both bags; pour in cooled brine. Seal bags, pressing out as much air as possible; turn to coat turkey. Place in a shallow roasting pan. Refrigerate for 18-24 hours, turning occasionally.

3. Remove turkey from brine; rinse and pat dry. Discard brine. Tuck wings under turkey; tie drumsticks together. Place on a rack in a shallow roasting pan, breast side up. Brush with melted butter; sprinkle with salt and pepper.

4. Bake, uncovered, at 325° for 3½ to 4 hours or until a thermometer inserted into thigh reads 180°, basting occasionally with pan drippings. Cover loosely with foil if turkey browns too quickly. Cover and let stand for 20 minutes before carving.
NOTE *It is best not to use a prebasted turkey for this recipe.*

Roast Turkey with Cider Gravy

We even used this basting sauce one year while camping on Thanksgiving Day and baked the turkey in a pan on the grill. It's such a great mix of ingredients!
—**KATHY KIRKLAND** MARYVILLE, TN

PREP: 25 MIN. • **BAKE:** 3 HOURS+ STANDING • **MAKES:** 12 SERVINGS (4 CUPS GRAVY)

- 1 quart apple cider
- 1 can (12 ounces) lemon-lime soda
- ½ cup chopped onion
- ½ cup chopped celery
- ¼ cup marinade for chicken
- 1 tablespoon Mrs. Dash Garlic & Herb seasoning blend
- 1 tablespoon Creole seasoning
- ¼ teaspoon dried thyme
- ¼ teaspoon dried rosemary, crushed
- 1 turkey (12 to 14 pounds)
- ¼ cup butter, softened
- ½ teaspoon salt
- ½ teaspoon pepper
- 1 tablespoon cornstarch
- 1 tablespoon cold water

1. In a large saucepan, combine the first nine ingredients; bring to a boil. Cook for 30 minutes or until mixture is reduced by almost half, about 4 cups. Strain, discarding vegetables.

2. Meanwhile, pat turkey dry. Rub butter over the outside and inside of turkey. Sprinkle salt and pepper over the outside and inside cavity. Place on a rack in a shallow roasting pan, breast side up.

3. Bake at 325° for 3 to 3¾ hours or until a thermometer inserted into thigh reads 180°, basting every 30 minutes with reduced cider mixture. Cover loosely with foil if turkey browns too quickly. Cover and let stand for 20 minutes before carving.

4. Pour drippings and loosened brown bits from roasting pan into a small saucepan; skim fat. Combine cornstarch and water until smooth; stir into drippings. Bring to a boil; cook and stir for 1-2 minutes or until thickened. Serve with turkey.

NOTE *This recipe was tested with Lea & Perrins Marinade for Chicken.*

Turkey Giblet Gravy

My mother used to make this old-fashioned, Southern-style gravy every holiday, and now I make it for my family. It's a tasty variation of a giblet gravy. You might be surprised how much you like it.
—**DUNYA JOHNSON** ROCHESTER, NY

START TO FINISH: 20 MIN. • **MAKES:** 1¾ CUPS

- Turkey giblets (liver and neck removed), chopped
- 1 carton (15 ounces) chicken stock
- ¼ teaspoon salt
- ¼ teaspoon pepper
- 4 hard-cooked eggs, finely chopped
- 2 tablespoons all-purpose flour

1. In a large saucepan, combine the giblets, chicken stock, salt and pepper. Bring to a boil; boil for 5-6 minutes. Remove from the heat. Strain giblets; return cooking juices to pan. Set aside 2 tablespoons juices. Finely chop giblets; add giblets and eggs to pan. Cook and stir for 1 minute.

2. In a small bowl, combine flour and reserved cooking juices; gradually stir into pan. Cook and stir 5-7 minutes longer or until thickened.

Mushroom Sour Cream Gravy

PICTURED ON PAGE 95

My grandma made this gravy every Thanksgiving to drizzle over sliced turkey and stuffing. When I have leftover turkey and mushroom gravy, I chop the turkey into small pieces and add it to the gravy. I serve it over a piece of bread, open-faced style.

—JOY MELLWIG NAPLES, FL

PREP: 15 MIN. • **COOK:** 25 MIN. • **MAKES:** ABOUT 4½ CUPS

1 pound small fresh mushrooms, thinly sliced
6 tablespoons butter, divided
1 large onion, finely chopped
2 celery ribs, chopped
⅓ cup all-purpose flour
¾ teaspoon salt
¾ teaspoon pepper
2 cups water
½ cup sour cream

1. In a large skillet, saute mushrooms in 3 tablespoons butter in batches; set aside. In the same pan, saute onion and celery in 1 tablespoon butter. Add the flour, salt, pepper and remaining butter; cook and stir until smooth.

2. Gradually add water. Bring to a boil; cook and stir for 2 minutes or until thickened. Stir in mushrooms and heat through. Remove from the heat; stir in sour cream.

Apple Butter & Onion Gravy

PICTURED ON PAGE 106

This gravy is so creamy and good I could eat it like soup. But it's best draped over mashed potatoes and other Thanksgiving fixings. For reheating the next day, if it's too thick, just stir in a bit of milk.

—MINDIE HILTON SUSANVILLE, CA

PREP: 15 MIN. • **COOK:** 25 MIN. • **MAKES:** 4½ CUPS

1 large sweet onion, finely chopped
3 tablespoons butter
1 tablespoon all-purpose flour
½ teaspoon salt
½ teaspoon garlic powder
½ teaspoon poultry seasoning
½ teaspoon pepper
¼ cup cornstarch
4 cups chicken stock

4 ounces cream cheese, cubed and softened
¼ cup apple butter

1. In a large saucepan, saute onion in butter. Stir in flour and seasonings. Whisk cornstarch and chicken stock until smooth; gradually stir into onion mixture. Bring to a boil; cook and stir for

2 minutes or until thickened. Cool slightly.

2. Transfer to a blender; cover and process until smooth. Return all to pan and heat through. Stir in cream cheese and apple butter; cook and stir just until blended.

MAKE YOUR OWN APPLE BUTTER

Peel and quarter 6 medium apples. Then place ¾ cup unsweetened apple cider or juice, ⅓ cup sugar, 1 teaspoon ground cinnamon and ¼ teaspoon ground cloves in a blender and blend, adding 3-4 apple pieces at a time until smooth. Pour into saucepan and bring to a boil. Reduce heat to low, cover and cook for 1 hour. Uncover and cook 1 more hour until thick. Store in airtight containers in the refrigerator. Makes 2 cups.

Foolproof Gravy

Make your Thanksgiving or other special-occasion dinner easy with this can't-miss recipe. Use the drippings from your roasted turkey, and the gravy is done in just 20 minutes.

—EDIE DESPAIN

LOGAN, UT

START TO FINISH: 20 MIN.
MAKES: 2⅓ CUPS

Drippings from 1 roasted turkey
½ **to 1 cup turkey or chicken broth**
¼ **cup plus 1 tablespoon all-purpose flour**
½ **cup fat-free milk**
1 **teaspoon chicken bouillon granules**
¼ **teaspoon poultry seasoning**
⅛ **teaspoon white pepper**

1. Pour drippings into a 2-cup measuring cup. Skim and discard fat. Add enough broth to the drippings to measure 2 cups; transfer to a small saucepan and bring to a boil.
2. In a small bowl, whisk flour and milk until smooth; gradually stir into drippings mixture. Stir in the bouillon granules, poultry seasoning and white pepper. Return to a boil, stirring constantly; cook and stir for 2 minutes or until thickened.

Pancetta Brioche Dressing

I crave this creamy and crunchy stuffing every year. And I suspect my guests do, too. It's usually gone before the turkey!
—**JAMIE BROWN-MILLER**
NAPA, CA

PREP: 15 MIN. • **BAKE:** 25 MIN.
MAKES: 12 CUPS (¾ CUP EACH)

- 16 **cups cubed brioche bread (about 1¾ pounds)**
- 2 **cups diced red onions**
- ¼ **teaspoon kosher salt**
- ⅛ **teaspoon pepper**
- 2 **tablespoons olive oil**
- 2 **cups chopped radicchio**
- 1½ **cups chicken broth**
- 5 **ounces pancetta, diced**
- 2 **eggs, lightly beaten**
- 2 **tablespoons minced fresh rosemary**
- ¼ **cup crumbled Roquefort or blue cheese**

1. Spread bread cubes on a baking sheet. Bake at 400° for 6-8 minutes or until dried (do not brown); set aside.

2. Meanwhile, in a large skillet, cook the onions, salt and pepper in oil over medium-high heat until onions begin to brown. Stir in radicchio; remove from the heat.

3. In a large bowl, combine the bread cubes, radicchio mixture, chicken broth, pancetta, eggs and rosemary; gently toss. Transfer to a greased 13-in. x 9-in. baking dish. Sprinkle with cheese. Bake, uncovered, at 400° for 25-30 minutes or until golden brown.

Vegetarian Dressing

PICTURED ON PAGE 104

Feast your eyes on this two-toned pumpernickel dressing.
It's my vegetarian version of the classic Thanksgiving staple.

—THOMAS ROEGER BLOOMINGTON, IN

PREP: 40 MIN. • **BAKE:** 35 MIN. • **MAKES:** 12 SERVINGS

- 8 slices pumpernickel bread, cubed (about 6 cups)
- 8 slices whole wheat bread, cubed (about 6 cups)
- 6 celery ribs, thinly sliced
- 1 large onion, chopped
- ¼ cup butter, cubed
- ½ cup dried cranberries
- 1 teaspoon salt
- 1 teaspoon dried rosemary, crushed
- 1 teaspoon dried thyme
- 1 teaspoon rubbed sage
- 1 teaspoon poultry seasoning
- ½ teaspoon pepper
- 2 cups vegetable stock

1. Place bread cubes in an ungreased 15-in. x 10-in. x 1-in. baking pan. Bake at 350° for 15 minutes, stirring twice. Set aside.

2. Meanwhile, in a large skillet, cook celery and onion in butter over medium heat until tender. Stir in the cranberries, salt, rosemary, thyme, sage, poultry seasoning and pepper; cook 2 minutes longer.

3. In a large bowl, combine bread cubes and celery mixture. Add stock and combine.

4. Transfer to a greased 13-in. x 9-in. baking dish. Cover and bake at 350° for 25 minutes. Uncover; bake 10-15 minutes longer or until lightly browned.

Pumpkin Bread & Pear Stuffing

Pumpkin quick bread and ginger ale give this stuffing a fun fall flavor. For me, this dish represents all the sweet and spicy aromas of Thanksgiving.

—CLAUDIA DIONNE NASHUA, NH

PREP: 20 MIN. • **BAKE:** 35 MIN. • **MAKES:** 16 SERVINGS (¾ CUP EACH)

- 3 medium pears, peeled and chopped
- 1 medium onion, chopped
- ⅓ cup butter, cubed
- 11 cups seasoned stuffing cubes
- 4 cups cubed pumpkin quick bread (about 12 ounces)
- 2¼ cups chicken broth
- 1 cup ginger ale

1. In a large skillet, saute pears and onion in butter until tender. Transfer to a large bowl. Add the stuffing cubes, bread cubes, broth and ginger ale; toss gently to coat. Transfer to a greased 13-in. x 9-in. baking dish.

2. Cover and bake at 350° for 20 minutes. Uncover; bake 15-20 minutes longer or until heated through.

Make-Ahead Corn Bread Dressing

Being from California, my family members have always been big veggie eaters. I wanted to share a little taste of home with my in-laws, so I created this dish for Thanksgiving. You don't have to let it sit overnight, but it's a nice make-ahead option and the flavors mesh more that way.
—**PATRICIA BROUSSARD** LAFAYETTE, LA

PREP: 1½ HOURS + CHILLING
BAKE: 55 MIN.
MAKES: 14 SERVINGS (¾ CUP EACH)

- 1 **medium spaghetti squash (about 4 pounds)**
- 1 **package (8½ ounces) corn bread/muffin mix**
- 1 **medium onion, finely chopped**
- 2 **celery ribs, thinly sliced**
- ½ **cup butter, cubed**
- 2 **garlic cloves, minced**
- ½ **pound bulk pork sausage, cooked and drained**
- 1 **cup frozen corn**
- 2 **tablespoons poultry seasoning**
- ¾ **teaspoon salt**
- ¼ **teaspoon pepper**
- 1 **cup chopped walnuts, toasted**
- 1 **cup chicken broth**
- ¼ **cup grated Parmesan cheese**

1. Cut squash lengthwise in half; remove and discard seeds. Place squash in a roasting pan, cut side down; add ½ in. of hot water. Bake, uncovered, at 375° for 45 minutes. Drain water from pan; turn squash cut side up. Bake 5 minutes longer or until squash is tender.

2. Prepare and bake corn bread mix according to package directions, using an 8-in.-square baking dish. Cool to room temperature; crumble bread. Place in an ungreased 13-in. x 9-in. baking pan. Bake at 350° for 8-13 minutes or until lightly browned, stirring twice.

3. In a large skillet, cook onion and celery in butter over medium heat for 4 minutes. Add garlic; cook 2 minutes longer. Stir in the sausage, corn, poultry seasoning, salt and pepper; heat through.

4. When squash is cool enough to handle, use a fork to separate strands. In a large bowl, combine the sausage mixture, corn bread, squash and walnuts. Stir in broth.

5. Transfer to a greased 13-in. x 9-in. baking dish. Cover and refrigerate for 8 hours or overnight. Remove from the refrigerator 30 minutes before baking. Cover and bake at 350° for 45 minutes. Uncover; sprinkle with cheese; bake 10-15 minutes longer or until heated through.

Artichoke Sausage Stuffing

I use spinach and artichoke dip to add creaminess and keep my stuffing from getting dry. Add to that sun-dried tomatoes and basil and this dish takes on a fresh Italian twist.
—**SALLY SIBTHORPE** SHELBY TOWNSHIP, MI

PREP: 15 MIN. • **BAKE:** 35 MIN. • **MAKES:** 13 CUPS

- 12 cups cubed day-old Italian bread
- 1 pound bulk Italian sausage
- 1 large onion, chopped
- ¾ cup finely chopped oil-packed sun-dried tomatoes
- 2 garlic cloves, minced
- ¼ cup butter, cubed
- 2 cups spinach and artichoke dip
- 1½ cups chicken stock
- 3 eggs
- ¼ cup chopped fresh parsley
- 2 tablespoons chopped fresh basil leaves
- 1 teaspoon salt
- ½ teaspoon pepper

1. Place bread cubes in large bowl; set aside. Crumble sausage into a large skillet; cook over medium heat until no longer pink; drain.

2. In the same skillet, cook the onion, tomatoes and garlic in butter for 4-5 minutes or until vegetables are tender. Add to bread mixture; stir in sausage.

3. In small bowl, combine artichoke dip, chicken stock, eggs, parsley, basil, salt and pepper. Pour over bread mixture; toss to combine.

4. Transfer to a greased 13-in. x 9-in. baking dish. Cover and bake at 350° for 20 minutes. Uncover and bake 15-20 minutes longer or until golden brown.

Herbed Garlic Mashed Potatoes

I call these the best mashed potatoes ever! The first time I made them was for Thanksgiving a few years ago. Everyone loved them so much that now whenever my family wants mashed potatoes for dinner, I make them this way.
—**SANDRA STOUT** SATELLITE BEACH, FL

PREP: 20 MIN. • **COOK:** 20 MIN. • **MAKES:** 12 SERVINGS (¾ CUP EACH)

- 10 medium Yukon Gold potatoes, peeled and cut into chunks (about 5 pounds)
- 4 garlic cloves, minced
- 2 tablespoons butter
- 1 tablespoon minced fresh thyme
- 1 tablespoon minced fresh rosemary
- 1½ teaspoons salt
- ¾ teaspoon pepper
- ½ cup heavy whipping cream
- ¼ to ⅓ cup 2% milk

1. Place potatoes in a Dutch oven and cover with water. Bring to a boil. Reduce heat; cover and cook for 15-20 minutes or until tender. Drain and return to pan.

2. Add garlic, butter, herbs, salt and pepper; mash potatoes. Gradually add cream and enough milk to reach desired consistency.

THANKSGIVING SHEPHERD'S PIE

Quickly turn leftovers into a shepherd's pie: In a greased 2-qt. baking dish, layer 2 cups cooked turkey, ¾ cup gravy, 1 cup shredded carrots, 2 cups prepared stuffing and 1 can (15¼ ounces) whole kernel corn, drained. Top with 2 cups warm mashed potatoes and bake, uncovered, at 325° for 45-50 minutes or until edges of potatoes are browned. Serves 4-5.

Spiced Sweet Potato Mash

One year my flight was canceled as I was traveling home. I finally arrived at 1 a.m. the morning of our holiday get-together. I was terribly tired when I woke up to prepare this dish, but it felt so good when I saw everyone smiling and enjoying what I'd made.

—ALLISON BRUMMET GLENARM, IL

START TO FINISH: 30 MIN.
MAKES: 10 SERVINGS

- 2 **pounds sweet potatoes, peeled and cubed**
- 1 **package (8 ounces) cream cheese, softened**
- ½ **cup 2% milk**
- ¼ **cup packed brown sugar**
- 1½ **teaspoons ground cinnamon**
- ½ **teaspoon salt**
- ½ **teaspoon ground ginger**
- ½ **teaspoon ground nutmeg**
- ¼ **teaspoon ground cardamom**
- ½ **cup chopped pecans, toasted**

1. Place sweet potatoes in a large saucepan; cover with water. Bring to a boil. Reduce heat; cover and cook for 15-20 minutes or until tender. Drain.

2. In a large bowl, mash potatoes. Add the cream cheese, milk, brown sugar and seasonings; beat until smooth. Top with pecans.

Parmesan-Romano Mashed Potatoes

My sister hates mashed potatoes, but for whatever reason, she likes when I prepare them this way. Boiling the potatoes with bay leaves gives them an extra herbed flavor without being overpowering.
—**SARAH CHRISTENSON** SAN DIEGO, CA

PREP: 20 MIN. • **COOK:** 15 MIN. • **MAKES:** 12 SERVINGS (¾ CUP EACH)

5 pounds potatoes, peeled and cubed
3 vegetable bouillon cubes
2 bay leaves
¾ cup heavy whipping cream
½ cup butter, cubed
1½ cups shredded Parmesan cheese
1½ cups shredded Romano cheese
1 garlic clove, minced
½ teaspoon salt
½ teaspoon pepper
½ teaspoon each dried basil, marjoram, oregano, tarragon and thyme

1. Place potatoes in a Dutch oven and cover with water. Add bouillon and bay leaves. Bring to a boil. Reduce heat; cover and cook for 10-15 minutes or until tender.
2. Drain potatoes; discard bay leaves. Mash potatoes with cream and butter. Stir in the cheeses, garlic and seasonings.

Potato Pumpkin Mash

PICTURED ON PAGE 93

I swirl fresh pumpkin into potatoes for a little extra holiday color.
No more plain white potatoes for us!
—**MICHELLE MEDLEY** DALLAS, TX

PREP: 20 MIN. • **COOK:** 25 MIN. • **MAKES:** 8 SERVINGS

8 cups cubed peeled pie pumpkin (about 2 pounds)
8 medium Yukon Gold potatoes, peeled and cubed (about 2 pounds)
½ to ¾ cup 2% milk, divided
8 tablespoons butter, softened, divided
1 teaspoon salt, divided
1 tablespoon olive oil
¼ teaspoon coarsely ground pepper

1. Place pumpkin in a large saucepan; add water to cover. Bring to a boil. Reduce heat; cook, uncovered, for 20-25 minutes or until tender.
2. Meanwhile, place potatoes in another saucepan; add water to cover. Bring to a boil. Reduce heat; cook, uncovered, for 10-15 minutes or until tender.
3. Drain potatoes; return to pan. Mash potatoes, adding ¼ cup milk, 4 tablespoons butter and ½ teaspoon salt. Add additional milk if needed to reach desired consistency. Transfer to a serving bowl; keep warm.
4. Drain pumpkin; return to pan. Mash pumpkin, gradually adding the remaining butter and salt and enough remaining milk to reach desired consistency; spoon evenly over the potatoes. Cut through mashed vegetables with a spoon or knife to swirl. Drizzle with olive oil; sprinkle with pepper. Serve immediately.

Smashed Potatoes Portobello

Having invited some friends for dinner, I decided I wanted to do something different with the potatoes. We all love portobello mushrooms, so I came up with the idea for Smashed Potatoes Portobello, and each of us thought it was a hit!
—**PATRICIA MANGUM** SIERRA VISTA, AZ

PREP: 35 MIN. • **BAKE:** 25 MIN. • **MAKES:** 12 SERVINGS (⅔ CUP EACH)

- 4 **pounds medium red potatoes, peeled and quartered**
- ½ **pound baby portobello mushrooms, chopped**
- 2 **garlic cloves, minced**
- 2 **tablespoons butter**
- 1 **tablespoon olive oil**
- 6 **green onions, chopped**
- ¾ **teaspoon salt**
- ¼ **teaspoon freshly ground pepper**
- ½ **cup butter, cubed**
- ½ **cup heavy whipping cream**

1. Place potatoes in a Dutch oven and cover with water. Bring to a boil. Reduce heat; cover and cook for 10-15 minutes or until tender.

2. Meanwhile, in a large skillet, saute mushrooms and garlic in butter and oil until tender. Stir in the green onions, salt and pepper.

3. Drain potatoes; return to pan. Mash, gradually adding the cubed butter, cream and mushroom mixture. Transfer to a greased 13-in. x 9-in. baking dish. Bake, uncovered, at 350° for 25-30 minutes or until heated through.

Mashed Potatoes with Garlic-Olive Oil

Garlic mashed potatoes are high on our love list. To intensify the flavor, I combine garlic and olive oil in the food processor and drizzle it on top of the potatoes.
—**EMORY DOTY** JASPER, GA

START TO FINISH: 30 MIN. • **MAKES:** 12 SERVINGS (¾ CUP EACH)

- 4 **pounds red potatoes, quartered**
- ½ **cup olive oil**
- 2 **garlic cloves**
- ⅔ **cup heavy whipping cream**
- ¼ **cup butter, softened**
- 2 **teaspoons salt**
- ½ **teaspoon pepper**
- ⅔ to ¾ **cup whole milk**
- 3 **green onions, chopped**
- ¾ **cup grated Parmesan cheese, optional**

1. Place potatoes in a Dutch oven; add water to cover. Bring to a boil. Reduce heat; cook, uncovered, for 15-20 minutes or until tender. Meanwhile, place oil and garlic in a small food processor; process until blended.

2. Drain potatoes; return to pan. Mash potatoes, gradually adding cream, butter, salt, pepper and enough milk to reach desired consistency. Stir in green onions. Serve with garlic olive oil and, if desired, cheese.

NOTE *For food safety purposes, prepare garlic olive oil just before serving; do not store leftover oil mixture.*

Loaded Smashed Potatoes

I love garlic, onions and bacon, and this dish has all three! After all, if mashed potatoes are a must at your family Thanksgiving, then why not go all out with the works?

—**KATHY HARDING** RICHMOND, MO

PREP: 40 MIN. • **BAKE:** 10 MIN.
MAKES: 15 SERVINGS

- 2 **whole garlic bulbs**
- 1 **tablespoon canola oil**
- 8 **bacon strips**
- 3 **green onions, chopped**
- 4 **pounds small red potatoes**
- 1 **container (16 ounces) sour cream**
- 1½ **cups (6 ounces) shredded cheddar cheese, divided**
- ⅓ **cup butter, softened**
- ¼ **cup 2% milk**
- ½ **teaspoon salt**
- ¼ **teaspoon pepper**
  Minced chives, optional

1. Remove papery outer skin from garlic (do not peel or separate cloves). Cut top off of garlic bulb. Brush with oil. Wrap each bulb in heavy-duty foil.

2. Bake at 425° for 30-35 minutes or until softened. Cool for 10 minutes.

3. Meanwhile, in a large skillet, cook bacon over medium heat until crisp. Remove to paper towels; drain, reserving 2 tablespoons drippings. In the same skillet, cook onions in reserved drippings for 2 minutes or until tender; set aside. Crumble bacon.

4. Place potatoes in a large saucepan and cover with water. Bring to a boil. Reduce heat; cover and cook for 10-15 minutes or until tender. Drain and transfer to a large bowl.

5. Mash potatoes. Squeeze softened garlic over top. Stir in the bacon, onions with drippings, sour cream, 1 cup cheese, butter, milk, salt and pepper; combine. Spoon mixture into a greased 13-in. x 9-in. baking dish; top with remaining cheese.

6. Bake, uncovered, at 350° for 10-15 minutes or until cheese is melted. Garnish with chives if desired.

Roasted Butternut Squash Salad with Caramelized Pumpkin Seeds

We had leftover roasted butternut squash one night, so I threw it on a salad and topped it with cheese. My family loved it! Since then we've added caramelized pumpkin seeds (my brother's idea) and a homemade dressing.

—NICOLE SADOWSKY RANCHO SANTA FE, CA

PREP: 30 MIN. • **BAKE:** 30 MIN. • **MAKES:** 8 SERVINGS

- 8 cups cubed peeled butternut squash
- 2 tablespoons olive oil
- ½ teaspoon salt
- ¼ teaspoon coarsely ground pepper

PUMPKIN SEEDS
- ⅓ cup fresh pumpkin seeds
- 1 teaspoon olive oil
- 2 teaspoons brown sugar
- 1 teaspoon balsamic vinegar
- ¼ teaspoon salt

DRESSING
- 3 tablespoons balsamic vinegar
- 3 tablespoons olive oil
- 1 shallot, finely chopped
- 4 teaspoons Dijon mustard
- ¼ teaspoon salt
- ¼ teaspoon coarsely ground pepper
- 1 package (10 ounces) fresh baby spinach
- ½ cup crumbled Gorgonzola cheese

1. Place squash in a greased 15-in. x 10-in. x 1-in. baking pan. Drizzle with oil and sprinkle with salt and pepper; toss to coat. Bake, uncovered, at 400° for 30-35 minutes or until tender, stirring occasionally.

2. In a large dry skillet, heat pumpkin seeds over medium heat for 4-6 minutes or just until seeds are golden brown, stirring constantly. Reduce heat to low. Add oil to seeds; toss to coat. Stir in the brown sugar, vinegar and salt. Cook and stir until brown sugar is melted and seeds are coated. Cool on waxed paper.

3. In a small bowl, whisk the first six dressing ingredients. Combine spinach and cheese; drizzle with dressing. Toss to coat. Transfer to a serving platter. Top with squash; sprinkle with pumpkin seeds.

Pear & Blue Cheese Salad

PICTURED ON PAGE 93

Always a reliable combination, sweet fruit, strong cheese and nuts over greens are the makings of a special-occasion salad.
—TASTE OF HOME TEST KITCHEN

START TO FINISH: 10 MIN. • **MAKES:** 10 SERVINGS

- 12 cups torn romaine
- ⅔ cup balsamic vinaigrette
- 2 medium pears, sliced
- ⅔ cup crumbled blue cheese
- ⅔ cup glazed pecans

Place romaine in a large bowl. Drizzle with vinaigrette; toss to coat. Top with pears, cheese and pecans. Serve immediately.

DIY DRESSING

If you don't have balsamic vinaigrette, try making your own dressing. In a bowl or jar with a tight-fitting lid, combine ½ cup white wine vinegar, ½ cup olive oil, 2 garlic cloves, minced, ½ teaspoon each of salt and pepper and 1 teaspoon dill weed. Mix or shake until well blended. Makes about 8 servings.

Pumpkin Soup with Sourdough Sage Croutons

We love soup in our home, and I'm a big fan of creamy-style soups. This Thanksgiving-inspired dish has all the traditional scents that fill the air during the holiday season. If you don't have pumpkin, you could also make this with butternut squash.

—JENN TIDWELL FAIR OAKS, CA

PREP: 35 MIN. • **COOK:** 30 MIN.
MAKES: 10 SERVINGS
(2½ QUARTS, 2 CUPS CROUTONS,
½ CUP SWEET CREAM)

- 1 **large onion, chopped**
- 2 **medium carrots, thinly sliced**
- 3 **tablespoons olive oil**
- 9 **cups cubed fresh pumpkin**
- 3 **cans (14½ ounces each) chicken broth**
- 2 **tablespoons minced fresh sage**
- 1½ **teaspoons garlic powder**
- ½ **teaspoon salt**
- ½ **teaspoon pepper**
- ⅛ **teaspoon ground nutmeg**

SWEET CREAM
- 1 **package (3 ounces) cream cheese, softened**
- ¼ **cup 2% milk**
- 2 **tablespoons confectioners' sugar**

CROUTONS
- 3 **slices sourdough bread, cubed**
- 2 **tablespoons olive oil**
- 2 **tablespoons butter, melted**
- 2 **tablespoons minced fresh sage**

1. In a Dutch oven, saute onion and carrots in oil for 5 minutes. Add pumpkin; cook 5-6 minutes longer. Stir in the broth, sage, garlic powder, salt, pepper and nutmeg; bring to a boil. Reduce heat; cover and simmer for 15-20 minutes or until pumpkin is tender.

2. Cool slightly. In a blender, process soup in batches until smooth. Return all to pan and heat through.

3. For sweet cream, combine ingredients until smooth. For croutons, place bread in a small bowl; drizzle with oil and butter. Sprinkle with sage and toss to coat. Transfer to a small skillet; cook and stir over medium heat for 4-6 minutes or until lightly toasted.

4. Garnish servings with sweet cream and croutons.

Maple-Glazed Parsnips on Kale

This recipe is special to me because it allows me to use delicious farm-fresh produce in a way my family loves.

—CHRISTINE WENDLAND
BROWNS MILLS, NJ

PREP: 20 MIN. • **COOK:** 25 MIN.
MAKES: 6 SERVINGS

- ¼ cup plus 1 tablespoon unsalted butter, divided
- 2 pounds medium parsnips, cut into ½-in. slices
- ⅔ cup maple syrup
- 1 medium shallot, thinly sliced
- 1 pound kale, stems removed, cut into 1-in. strips
- ½ teaspoon salt
- 1 tablespoon apple cider or juice

1. In a large skillet, melt ¼ cup butter over medium heat. Add parsnips and maple syrup. Cook, uncovered, for 15-20 minutes or until syrup is almost evaporated and parsnips are caramelized, stirring frequently.

2. Meanwhile, in a Dutch oven, melt remaining butter over medium heat. Add shallot; cook for 4-5 minutes or until tender. Add kale; sprinkle with salt. Cook and stir for 3-5 minutes or until slightly wilted. Add cider; reduce heat to low. Cover and steam for 5 minutes.

3. To serve, spoon kale onto a large plate; top with parsnips.

Apricot-Apple Cranberry Sauce

PICTURED AT LEFT

Though I prefer this as a side dish, my sister swears it makes the best topping in the world for a slice of Thanksgiving turkey.

—AYSHA SCHURMAN AMMON, ID

PREP: 15 MIN. • **COOK:** 15 MIN. + CHILLING • **MAKES:** 5 CUPS

- 4 **cups fresh or frozen cranberries**
- 1⅔ **cups sugar**
- 1⅔ **cups water**
- ¾ **cup orange juice**
- ¼ **cup chopped dried apricots**
- ¼ **cup chopped dried apples**
- ¼ **cup dried cranberries**
- 1 **teaspoon grated lemon peel**
- 1 **teaspoon grated orange peel**

In a large saucepan, combine the first seven ingredients. Cook over medium heat until berries pop, about 15 minutes. Remove from the heat; stir in lemon and orange peels. Transfer to a bowl; refrigerate until chilled.

Roasted Brussels Sprouts & Apples

Brussels sprouts are one of our favorite vegetables, especially when roasted together with tart apples, such as Granny Smith. Topped with toasted nuts and feta cheese, this is an attractive dish for us to serve during the holidays.

—BARBARA ESTABROOK RHINELANDER, WI

START TO FINISH: 30 MIN. • **MAKES:** 8 SERVINGS

- 1½ **pounds fresh Brussels sprouts, trimmed and quartered**
- 1½ **cups cubed tart apples**
- 2 **tablespoons plus 1 teaspoon olive oil, divided**
- ½ **teaspoon salt**
- ¼ **teaspoon pepper**
- ½ **cup crumbled feta cheese**
- ⅓ **cup toasted walnuts, coarsely chopped**

1. In a large bowl, combine the Brussels sprouts and apples. Drizzle with 2 tablespoons oil; toss to coat. Transfer to a greased 15-in. x 10-in. x 1-in. baking pan.

2. Bake, uncovered, at 400° for 15-20 minutes or until tender, stirring occasionally. Transfer to a serving bowl; sprinkle with salt and pepper. Top with cheese and walnuts; drizzle with the remaining oil.

Holiday Glazed Carrots

When I took over the holiday cooking in my house a few years ago, these brandy-glazed carrots became a new Thanksgiving tradition.
—**PAM FOX** DANE, WI

PREP/TOTAL 25 MIN. • **MAKES:** 8 SERVINGS

- 2 **pounds fresh baby carrots**
- 2 **tablespoons sugar**
- 2 **teaspoons salt**
- **GLAZE**
- 3 **tablespoons butter**
- 3 **tablespoons brandy**
- 3 **tablespoons honey**
- 1 **tablespoon brown sugar**

1. Place the carrots, sugar and salt in a large saucepan; add 1 in. of water. Bring to a boil. Reduce heat; cover and simmer for 8-10 minutes or until crisp-tender. Drain and set aside.

2. In the same pan, combine the glaze ingredients; cook and stir over medium heat until blended. Return carrots to pan; bring to a boil. Reduce heat; simmer, uncovered, for 4-6 minutes or until carrots are glazed, stirring occasionally.

WHERE DO BABY CARROTS COME FROM?

Baby carrots aren't babies at all. They're harvested from a carrot variety that grows into a slender shape and cut into 2-inch pieces. They typically come packaged in 1-pound bags containing filtered tap water to keep the little guys well hydrated.

Smashed Root Vegetables with Crispy Shallots

One of the many reasons I love this dish: Roasted potatoes always remind me of Sunday suppers at my grandma's house—delicious and comforting!
—**KATHI JONES-DELMONTE** ROCHESTER, NY

PREP: 35 MIN. • **BAKE:** 40 MIN. • **MAKES:** 8 SERVINGS

- 3 **medium potatoes, peeled and cubed**
- 2 **large sweet potatoes, peeled and cubed**
- 1 **large rutabaga, peeled and cubed**
- 2 **medium carrots, sliced**
- 1 **medium turnip, peeled and cubed**
- 1 **medium parsnip, peeled and cubed**
- 5 **tablespoons olive oil, divided**
- 1½ **teaspoons dried thyme**
- 1 **teaspoon salt**
- 1 **teaspoon coarsely ground pepper**
- 1 **teaspoon paprika**
- 5 **shallots, peeled and thinly sliced**
- ½ **teaspoon sugar**
- ½ **teaspoon balsamic vinegar**
- ¼ **cup butter, cubed**
- ¼ **cup 2% milk**
- ⅛ **teaspoon ground nutmeg**

1. In a large bowl, combine the first six ingredients. Drizzle with 3 tablespoons oil. Combine the thyme, salt, pepper and paprika. Sprinkle over vegetables; toss to coat. Divide between two 15-in. x 10-in. x 1-in. baking pans.

2. Bake, uncovered, at 400° for 40-45 minutes or until tender and golden brown, stirring occasionally.

3. Meanwhile, in a small skillet, saute shallots in remaining oil until golden brown and crispy. Stir in sugar and vinegar; cook 1 minute longer. Drain; set aside.

4. Transfer vegetables to a large bowl. Coarsely mash with butter, milk and nutmeg. Sprinkle with shallots; serve immediately.

Thanksgiving Baked Apples

We have always loved applesauce but wanted to do something a little bit more elegant for Thanksgiving. Over the years, I have adjusted this recipe, using different fruits and types of alcohol, but this is the most enjoyable combination.

—HEATHER EDWARDS HOPEWELL, NJ

PREP: 30 MIN. • **BAKE:** 45 MIN.
MAKES: 8 SERVINGS

- 1 **cup butter, melted**
- ⅔ **cup packed brown sugar**
- ½ **cup cranberry-apple juice**
- ½ **cup whiskey**
- 2 **chopped ripe pears**
- ½ **cup pitted dried plums, chopped**
- ½ **cup raisins**
- 8 **medium Gala apples**

1. In a large bowl, mix the butter, brown sugar, juice and whiskey until blended. Stir in the pears, dried plums and raisins.

2. Cut a ½-in. slice off the top of each apple. Hollow out remaining apple, reserving centers and leaving a ½-in.-thick shell. Chop centers, discarding center cores and seeds. Add chopped apple to pear mixture; toss to combine.

3. Place hollowed-out apples in a greased 13-in. x 9-in. baking dish. Fill with pear mixture; spoon remaining mixture around apples.

4. Bake at 350°, uncovered, for 45-50 minutes or until apples are tender. Remove apples to dessert plates. Transfer remaining fruit mixture to a small saucepan. Bring to a boil; cook for 10-15 minutes or until liquid is syrupy. Spoon over apples.

Sweet Potato Patties with Orange Relish

For an alternative to sweet potato casserole, we serve sweet potato croquettes as a unique side dish. They're easier to make than you would think, and the relish can be prepared ahead and served chilled.

—RADELLE KNAPPENBERGER OVIEDO, FL

PREP: 20 MIN. + CHILLING
BAKE: 25 MIN.
MAKES: 12 SERVINGS

4 **cups mashed sweet potatoes**
2 **eggs, lightly beaten**
2 **tablespoons brown sugar**
2 **tablespoons butter, melted**
1 **teaspoon salt**
1½ **cups finely chopped walnuts**

RELISH
⅔ **cup dried cranberries**
½ **cup orange juice**
¼ **cup packed brown sugar**
2 **tablespoons honey**
3 **medium navel oranges, peeled and chopped**
½ **cup chopped walnuts, optional**

1. In a large bowl, combine the sweet potatoes, eggs, brown sugar butter and salt. Refrigerate for 1 hour. Shape into 12 oval patties; flatten to ½-in. thickness. Place walnuts in a shallow bowl; coat patties in nuts.

2. Place on greased baking sheets. Bake, uncovered, at 425° for 25-30 minutes or until golden brown.

3. Meanwhile, in a small saucepan, combine the cranberries, orange juice, brown sugar and honey. Cook and stir over medium heat until thickened, about 5 minutes. Stir in oranges and walnuts if desired. Serve with patties.

Lemon Chess Pie with Berry Sauce

Chess pie is one of those Southern desserts that just make you feel good.
This variation has a tangy lemon custard, coconut crust and fruit compote to top it off.
—**APRIL HEATON** BRANSON, MO

PREP: 45 MIN. + CHILLING • **BAKE:** 35 MIN. + CHILLING • **MAKES:** 8 SERVINGS (1½ CUPS SAUCE)

1 cup all-purpose flour
½ cup flaked coconut
¼ teaspoon salt
⅓ cup cold butter, cubed
3 to 4 tablespoons ice water

FILLING
6 eggs
1½ cups sugar
⅓ cup buttermilk
⅓ cup lemon juice
3 tablespoons cornmeal
2 tablespoons grated lemon peel
¼ teaspoon salt
Dash ground nutmeg
½ cup butter, melted

BERRY SAUCE
⅔ cup water
⅓ cup sugar
1 package (12 ounces) frozen unsweetened mixed berries, thawed and drained
2 teaspoons lemon juice

1. Place the flour, coconut and salt in a food processor; process until blended. Add butter; pulse until mixture is the size of peas. While pulsing, add just enough ice water to form moist crumbs. Shape dough into a disk; wrap in plastic wrap. Refrigerate for 30 minutes or overnight.

2. On a lightly floured surface, roll dough to a ⅛-in.-thick circle; transfer to a 9-in. pie plate. Trim pastry to ½ in. beyond rim of plate; flute edge. Line unpricked pastry with a double thickness of foil. Fill with pie weights, dried beans or uncooked rice.

3. Bake at 400° on a lower oven rack for 8 minutes. Remove foil and weights; bake 6-9 minutes longer or until crust is light brown. Cool on a wire rack. Reduce oven setting to 325°.

4. In a large bowl, whisk the eggs, sugar, buttermilk, lemon juice, cornmeal, lemon peel, salt and nutmeg. Gradually whisk in butter. Pour into crust. Cover edge with foil to prevent overbrowning.

5. Bake at 325° for 35-40 minutes or until a knife inserted near the center comes out clean. Remove foil. Cool on a wire rack. Refrigerate, covered, for 3 hours or until chilled.

6. For sauce, in a small saucepan, bring water and sugar to a boil. Cook until syrup is reduced to ¼ cup; transfer to a small bowl. Cool completely. Just before serving, stir in berries and lemon juice; serve with pie.

MY, MY, WHY DO THEY CALL IT CHESS PIE?

While there may be no definitive answer to this question, there sure are a lot of fun explanations on why we call this sugary treat chess pie. Like many Southern desserts, chess pie was born from common pantry ingredients, especially sugar, which was widely available in the South during the Colonial days. Southern cooks learned that foods prepared with large amounts of sugar kept longer in the chest. And so, with a little help from a Southern drawl, chest pie became "chess" pie. Others say its name is derived from "cheese pie," a traditional English lemon curd pie. Or perhaps it earned its title because it was served to gentlemen who retreated to a room to play chess. But our favorite reasoning is that it was misinterpreted when a cook referred to it in Southern dialect, saying, "It's jes' pie."

Gingersnap-Crusted Sweet Potato Cake

I like to bring one of these glazed sweet potato Bundt cakes as a special hostess gift during the holiday season. The icing looks pretty draping down the sides and remains glossy even after it dries.
—CATHERINE WILKINSON DEWEY, AZ

PREP: 25 MIN. • BAKE: 65 MIN. + COOLING • MAKES: 12 SERVINGS

- 2 teaspoons plus 1 cup butter, softened, divided
- ⅓ cup finely crushed gingersnap cookies (about 6 cookies)
- 2 cups sugar
- 2 eggs
- 2 cans (15¾ ounces each) sweet potatoes, drained and pureed
- 3½ cups all-purpose flour
- 2 teaspoons baking soda
- 2 teaspoons ground ginger
- 1 teaspoon salt
- ½ teaspoon ground cloves
- 2¼ cups confectioners' sugar
- ½ cup maple syrup
- ¾ teaspoon vanilla extract

1. Grease a 10-in. tube pan with 2 teaspoons butter and coat with crushed cookies; set aside.
2. In a large bowl, cream sugar and remaining butter until light and fluffy. Add eggs, one at a time, beating well after each addition. Beat in sweet potatoes. Combine the flour, baking soda, ginger, salt and cloves; gradually add to the creamed mixture.
3. Transfer to prepared pan. Bake at 350° for 65-75 minutes or until a toothpick inserted near the center comes out clean. Cool for 10 minutes before removing from the pan to a wire rack to cool completely.
4. For glaze, in a small bowl, combine the confectioners' sugar, maple syrup and vanilla. Pour over top of cake, allowing glaze to drape over sides.

Cranberry Ginger Tart

I love desserts that look impressive but are actually simple to make. This almond-crusted tart will charm guests, especially when served with fresh, orange-infused whipped cream.
—ROXANNE CHAN ALBANY, CA

PREP: 30 MIN. • BAKE: 20 MIN. + COOLING • MAKES: 12 SERVINGS

- 2 cups ground almonds
- ¼ cup butter, melted
- 2 tablespoons sugar

FILLING
- 2 cups fresh or frozen cranberries
- 2 teaspoons cornstarch
- 1 teaspoon minced fresh gingerroot
- 3 egg whites
- ¾ cup confectioners' sugar

TOPPING
- 1 cup heavy whipping cream
- 1 tablespoon confectioners' sugar
- ½ teaspoon grated orange peel
- ¼ cup finely chopped crystallized ginger

1. In small bowl, combine the almonds, butter and sugar; press onto bottom and up sides of an ungreased 9-in. fluted tart pan with removable bottom. Bake at 375° for 10-12 minutes or until edges are golden brown. Cool on wire rack.
2. Meanwhile, in large bowl, combine cranberries, cornstarch and ginger. In another bowl with clean beaters, beat egg whites on medium speed until soft peaks form. Slowly beat in confectioners' sugar, 1 tablespoon at a time, on high until stiff peaks form; gently fold in cranberry mixture.
3. Spread cranberry mixture into prepared crust. Bake at 375° for 18-22 minutes or until meringue is lightly browned. Cool completely on a wire rack.
4. In a small bowl, beat cream until it begins to thicken. Add confectioners' sugar and orange peel; beat until stiff peaks form. Stir in crystallized ginger. To cut tart, use a knife dipped in hot water; serve with whipped cream. Store in the refrigerator.

Peach-Blueberry Crumble Tart

Fresh out of the oven or at room temperature with a scoop of vanilla ice cream, this easy-to-prepare tart is a family favorite in our home.

—JAMES SCHEND PLEASANT PRAIRIE, WI

PREP: 30 MIN. + COOLING
BAKE: 35 MIN.
MAKES: 12 SERVINGS

- 1⅓ cups all-purpose flour
- ¼ cup sugar
- ¼ teaspoon ground cinnamon
- ½ cup butter, melted
- 2 cups frozen unsweetened blueberries, thawed
- 2 cups frozen unsweetened sliced peaches, thawed
- 1 tablespoon honey

CRUMB TOPPING

- ¼ cup all-purpose flour
- ¼ cup packed brown sugar
- ¼ cup old-fashioned oats
- ¼ cup chopped pecans
- ⅛ teaspoon ground cloves
- 2 tablespoons butter, melted

1. Preheat oven to 350°. In a small bowl, mix flour, sugar and cinnamon; stir in butter just until blended. Press onto the bottom and up the sides of a 9-in. fluted tart pan with removable bottom. Bake 15-20 minutes or until lightly browned. Cool on a wire rack.

2. In a large bowl, combine blueberries, peaches and honey; toss to coat. In a small bowl, combine first five topping ingredients; stir in butter.

3. Spoon fruit mixture into crust; sprinkle with topping. Bake at 350° for 35-40 minutes or until topping is golden brown and filling is bubbly. Cool on a wire rack at least 15 minutes before serving.

Cranberry-Apple Lattice Pie

Two favorite fall fruits bring out the best in each other—while rum works its own mellow magic. You won't meet too many folks who can pass up a piece of this!
—ADRI BARR CROCETTI SHERMAN OAKS, CA

PREP: 40 MIN. + CHILLING • **BAKE:** 1 HOUR 5 MIN. + COOLING
MAKES: 8 SERVINGS

2½ cups all-purpose flour
1 tablespoon sugar
¾ teaspoon salt
½ cup cold unsalted butter, cubed
⅓ cup cold shortening
5 to 7 tablespoons ice water

FILLING
½ cup dried currants or raisins
2 tablespoons dark rum or water
1 cup fresh or frozen cranberries, divided
¾ cup sugar, divided
6 medium baking apples, such as Fuji or Braeburn (about 2 pounds), peeled and cut into ¼-inch slices
2 tablespoons quick-cooking tapioca
1 tablespoon lemon juice
2 teaspoons grated lemon peel
½ teaspoon ground cinnamon

GLAZE
2 teaspoons sugar
Dash ground cinnamon
1 egg
1 tablespoon 2% milk or heavy whipping cream

1. In a small bowl, mix the flour, sugar and salt; cut in butter and shortening until crumbly. Gradually add water, tossing with a fork until dough holds together when pressed. Divide dough in half. Shape each half into a disk; wrap in plastic wrap. Refrigerate for 30 minutes or overnight.

2. In a small bowl, combine currants and rum; let stand for 20 minutes.

3. Place ¾ cup cranberries and ¼ cup sugar in a food processor; pulse until the cranberries are coarsely chopped. Transfer to a large bowl. Add the apples, tapioca, lemon juice, lemon peel, cinnamon, remaining sugar and currant mixture; toss to combine. Let stand for 15 minutes.

4. On a lightly floured surface, roll one half of dough to a ⅛-in.-thick circle; transfer to a 9-in. deep-dish pie plate. Trim pastry to ½ in. beyond rim of plate. Add filling.

5. Roll remaining dough to a ⅛-in.-thick circle; cut into ½-in.-wide strips. Arrange over filling in a lattice pattern. Trim and seal strips to edge of bottom pastry; flute edge. Place remaining cranberries in spaces between lattice strips.

6. For glaze, in a small bowl, mix sugar and cinnamon; set aside. In another bowl, whisk egg and milk; brush over lattice top. Sprinkle with sugar mixture.

7. Bake on a lower oven rack at 400° for 25 minutes. Reduce oven temperature to 325°; bake 40-45 minutes longer or until crust is golden brown and filling is bubbly.

8. Cool on a wire rack for 30 minutes; serve warm.

CREATING A LATTICE CRUST

1. Roll out pastry to a 12-inch circle. With a fluted pastry wheel, pizza cutter or sharp knife, cut pastry into strips ½ inch wide. Lay strips in rows about ½ inch apart. (Use longer strips for center of pie.) Fold every other strip halfway back. Starting at the center, add strips at right angles, lifting every other strip as the cross strips are put down.

2. Continue to add strips, lifting and weaving until lattice top is completed.

3. Trim strips even with pastry edge. Fold bottom pastry up and over ends of strips and seal. Flute edges.

Sticky Toffee Rice Pudding with Caramel Cream

Once-homely rice pudding gets the Cinderella treatment in this comforting dessert that delivers on sticky toffee flavor. It has just the right amount of thickness for soaking up a hot caramel topping.

—JANICE ELDER CHARLOTTE, NC

PREP: 45 MIN.
BAKE: 35 MIN. + COOLING
MAKES: 16 SERVINGS

- 3 cups water
- 1 cup uncooked medium grain rice
- ¼ teaspoon salt
- 3 cups pitted dates, chopped
- 3 cups 2% milk
- 2 teaspoons vanilla extract
- 1 cup packed brown sugar
- 1½ cups heavy whipping cream, divided
- ¼ cup butter, cubed
- ½ cup sour cream
- ¼ cup hot caramel ice cream topping

1. In a large saucepan, bring the water, rice and salt to a boil. Reduce heat; cover and simmer for 12-15 minutes or until rice is tender. Add dates and milk; cook and stir for 10 minutes. Remove from the heat; stir in vanilla. Set aside.

2. In a small saucepan, combine the brown sugar, 1 cup cream and butter. Bring to a boil. Reduce heat; simmer, uncovered, for 2 minutes, stirring constantly. Stir into rice mixture. Transfer to a greased 13-in. x 9-in. baking dish. Bake, uncovered, at 350° for 35-40 minutes or until bubbly. Cool for 15 minutes.

3. Meanwhile, in a small bowl, beat the sour cream, caramel topping and remaining cream until slightly thickened. Serve with warm rice pudding. Refrigerate leftovers.

Pumpkin Pie Cannoli

I love to play around with different fillings in these cannoli. I've used pumpkin pie pudding (when it's in season at the store), but you can also make it with canned pumpkin and vanilla pudding.

—**BARBARA CARLUCCI** ORANGE PARK, FL

PREP: 30 MIN.
COOK: 5 MIN./BATCH
MAKES: 1 DOZEN

- 1 **cup all-purpose flour**
- 1 **tablespoon sugar**
- ¼ **teaspoon salt**
- 1 **egg, separated**
- ¼ **cup white wine**
- 2 **teaspoons canola oil**
  Oil for deep-fat frying

FILLING
- 1 **carton (15 ounces) ricotta cheese**
- ¾ **cup canned pumpkin**
- 1 **package (3.4 ounces) instant vanilla pudding mix**
- ⅓ **cup 2% milk**
- ¾ **teaspoon pumpkin pie spice**
- ¼ **cup miniature semisweet chocolate chips**
- ¼ **cup chopped hazelnuts**
  Confectioners' sugar, optional

1. In small bowl, combine flour, sugar and salt. Stir in egg yolk, wine and canola oil. Turn onto a floured surface; knead until smooth. Divide dough into 12 portions; roll each into a 4-in. circle (dough will be thin). Curl around a metal cannoli tube to shape. Moisten edges with egg white; press to seal.

2. In electric skillet or deep fryer, heat oil to 375°. Fry cannoli shells, a few at a time, until golden brown on all sides. Drain on paper towels.

3. For filling, in a small bowl, combine the ricotta, pumpkin, pudding mix, milk and pie spice. Stir in chocolate chips.

4. Spoon or pipe filling into shells. Dip each side in hazelnuts. Sprinkle with confectioners' sugar if desired. Serve immediately.

In a Nutshell

Turn walnut shells into decorative floating candles.

MATERIALS

Halved walnut shells
4-inch pre-waxed wire wicks
Candle mold or putty
Microwavable soy wax or
    beeswax
Microwavable container
    for soy wax or
    double boiler for beeswax

DIRECTIONS

1. Clean out halved walnut shells.
2. Place a wick in the center of each walnut shell. Use a pinch of candle mold or putty on the bottom of the wick and press onto shell to hold in place.
3. Following manufacturer's instructions, melt soy wax in microwave or melt beeswax in a double boiler on stovetop.
4. Pour melted wax into each walnut shell, filling to top edge. Let solidify.
5. Trim wicks to about ½ in. above solidified wax.

Carefully place nutshell candles in water in decorative bowl, being sure not to get the wick wet. Light each candle. (Approximate burn time per candle is one hour.)

NOTE *To make perfectly split walnut shells, use a rotary tool such as a Dremel with a cutting attachment. Use a wide clamp or long-handled pliers to hold each nut, then cut along seam. You need to cut only part way. Then use a flat screwdriver or spatula to gently pry the shell apart.*

Thanksgiving doesn't have to attract a large crowd to be memorable. Choose from an assortment of scaled-down fare to create an intimate dinner for you and someone special. You'll get all the traditional aromas and flavors in custom-sized portions—from sourdough stuffing in ramekins to adorably irresistible li'l pies.

Best of all, you get to decide the amount of leftovers you want. Simply double a recipe to serve 4 to 6, depending on how many Mashed Sweet Potato Mounds or how much Honey Mustard Green Beans you want the next day.

Orange-Glazed Carrots & Parsnips (p. 131)
Honey Mustard Green Beans (p. 127)
Mahogany-Glazed Cornish Hens (p. 128)

THANKSGIVING **FOR TWO**

Amber's Sourdough Stuffing

All my kids and grandkids absolutely love this stuffing, but especially my daughter-in-law, Amber. I usually have to make a big batch at Thanksgiving so I will have leftovers for my husband. Otherwise, you can use this recipe to make it for two.

—KATHY KATZ OCALA, FL

PREP: 20 MIN. • **BAKE:** 20 MIN.
MAKES: 2 SERVINGS

- 1 tablespoon olive oil
- ⅓ cup sliced fresh mushrooms
- ⅓ cup chopped celery
- ⅓ cup finely chopped carrot
- ⅓ cup finely chopped onion
- 2½ cups cubed sourdough bread
- ½ teaspoon poultry seasoning
- ¼ teaspoon salt
- ⅛ teaspoon pepper
- 2 tablespoons beaten egg
- ½ to ¾ cup chicken broth

1. Preheat oven to 350°. In a large skillet, heat oil over medium-high heat. Add mushrooms, celery, carrot and onion; cook and stir until tender.

2. Transfer to a large bowl. Add bread cubes and seasonings; toss to combine. Stir in egg and enough broth to reach desired moistness.

3. Transfer to two greased 10-oz. ramekins or a 1-qt. baking dish. Bake 20-25 minutes or until top is lightly browned and a thermometer reads 160°.

Pureed Butternut Squash Soup

For several years, we've been enjoying this velvety yet healthy soup at Thanksgiving. Butternut squash isn't the easiest thing to cut into, so I go ahead and buy mine pre-chopped.
—**CHRISTEN CHALMERS** HOUSTON, TX

START TO FINISH: 30 MIN. • **MAKES:** 2 SERVINGS

1 teaspoon butter
1 teaspoon olive oil
¼ cup chopped onion
¼ cup chopped carrot
1 garlic clove, minced
1½ cups cubed peeled butternut squash
1½ cups chicken stock
¼ teaspoon dried sage leaves
¼ teaspoon salt
⅛ teaspoon pepper
   Pinch crushed red pepper flakes

1. In a small saucepan, heat butter and oil over medium heat. Add onion and carrot; cook and stir until tender. Add garlic; cook 1 minute longer.

2. Stir in squash, stock, sage, salt and pepper; bring to a boil. Reduce heat; simmer, covered, 10-15 minutes or until squash is tender. Remove from heat; cool slightly. Process in a blender until smooth. Sprinkle servings with pepper flakes.

Honey Mustard Green Beans

PICTURED ON PAGE 125

I love fresh beans but was getting tired of just steaming them and eating them plain. So I whipped up this easy honey-mustard combination as a simple side dish.
—**CAROL TRAUPMAN-CARR** BREINIGSVILLE, PA

START TO FINISH: 20 MIN. • **MAKES:** 2 SERVINGS

½ pound fresh green beans, trimmed
¼ cup thinly sliced red onion
2 tablespoons spicy brown mustard
2 tablespoons honey
1 tablespoon snipped fresh dill or 1 teaspoon dill weed

1. In a large saucepan, bring 6 cups water to a boil. Add beans; cook, uncovered, 3-4 minutes or just until crisp-tender. Drain beans and immediately drop into ice water. Drain and pat dry; transfer to a small bowl.

2. In another bowl, combine onion, mustard, honey and dill. Pour over beans; toss to coat.

HOW DO YOU LIKE YOUR STUFFING?

For a more crisp stuffing, use prepackaged dry bread crumbs or cubes and limit the amount of liquid. For a denser stuffing, add stock, broth or juice until the mixture begins to stick together when pinched. For fluffier stuffing, stir in a beaten egg before baking.

Mahogany-Glazed Cornish Hens

PICTURED ON PAGE 125

My husband and I enjoy this for Thanksgiving dinner.
It's an elegant tradition custom-fit for two.

—JEANNETTE SABO LEXINGTON PARK, MD

PREP: 15 MIN. • **BAKE:** 20 MIN. • **MAKES:** 2 SERVINGS

1 **Cornish game hen (20 to 24 ounces), split lengthwise**
1 **tablespoon butter**
½ **teaspoon minced fresh gingerroot**
½ **teaspoon grated orange peel**
2 **tablespoons apricot preserves**
1 **tablespoon balsamic vinegar**
1 **tablespoon reduced-sodium soy sauce**
2 **teaspoons Dijon mustard**
¼ **teaspoon salt**
⅛ **teaspoon pepper**
1 **to 1½ cups chicken broth, divided**

1. Preheat oven to 450°. Place hen in a greased shallow roasting pan, skin side up. Combine butter, ginger and orange peel; rub under skin.

2. In a small bowl, whisk preserves, vinegar, soy sauce and mustard. Reserve half of the mixture for basting. Spoon remaining mixture over hen; sprinkle with salt and pepper. Pour ½ cup chicken broth into pan.

3. Roast 20-25 minutes or until a thermometer inserted in thigh reads 180°, adding broth to pan as necessary and basting with remaining glaze halfway through cooking. Serve with pan juices.

Mashed Sweet Potato Mounds

I have made these potato bundles for several Thanksgiving dinners. I think it's a nice, different way to prepare sweet potatoes, and the serving is just right for a couple.

—PAMELA SHANK PARKERSBURG, WV

PREP: 30 MIN. • **BAKE:** 15 MIN. • **MAKES:** 2 SERVINGS

3 **cups cubed peeled sweet potatoes (about 2 small)**
¼ **cup packed brown sugar**
2 **tablespoons butter**
2 **tablespoons beaten egg**
4 **tablespoons finely chopped pecans, divided**
¼ **teaspoon ground cinnamon**
⅛ **teaspoon salt**

1. Preheat oven to 350°. Place sweet potatoes in a small saucepan; add water to cover. Bring to a boil. Reduce heat; cook, uncovered, 10-15 minutes or until tender.

2. Drain; return to pan. Mash potatoes, gradually adding brown sugar and butter. Mix in egg, 2 tablespoons pecans, cinnamon and salt.

3. Spoon or pipe potatoes onto a parchment paper-lined baking sheet, forming two mounds. Sprinkle with remaining pecans. Bake 15-20 minutes or until lightly browned and heated through.

Fennel Wild Rice Salad

This is a salad I invented years ago when my sister's family had to go gluten-free. It has since become a favorite, and Thanksgiving just isn't the same without our wild rice salad!
—**AIMEE DAY** FERNDALE, WA

PREP: 15 MIN. • **COOK:** 55 MIN.
MAKES: 2 SERVINGS

- ⅓ cup uncooked wild rice
- 1 cup water
- 1½ teaspoons lemon juice
- 1½ teaspoons olive oil
- ¼ cup thinly sliced fennel bulb
- 2 tablespoons salted pumpkin seeds or pepitas
- 2 tablespoons dried cherries
- 1 green onion, sliced
- 1 tablespoon minced fresh parsley
- ⅛ teaspoon salt
  Dash pepper

1. Rinse wild rice thoroughly; drain. In a small saucepan, combine water and rice; bring to a boil. Reduce heat; simmer, covered, 50-55 minutes or until rice is fluffy and tender. Drain if necessary.

2. Transfer rice to a small bowl. Drizzle with lemon juice and oil; toss to coat. Stir in remaining ingredients.

Pumpkin Pie Martinis

This is an amazing treat! My girlfriends start asking me to make this in the fall and continue to request it through the holidays. Dessert martinis are always a fun way to end a special evening.

—CATHLEEN BUSHMAN GENEVA, IL

START TO FINISH: 5 MIN.
MAKES: 2 SERVINGS

- 1 vanilla wafer, crushed, optional
  Ice cubes
- 2 ounces vanilla-flavored vodka
- 2 ounces milk
- 2 ounces heavy whipping cream
- 1 ounce simple syrup
- 1 ounce hazelnut liqueur
- ⅛ teaspoon pumpkin pie spice
  Dash ground cinnamon

1. If a cookie-crumb rim is desired, wet the rims of two cocktail glasses with water. Place cookie crumbs on a plate; dip rims in crumbs. Set aside.

2. Fill a mixing glass or tumbler three-fourths full with ice. Add the remaining ingredients; stir until condensation forms on outside of glass. Strain into two chilled cocktail glasses.

PUMPKIN SPICE & EVERYTHING NICE

During the holiday season, some grocery stores sell pumpkin spice syrup, a flavoring used in coffee drinks. You can use 1 ounce of this syrup to replace the simple syrup and pumpkin pie spice in the martini above.

Orange-Glazed Carrots and Parsnips

PICTURED ON PAGE 124

Ribbons of buttery carrots and parsnips play double duty as a vibrant visual and tasty side dish—a perfect way to round out a special Thanksgiving for two.

—**DEIRDRE COX** KANSAS CITY, KS

START TO FINISH: 30 MIN. • **MAKES:** 2 SERVINGS

1 cup orange juice
2 tablespoons sugar
1 tablespoon minced fresh gingerroot
¼ teaspoon salt
¼ cup butter, cubed
2 large carrots
1 large parsnip
1 green onion, thinly sliced

1. In a large nonstick skillet, whisk orange juice, sugar, ginger and salt. Bring to a boil over medium-high heat; cook until liquid is reduced by half. Stir in butter until melted.
2. Meanwhile, using a vegetable peeler, shave carrots and parsnip lengthwise into very thin strips (about 4 cups carrot strips and 2 cups parsnip strips).
3. Add vegetables to skillet; stir to coat. Bring to a boil. Reduce heat; simmer, covered, 3 minutes.
4. Uncover; cook 8-10 minutes or until vegetables are tender and glazed, stirring frequently. Sprinkle with green onion.

Blue Cheese Pear Salad

It's the maple-raspberry dressing that brings this sweet and tangy salad together. You can easily double the recipe so you'll have some on hand for lunch the next day.

—**ANNE BENNETT** DELMAR, MD

START TO FINISH: 15 MIN. • **MAKES:** 2 SERVINGS

3 cups torn leaf lettuce
1 can (8½ ounces) pear halves, drained
2 thin slices red onion, separated into rings
3 tablespoons crumbled blue cheese
3 tablespoons chopped walnuts

DRESSING
¼ cup olive oil
2 tablespoons raspberry vinegar
2 teaspoons maple syrup
¼ teaspoon Dijon mustard
⅛ teaspoon garlic powder
⅛ teaspoon onion powder

1. Divide lettuce between two salad plates. Top with pears, onion, blue cheese and walnuts.
2. In a small bowl, whisk oil, vinegar, syrup, mustard, garlic powder and onion powder until blended. Drizzle over salads.

OLIVE OIL—MAKING THE GRADE

When choosing olive oil, it may help to know that the oils are graded according to acidity. Extra-virgin olive oil is the top grade and is extremely low in acidity (1%). It's produced by the first crushing and pressing of tree-ripened olives and has a deep color and rich olive flavor. Virgin olive oil has a slightly higher acidity (2%), lighter color and less fruity flavor. Plain olive oil usually contains a blend of refined oil and virgin or extra-virgin oil.

Mashed Cauliflower

This is our choice for a side dish that's lower in carbs than mashed potatoes, but just as flavorful and satisfying. I suggest garnishing it with chopped green onions.
—**TINA MARTINI** SPARKS, NV

START TO FINISH: 25 MIN. • **MAKES:** 2½ CUPS

1 medium head cauliflower, broken into florets
½ cup shredded Swiss cheese
1 tablespoon butter
¾ teaspoon salt
¼ teaspoon pepper
⅛ teaspoon garlic powder
2 to 3 tablespoons 2% milk

1. In a large saucepan, bring 1 in. of water to a boil. Add cauliflower; cook, covered, 8-12 minutes or until very tender. Drain.

2. Mash cauliflower, adding cheese, butter, seasonings and enough milk to reach desired consistency.

Whiskey-Glazed Pecans

I call these my Jack Daniels Pecans. The subtly spiked buttery coating makes them an addictive little nosh during a holiday cocktail hour.
—**JENNIFER SCHOONOVER** TRIMBLE, MO

PREP: 10 MIN. • **BAKE:** 30 MIN. + COOLING • **MAKES:** 2 CUPS

¼ cup butter, cubed
3 tablespoons brown sugar
5 teaspoons whiskey
2 cups pecan halves
¼ teaspoon kosher salt

1. Preheat oven to 300°. In a microwave-safe bowl, combine butter, brown sugar and whiskey. Microwave, covered, on high for 30-60 seconds or until butter is melted; stir until smooth.

2. Place pecans in a small bowl; drizzle with butter mixture and toss to coat. Transfer to a greased 15x10x1-in. baking pan. Bake 30-35 minutes or lightly browned, stirring occasionally. Sprinkle with salt. Cool completely. Store in an airtight container.

YOU SAY PECAN, I SAY...

So what's the proper way to pronounce pecan? If you bet that your way is right, you might want to think twice, or thrice. According to the Merriam-Webster dictionary, there are three correct pronunciations: pi-ˈkän, pi-ˈkan and ˈpē-kan. Any other way would be nutty.

Li'l Pecan Pies

I love having all the rich, traditional flavors of a full-size pecan pie in an adorable li'l size—just perfect for my husband and me.
—**CHRISTINE BOITOS** LIVONIA, MI

PREP: 15 MIN. + CHILLING
BAKE: 35 MIN. + COOLING
MAKES: 2 SERVINGS

- ½ **cup all-purpose flour**
- ⅛ **teaspoon salt**
- 3 **tablespoons shortening**
- 4 **teaspoons cold water**

FILLING
- ⅓ **cup pecan halves**
- 1 **egg**
- ⅓ **cup packed brown sugar**
- ⅓ **cup corn syrup**
- ½ **teaspoon vanilla extract**
- **Whipped cream, optional**

1. In a small bowl, combine flour and salt; cut in shortening until crumbly. Gradually add water, tossing with fork until dough forms a ball. Cover and refrigerate for at least 30 minutes.

2. Divide dough in half. Roll each half into a 6-in. circle. Transfer to two 4½-in. tart pans; fit pastry into pans, trimming if necessary. Arrange pecans in shells.

3. In another small bowl, whisk egg, brown sugar, corn syrup and vanilla. Pour over pecans. Place shells on a baking sheet. Bake at 375° for 35-40 minutes or until a knife inserted near the center comes out clean. Cool on a wire rack. Top with whipped cream if desired.

eastergatherings

Some consider the perfect Easter get-together to be an elegant feast, while others cherish the sweeter side. No matter your preference, the unique variety of entertaining ideas in this section will help make your springtime celebration as bright and joyous as the season itself.

After months of waiting in sweet anticipation for warm breezes and the first delicate bud to sprout, it's time to celebrate with an elegant Easter feast.

But if the traditional ham sounds a little ho-hum, shake things up with a regal entree that puts the flair in fancy. Basted with apple juice and slowly baked to perfection, Crown Roast with Wild Rice Stuffing will have everyone's taste buds reeling.

With a wonderful blend of ingredients, Pecan-Coconut Sweet Potatoes gives a favorite vegetable a deliciously different taste twist. A refreshingly sweet fruit medley, golden brown herbed rolls and a lighter-than-air lemon angel food cake are just a few of the impressive accompaniments that round out the meal.

FORMAL **EASTER DINNER**

Lemony Cooler

I like to freeze a combination of lemon juice, water and mint leaves in ice cube trays to serve with this drink.
—**BONNIE HAWKINS** ELKHORN, WI

PREP: 15 MIN. + CHILLING
MAKES: 8 SERVINGS (2 QUARTS)

- 3 **cups white grape juice**
- ½ **cup sugar**
- ½ **cup lemon juice**
- 1 **bottle (1 liter) club soda, chilled**
  Ice cubes
  Assorted fresh fruit, optional

1. In a pitcher, combine the grape juice, sugar and lemon juice; stir until sugar is dissolved. Refrigerate until chilled.

2. Just before serving, stir in club soda. Serve over ice. Garnish with fruit if desired.

Parmesan Artichoke Soup

Showcase colorful carrots, celery, sun-dried tomatoes and artichoke hearts by serving this spring-fresh soup in little glass bowls. Rich and creamy, a small serving goes a long way.
—**MALEE JERGENSEN** MURRAY, UT

PREP: 25 MIN. • **COOK:** 30 MIN. • **MAKES:** 12 SERVINGS (3 QUARTS)

- 4 **celery ribs, finely chopped**
- 1 **medium onion, finely chopped**
- ½ **cup finely chopped carrot**
- ½ **cup butter, cubed**
- 3 **garlic cloves, minced**
- 1 **cup all-purpose flour**
- 4½ **teaspoons minced fresh thyme or 1½ teaspoons dried thyme**
- ¾ **teaspoon salt**
- ½ **teaspoon pepper**
- 2 **cartons (32 ounces each) reduced-sodium chicken broth**
- 3 **bay leaves**
- 1 **quart heavy whipping cream**
- 1½ **cups shredded Parmesan cheese**
- 1 **jar (7½ ounces) marinated quartered artichoke hearts, drained and coarsely chopped**
- ¼ **cup sun-dried tomatoes (not packed in oil), chopped**

1. In large saucepan, saute celery, onion and carrot in butter until tender. Add garlic; cook 1 minute longer. Stir in flour, thyme, salt and pepper until blended; gradually add broth. Add bay leaves. Bring to a boil. Cook and stir for 2 minutes or until thickened.

2. Reduce heat; whisk in the cream, cheese, artichokes and tomatoes. Bring to a gentle boil. Simmer, uncovered, for 5-10 minutes or until flavors are blended. Discard bay leaves.

Spinach Artichoke-Stuffed Tomatoes

These mingle-friendly bites are sure to be a delicious addition to any buffet table. If you don't stuff all the tomatoes, use the leftover filling as a dip or to spread on crostini or crackers.

—AMY GAISFORD SALT LAKE CITY, UT

PREP: 40 MIN. + CHILLING • **MAKES:** 6½ DOZEN

- 1 package (3 ounces) cream cheese, softened
- ½ cup mayonnaise
- ½ cup sour cream
- 1 can (14 ounces) water-packed artichoke hearts, rinsed, drained and chopped
- 1 package (10 ounces) frozen chopped spinach, thawed and squeezed dry
- ⅓ cup shredded part-skim mozzarella cheese
- 4 tablespoons shredded Parmesan cheese, divided
- ¾ teaspoon garlic salt
- 78 cherry tomatoes

1. In a small bowl, beat the cream cheese, mayonnaise and sour cream. Stir in artichokes, spinach, mozzarella cheese, 3 tablespoons Parmesan and garlic salt.

2. Cut a thin slice off the top and bottom of each tomato. Scoop out pulp, leaving a ½-in. shell. Invert onto paper towels to drain. Fill each tomato with about 2 teaspoons filling. Sprinkle with remaining Parmesan cheese.

3. Serve chilled, or place on foil-lined baking sheets; bake at 400° for 5 minutes to warm.

Layered Spinach & Orange Salad

PICTURED ON PAGE 136

Good-for-you spinach is the perfect backdrop for juicy mandarin oranges, red onion and Parmesan cheese in this refreshing salad. The tangy homemade vinaigrette features a perfect sweet-tart balance, and it couldn't be easier to prepare.

—JIM GALES GLENDALE, WI

START TO FINISH: 25 MIN. • **MAKES:** 10 SERVINGS

- 6 cups fresh baby spinach
- 1 can (15 ounces) mandarin oranges, drained
- ½ cup chopped red onion

VINAIGRETTE
- ⅓ cup olive oil
- 2 tablespoons red wine vinegar
- 4 teaspoons orange marmalade
- ¼ teaspoon salt
- ⅛ teaspoon pepper
- ¾ cup shaved Parmesan cheese

Arrange the spinach, oranges and onion on a serving plate. In a small bowl, whisk the oil, vinegar, marmalade, salt and pepper. Pour over salad. Top with cheese.

PLATTER UP

Think outside the bowl and arrange this colorful layered salad on a 15-in. x 9½-in. serving platter. Drizzled with orange dressing and finished with a shaved Parmesan topping, your guests are in for a visually stunning feast for the eyes.

Peas a la Francaise

I love peas, and this recipe is a favorite. It features tiny pearl onions touched with thyme and chervil, and its presentation is beyond lovely.
—**CHRISTINE FRAZIER** AUBURNDALE, FL

START TO FINISH: 30 MIN. • **MAKES:** 12 SERVINGS (½ CUP EACH)

1½ cups pearl onions, trimmed
¼ cup butter, cubed
¼ cup water
1 tablespoon sugar
1 teaspoon salt
¼ teaspoon dried thyme
¼ teaspoon dried chervil
¼ teaspoon pepper

2 packages (16 ounces each) frozen peas, thawed
2 cups shredded lettuce

1. In a Dutch oven, bring 6 cups water to a boil. Add pearl onions; boil for 3 minutes. Drain and rinse in cold water; peel and set aside.

2. In the same saucepan, melt butter over medium heat. Stir in the onions, water, sugar and seasonings. Add peas and lettuce; stir until blended. Cover and cook for 6-8 minutes or until vegetables are tender. Serve with a slotted spoon.

Spinach Orzo Salad

This incredibly tasty salad couldn't be any easier to toss together, and since it feeds a bunch, you won't have to double the recipe if you're hosting a crowd. Chill it for about an hour to bring out all the fresh flavors.
—**DONNA BARDOCZ** HOWELL, MI

START TO FINISH: 30 MIN. • **MAKES:** 10 SERVINGS

1 package (16 ounces) orzo pasta
1 package (6 ounces) fresh baby spinach, finely chopped
¾ cup crumbled feta cheese
¾ cup finely chopped red onion
¾ cup reduced-fat balsamic vinaigrette

½ teaspoon dried basil
¼ teaspoon white pepper
¼ cup pine nuts, toasted

1. Cook orzo according to package directions. Drain and rinse in cold water.

2. In a large bowl, combine the spinach, cheese, onion and orzo. In a small bowl, combine the vinaigrette, basil and pepper. Pour over orzo; toss to coat. Chill until serving. Just before serving, stir in pine nuts.

WHITE PEPPER VS. BLACK PEPPER

White pepper is prepared from the husked dried berries of the pepper plant and can be used either whole or ground. It's considered less pungent than black pepper and does not last as long. It's mainly used in light-colored dishes where the black pepper speckles might be considered objectionable.

Herb-Swirled Rolls

Frozen bread dough gives you a head start for these rolls. Sprinkled with fresh herbs and sesame seeds, they're a nice addition to an Easter spread.

—LOIS GALLUP EDWARDS
WOODLAND, CA

PREP: 20 MIN. + RISING
BAKE: 15 MIN.
MAKES: 1 DOZEN

- 1 loaf (1 pound) frozen bread dough, thawed
- 3 tablespoons butter, melted
- 2 tablespoons minced chives
- 2 tablespoons dried parsley flakes
- ½ teaspoon dill weed or dried thyme
- ¼ teaspoon salt
- ⅛ teaspoon pepper
- 1 egg
- 2 tablespoons water
  Sesame and/or poppy seeds

1. On a floured surface, roll dough into a 14-in. x 12-in. rectangle; brush with butter. Sprinkle with chives, parsley, dill, salt and pepper. Roll up jelly-roll style, starting with a long side; pinch seam to seal. Cut into 12 slices.

2. Place cut side down in greased muffin cups. Cover and let rise until doubled, about 45 minutes.

3. Combine egg and water; brush over tops. Sprinkle with seeds. Bake at 375° for 12-15 minutes or until golden brown. Remove from pan to a wire rack.

Roasted Asparagus Salad

Now that my six children are grown, they've started sharing recipes with me.
This tasty way to prepare fresh asparagus came from my daughter.
—**ANNA KREYMBORG** LOUISVILLE, KY

PREP: 10 MIN.
BAKE: 20 MIN. + COOLING
MAKES: 12 SERVINGS

- 3 **pounds fresh asparagus, trimmed**
- ¼ **cup olive oil**
- 2 **garlic cloves, minced**

DRESSING

- ¼ **cup olive oil**
- 1 **tablespoon snipped fresh tarragon or 1 teaspoon dried tarragon**
- 1 **tablespoon cider or red wine vinegar**
- 1 **tablespoon Dijon mustard**
- 1 **teaspoon lemon juice**
- ½ **teaspoon salt**
- ⅛ **teaspoon pepper**

1. Place asparagus in a 13-in. x 9-in. baking dish coated with cooking spray. Combine oil and garlic; pour over asparagus and turn to coat. Bake, uncovered, at 400° for 20-25 minutes or until tender, turning after 10 minutes. Cool completely.

2. In a small bowl, whisk the dressing ingredients; pour over asparagus and turn to coat. Serve immediately or allow to marinate. Serve at room temperature.

Crown Roast with Wild Rice Stuffing

PICTURED ON PAGE 137

Are you looking for a fresh approach to Easter dinner? Family and friends
will feel like royalty when you set this tender, juicy crown roast on your holiday table.
The wild rice stuffing is a welcome change of pace from traditional stuffing.
—**CHRISTINE FRAZIER** AUBURNDALE, FL

PREP: 15 MIN. • **BAKE:** 2 HOURS + STANDING • **MAKES:** 16 SERVINGS (12 CUPS STUFFING)

1 teaspoon salt
1 teaspoon dried thyme
1 teaspoon fennel seed, crushed
½ teaspoon pepper
1 pork crown roast (16 ribs and
   about 9 pounds)
1 cup unsweetened apple juice

STUFFING
2 quarts water
2 cups uncooked wild rice
2 teaspoons salt, optional
½ pound sliced fresh mushrooms
2 medium onions, chopped
2 tablespoons butter
2 pounds seasoned bulk pork
   sausage

OPTIONAL GARNISH
   **Fresh kale and pickled whole
   beets**

1. Combine the salt, thyme,
fennel and pepper; sprinkle over
roast. Place on a rack in a large
shallow roasting pan. Cover rib
ends with foil. Bake, uncovered, at
350° for 2 to 2½ hours or until a
thermometer reads 145°, basting
occasionally with apple juice.

2. Meanwhile, in a large saucepan,
bring water, rice and salt if desired
to a boil. Reduce heat; cover and
simmer for 45-60 minutes or until
rice is tender.

3. In a large skillet, saute
mushrooms and onions in butter
until tender. Transfer to a large
bowl. In same skillet, cook sausage
over medium heat until no longer
pink; drain. Drain rice; add rice
and sausage to mushroom mixture
and stir until blended.

4. Remove roast from oven; tent
with foil. Let stand 15 minutes.
Remove foil. Spoon stuffing into
center of roast. Garnish platter
with kale and beets if desired. To
serve, carve between ribs.

Pecan-Coconut Sweet Potatoes

It's such an advantage to be able to make a tempting sweet potato dish well ahead by putting it
in the slow cooker. This tasty recipe includes sweet coconut and crunchy pecans.
—**REBECCA CLARK** WARRIOR, AL

PREP: 20 MIN. • **COOK:** 5 HOURS • **MAKES:** 6 SERVINGS

2 pounds sweet potatoes, peeled
   and cut into ¾-inch cubes
¼ cup packed brown sugar
2 tablespoons flaked coconut
2 tablespoons chopped pecans,
   toasted
1 teaspoon vanilla extract
½ teaspoon salt
¼ teaspoon ground cinnamon
1 tablespoon butter, melted
½ cup miniature marshmallows

1. Place sweet potatoes in a 3-qt.
slow cooker coated with cooking
spray. In a small bowl combine the
brown sugar, coconut, pecans,
vanilla, salt and cinnamon;
sprinkle over sweet potatoes.
Drizzle with butter.

2. Cover and cook on low for
5-6 hours or until potatoes
are tender, sprinkling with
marshmallows during the last
5 minutes of cooking.

Fruit with Honey-Ginger Dressing

This colorful medley of strawberries, blueberries and grapes gets its refreshing flavor from a honey-ginger dressing. Drizzle the dressing over any bounty of fresh fruit for an eye-appealing salad that's perfect for a sit-down dinner or brunch.

—CHERYL PERRY HERTFORD, NC

START TO FINISH: 15 MIN. • **MAKES:** 8 SERVINGS

1½ cups plain yogurt
2 tablespoons honey
2 teaspoons lemon juice
½ teaspoon ground ginger
½ teaspoon vanilla extract
2 cups cantaloupe balls or additional seedless red grapes

2 cups seedless red grapes
2 cups sliced fresh strawberries
2 cups fresh blueberries

For dressing, in a small bowl, whisk the first five ingredients until smooth. In a large bowl, combine the cantaloupe, grapes, strawberries and blueberries; spoon into serving bowls. Drizzle with dressing.

Lemon Meringue Angel Cake

PICTURED AT RIGHT

This heavenly angel food cake makes a sweet ending to a special Easter dinner. Its soft and airy texture is complemented by a lovely lemon curd filling and crisp meringue topping. Each slice melts in your mouth.

—SHARON KURTZ EMMAUS, PA

PREP: 40 MIN. + STANDING • **BAKE:** 35 MIN. + COOLING • **MAKES:** 14 SERVINGS

12 egg whites
1½ cups sugar, divided
1 cup cake flour
2 teaspoons cream of tartar
1½ teaspoons vanilla extract
¼ teaspoon salt
1 jar (10 ounces) lemon curd

MERINGUE TOPPING
4 egg whites
¾ teaspoon cream of tartar
½ cup sugar

1. Place egg whites in a large bowl; let stand at room temperature for 30 minutes. Sift ½ cup sugar and the flour together twice; set aside.

2. Add cream of tartar, vanilla and salt to egg whites; beat on medium speed until soft peaks form. Gradually beat in remaining sugar, 2 tablespoons at a time, on high until stiff glossy peaks form and sugar is dissolved. Gradually fold in flour mixture, about ½ cup at a time.

3. Gently spoon batter into an ungreased 10-in. tube pan. Cut through batter with a knife to remove air pockets. Bake on lowest oven rack at 350° for 35-40 minutes or until golden brown and entire top appears dry. Immediately invert pan; cool completely, about 1 hour.

4. Run a knife around side and center tube of pan. Remove cake; split into two horizontal layers. Place cake bottom on an ovenproof plate. Spread with lemon curd; replace cake top.

5. For meringue, in a small bowl, beat egg whites and cream of tartar on medium until soft peaks form. Gradually beat in sugar, 1 tablespoon at a time, on high until stiff glossy peaks form and sugar is dissolved. Spread over top and sides of cake. Bake at 350° for 15-18 minutes or until golden brown. Refrigerate leftovers.

Rhubarb Ice Cream

Years ago we had a big rhubarb patch, so a neighbor who knew I loved ice cream shared this recipe with me. You don't need any special equipment to make it.
—**JAN DOUGLAS** DENT, MN

PREP: 15 MIN. + CHILLING
COOK: 10 MIN. + FREEZING
MAKES: ABOUT 2 QUARTS

- 4 **cups sliced rhubarb**
- 2 **cups sugar**
- 2 **cups water**
- 3 **cups miniature marshmallows**
- 3 **tablespoons lemon juice**
- 5 **to 7 drops red food coloring, optional**
- 2 **cups heavy whipping cream, whipped**

1. In a large saucepan, bring rhubarb, sugar and water to a boil. Reduce heat; cover and simmer for 10-12 minutes or until rhubarb is soft.

2. Stir in marshmallows, lemon juice and food coloring if desired; cook and stir until marshmallows are melted. Cover and refrigerate for 1 hour.

3. Fold in the whipped cream. Transfer to a freezer container; cover and freeze for up to 2 months. Remove from the freezer 20 minutes before serving.

As gardens everywhere awake from a cozy winter slumber, markets are stocking up on fresh asparagus, carrots, peas and spinach.

It won't be long now before Peter Rabbit arrives and the Easter celebration begins. Maybe you're planning to dish up a honey-glazed ham, grilled leg of lamb or crown roast—whatever you choose, let these fresh-from-the-garden sides reward you for your winter patience. Welcome to spring.

Dijon Scalloped Potatoes (p. 148)

Marinated Cheese-Topped Salad

If you want to make a salad that stands out for a special celebration, top it off with melt-in-your-mouth marinated cream cheese cubes.

—BARBARA ESTABROOK RHINELANDER, WI

PREP: 25 MIN. + MARINATING • **MAKES:** 6 SERVINGS

½ cup olive oil
2 tablespoons minced fresh Italian parsley
2 tablespoons lemon juice
1 tablespoon minced fresh oregano
1 tablespoon red wine vinegar
1 large garlic clove, minced
¼ teaspoon salt
⅛ teaspoon pepper
1 package (8 ounces) cream cheese, chilled

4 cups torn romaine
2 cups fresh arugula or baby spinach
1½ cups grape tomatoes, halved
2 shallots, thinly sliced
½ cup medium pitted green olives

1. For dressing, in a small bowl, combine the first eight ingredients. Cut cream cheese into ½-in. cubes; toss with half of the dressing. Cover and refrigerate for 30 minutes.

2. In a large bowl, combine the romaine, arugula, tomatoes, shallots and olives. Drizzle with remaining dressing; toss to coat. Top with marinated cheese. Serve immediately.

Dijon Scalloped Potatoes

PICTURED ON PAGE 146

My family loves cheesy potatoes. I was so happy to find this recipe using both sweet potatoes and russet potatoes for something a little different.

—CAROLYN PUTNAM NORWALK, OH

PREP: 25 MIN. • **BAKE:** 50 MIN. + STANDING • **MAKES:** 8 SERVINGS

⅔ cup chopped onion
2 teaspoons canola oil
1 can (14½ ounces) chicken broth
2 packages (3 ounces each) cream cheese, cubed
1 tablespoon Dijon mustard
3 medium russet potatoes, peeled and thinly sliced
2 medium sweet potatoes, peeled and thinly sliced
1½ to 2 cups crushed butter-flavored crackers
3 tablespoons grated Parmesan cheese
2 tablespoons butter, melted
2 teaspoons minced fresh parsley

1. In a Dutch oven, saute onion in oil until tender. Reduce heat to medium; stir in the broth, cream cheese and mustard until blended. Remove from the heat. Stir in the potatoes.

2. Transfer to a 13-in. x 9-in. baking dish coated with cooking spray. In a small bowl, combine the crushed crackers, Parmesan cheese and butter; sprinkle over the top.

3. Bake, uncovered, at 350° for 50-60 minutes or until potatoes are tender. Sprinkle with the parsley. Let stand for 10 minutes before serving.

SCALLOPED POTATO SOUP

On a cold winter day, my family and I love this heartwarming soup made with leftover scalloped potatoes: I place the potatoes in a saucepan and add milk, chicken bouillon and grated carrots. I sprinkle a few parsley flakes over the top and let the soup simmer for 20 minutes. Before I know it, I have a great-tasting homemade soup.

—MARY LANDAAS
GLENVILLE, MN

Decadent Broccoli Souffle

Don't be afraid to serve a souffle for holiday dinners. This so-easy recipe can be whipped up in minutes and prepared in a large souffle dish or individual ramekins.

—ELAINE LUTHER HOMOSASSA, FL

PREP: 20 MIN.
BAKE: 35 MIN. + STANDING
MAKES: 10 SERVINGS

3 eggs
4 tablespoons butter, divided
2 bunches broccoli
2 tablespoons all-purpose flour
¼ teaspoon salt
¼ teaspoon pepper
1½ cups 2% milk
2 cups (8 ounces) shredded cheddar cheese, divided
1 teaspoon Dijon mustard
2 tablespoons dry bread crumbs

1. Separate eggs; let stand at room temperature for 30 minutes. Grease a 2½-qt. souffle dish with 1 tablespoon butter; set aside.
2. Cut broccoli into florets; peel and chop stems. Place broccoli in a steamer basket; place in a Dutch oven over 1 in. of water. Bring to a boil; cover and steam for 4-6 minutes or until crisp-tender.
3. In a large saucepan, melt remaining butter. Stir in the flour, salt and pepper until smooth. Gradually add milk. Bring to a boil; cook and stir for 2 minutes or until thickened. Add 1½ cups cheese and mustard; stir until cheese is melted.
4. Remove from the heat. Stir a small amount of hot mixture into egg yolks; return all to the pan, stirring constantly. Stir in the broccoli. Allow to cool slightly.
5. In a large bowl, beat egg whites until stiff peaks form. With a spatula, stir a fourth of the egg whites into broccoli mixture until no white streaks remain. Fold in remaining egg whites until combined. Transfer to prepared dish. Sprinkle with remaining cheese and bread crumbs.
6. Bake at 350° for 35-40 minutes or until the top is puffed and center appears set. Let stand for 15 minutes before serving.
NOTE *To bake in 10-oz. ramekins, divide among six greased ramekins. Bake at 350° for 20-25 minutes or until top is puffed and center appears set.*

Garden Risotto

A trio of the season's best—peas, asparagus and spinach—tucked inside a creamy white wine risotto is one of the reasons we love spring.
—**KENDRA DOSS** COLORADO SPRINGS, CO

PREP: 20 MIN. • **COOK:** 25 MIN.
MAKES: 8 SERVINGS

- ½ **pound fresh asparagus, trimmed and cut into ¾-inch pieces**
- 4½ **cups reduced-sodium chicken broth**
- 1 **medium onion, chopped**
- 2 **teaspoons olive oil**
- 1½ **cups uncooked arborio rice**
- ½ **cup dry white wine or additional reduced-sodium chicken broth**
- ½ **teaspoon salt**
- ¼ **teaspoon pepper**
- 3 **cups fresh baby spinach**
- 1 **cup frozen peas**
- ¼ **cup grated Parmesan cheese**

1. Place asparagus in a steamer basket; place in a small saucepan over 1 in. of water. Bring to a boil; cover and steam for 2-3 minutes or until crisp-tender. Set aside.

2. Meanwhile, in a small saucepan, heat broth and keep warm. In a large nonstick skillet coated with cooking spray, saute onion in oil until tender. Add rice; cook and stir for 2-3 minutes. Reduce heat; stir in the wine, salt and pepper. Cook and stir until all of the liquid is absorbed.

3. Add heated broth, ½ cup at a time, stirring constantly. Allow the liquid to absorb between additions. Cook just until risotto is creamy and rice is almost tender. (Cooking time is about 20 minutes.)

4. Add the spinach, peas, cheese and reserved asparagus; cook and stir until heated through. Serve immediately.

Crumb-Topped Asparagus Casserole

We used to live on a farm and had plenty of fresh vegetables to make casseroles like this. You can use green beans or broccoli, but in spring, this creamy asparagus bake is our family's favorite.

—**MRS. E. ALLEN OREM** ROCHESTER, NY

PREP: 20 MIN. • **BAKE:** 20 MIN. • **MAKES:** 8 SERVINGS

- 2 pounds fresh asparagus, trimmed and cut into 1-inch pieces
- 2 cans (10¾ ounces each) condensed cream of celery soup, undiluted
- ½ cup heavy whipping cream
- ½ cup mayonnaise
- 1 tablespoon Heinz 57 steak sauce
- ¼ teaspoon ground cloves
- ¼ teaspoon ground nutmeg
- 1 cup (4 ounces) shredded cheddar cheese
- 2½ cups crushed seasoned stuffing
- 5 tablespoons butter, melted

1. In a large saucepan, bring ½ in. of water to a boil. Add asparagus; cover and boil for 3-5 minutes or until crisp-tender. Drain well. Place in a greased 11-in. x 7-in. baking dish; set aside.

2. In a small bowl, combine the soup, cream, mayonnaise, steak sauce, cloves and nutmeg. Spread over asparagus; sprinkle with cheese.

3. In another small bowl, toss stuffing with butter; sprinkle over casserole. Bake, uncovered, at 350° for 20-25 minutes or until bubbly.

Sunny Snow Peas

I enjoy serving fresh vegetables, especially when I can prepare a sauce that adds a bright taste of sunshine.

—**KATHLEEN BAILEY** CHESTER SPRINGS, PA

START TO FINISH: 25 MIN. • **MAKES:** 6 SERVINGS

- ½ cup orange juice
- 2 tablespoons honey
- 1 tablespoon butter
- 1 to 2 teaspoons grated orange peel
- ½ teaspoon salt
- ⅛ teaspoon ground cardamom
- 1 pound fresh snow peas or sugar snap peas

1. In a small saucepan, combine the first six ingredients; bring to a boil. Reduce heat; simmer, uncovered, until the mixture is reduced by half, about 15 minutes.

2. Meanwhile, in another saucepan, bring 1 in. of water to a boil. Add peas. Reduce heat; cover and simmer for 3-4 minutes or until crisp-tender. Drain and transfer to a serving bowl. Add orange juice mixture and toss to coat.

THREE PEAS IN A POD

Do you know the difference between garden peas, snow peas and sugar snap peas? Garden peas must be shelled before eating and are mostly sold frozen or canned. Snow peas are never shelled and have flat, edible pods. Sugar snap peas are also not shelled but are slightly sweeter and have plump, crisp, edible pods.

Herbed Garlic Potatoes

I learned to cook from my mom, using a pinch of this and a dash of that, but it was actually my father who came up with this recipe. It's a tasty treatment for potatoes that can go with a special-occasion meal or a casual cookout.
—**SHERRY DESJARDIN** FAIRBANKS, AK

START TO FINISH: 30 MIN. • **MAKES:** 8 SERVINGS

15 small red potatoes (about 2 pounds), cut in half
⅓ cup butter, cubed
¼ cup minced fresh parsley
2 tablespoons minced chives
1½ teaspoons minced fresh tarragon or ½ teaspoon dried tarragon
2 to 3 garlic cloves, minced
3 bacon strips, cooked and crumbled
½ teaspoon salt
¼ teaspoon pepper

1. Place potatoes in a large saucepan and cover with water. Bring to a boil. Reduce heat; cover and cook for 15-20 minutes or until tender. Drain well.

2. In a large skillet, melt butter. Add the parsley, chives, tarragon and garlic; cook and stir over low heat for 1-2 minutes. Add the potatoes, bacon, salt and pepper; toss to coat. Cook until heated through, about 5 minutes.

Creamy Vegetable Casserole

I've also used an Italian cheese blend instead of Swiss to prepare this family-friendly veggie bake. I like to add extra white pepper for a little kick.
—**CHRISTIE NELSON** TAYLORVILLE, IL

PREP: 25 MIN. • **BAKE:** 20 MIN. • **MAKES:** 8 SERVINGS

2 cups fresh baby carrots
2 cups fresh broccoli florets
2 cups fresh cauliflowerets
1¾ cups sliced fresh mushrooms
2 tablespoons butter
2 tablespoons all-purpose flour
2 cups half-and-half cream
1 teaspoon chicken bouillon granules
½ teaspoon onion powder
¼ teaspoon white pepper
1 cup (4 ounces) shredded Swiss cheese
½ cup crushed butter-flavored crackers (about 15 crackers)

1. Place carrots in a steamer basket; place in a large saucepan over 1 in. of water. Bring to a boil; cover and steam for 3 minutes.

2. Add broccoli and cauliflower; steam 5 minutes longer or until vegetables are tender. Transfer to a greased 2½-qt. baking dish.

3. In a large skillet, saute the mushrooms in butter until tender. Stir in flour until blended. Gradually stir in the cream, bouillon, onion powder and pepper. Bring to a boil; cook and stir for 2 minutes or until thickened. Stir in cheese.

4. Pour over vegetables and stir to coat. Sprinkle with cracker crumbs. Bake, uncovered, at 350° for 20-25 minutes or until bubbly.

Marmalade Candied Carrots

Drizzled with a thick glaze bursting with sweet orange flavors—fresh baby carrots are my favorite thing to prepare in spring.
—HEATHER CLEMMONS SUPPLY, NC

START TO FINISH: 30 MIN.
MAKES: 8 SERVINGS

2 **pounds fresh baby carrots**
⅔ **cup orange marmalade**
3 **tablespoons brown sugar**
2 **tablespoons butter**
½ **cup chopped pecans, toasted**
1 **teaspoon rum extract**

1. Place carrots in a steamer basket; place in a large saucepan over 1 in. of water. Bring to a boil; cover and steam for 12-15 minutes or until crisp-tender.
2. Meanwhile, in a small saucepan, combine the marmalade, brown sugar and butter; cook and stir over medium heat until mixture is thickened and reduced to about ½ cup. Stir in pecans and extract.
3. Place carrots in a large bowl; drizzle with glaze and stir gently to coat.

Stuffed Sweet Onions

I must say, I think this side dish is almost a meal in itself. Sometimes I serve it with a white sauce ladled over the top. It's certainly a nice change from meat and potatoes.

—JEANNE ALLEN RYE, CO

PREP: 30 MIN. • **COOK:** 5 MIN.
MAKES: 4 SERVINGS

- 3 **quarts water**
- 4 **medium sweet onions, peeled**
- 1 **tablespoon chopped green onion**
- 1½ **teaspoons minced fresh parsley**
- 6 **teaspoons butter, divided**
- ½ **cup chopped fully cooked lean ham**
- ¼ **teaspoon salt**
- ¼ **teaspoon celery seed**
- ¼ **teaspoon pepper**
- ⅛ **teaspoon garlic powder**
- ½ **cup soft bread crumbs, divided**

1. In a large saucepan, bring water to a boil. Add onions; cover and boil for 9-11 minutes or until tender. Drain; cool for 5 minutes. Cut a thin slice off the top of each onion; carefully hollow out, leaving a ½-in. shell. Chop removed onion.

2. In a nonstick skillet coated with cooking spray, cook the chopped onion, green onion and parsley in 4 teaspoons butter for 3 minutes. Add the ham, salt, celery seed, pepper and garlic powder; cook until onions are tender and ham is lightly browned. Stir in ¼ cup bread crumbs; heat through. Stuff into onion shells.

3. Melt remaining butter; toss with remaining bread crumbs. Sprinkle over stuffing. Broil 6 in. from the heat for 3-4 minutes or until crumbs are lightly browned and onions are heated through.

International Potato Cake

I once prepared food for an embassy function in Turkey, where diplomats from most European and Middle Eastern countries were present. And this International Potato Cake was devoured by all!

—**JUDY BATSON** TAMPA, FL

PREP: 40 MIN. • **BAKE:** 35 MIN. + COOLING • **MAKES:** 12 SERVINGS

- ¼ **cup seasoned bread crumbs**
- 3 **pounds potatoes (about 9 medium), peeled and cubed**
- ½ **cup heavy whipping cream**
- ¼ **cup butter, cubed**
- 3 **eggs, beaten**
- 1 **teaspoon Greek seasoning**
- ¼ **teaspoon garlic salt**
- ¼ **teaspoon lemon-pepper seasoning**
- ¼ **pound thinly sliced fontina cheese**
- ¼ **pound thinly sliced hard salami, coarsely chopped**

TOPPING
- ⅓ **cup grated Parmesan cheese**
- 1 **tablespoon seasoned bread crumbs**
- 1 **tablespoon butter, melted**

1. Sprinkle bread crumbs onto the bottom of a greased 9-in. springform pan; set aside.

2. Place potatoes in a large saucepan and cover with water. Bring to a boil. Reduce heat; cover and simmer for 10-15 minutes or until tender. Drain; transfer to a large bowl. Mash potatoes with cream, butter, eggs and seasonings.

3. Spoon half of potatoes into prepared pan. Layer with cheese and salami; top with remaining potatoes. Combine the topping ingredients; spoon over potatoes.

4. Cover and bake at 350° for 30 minutes. Uncover; bake 5-10 minutes longer or until topping is golden brown and a thermometer reads 160°. Cool on a wire rack for 10 minutes. Carefully run a knife around edge of pan to loosen; remove sides of pan. Serve warm.

Easter dinner just isn't complete without a little something sweet to end the meal. But amid the frenzy of holiday preparations, you want something that will get you out of the kitchen fast. Whether you're hosting a lavish party or simply seeking the perfect grand finale to a casual brunch, any one of these no-bake desserts will save the day.

PEEPS STICK TOGETHER

These chicks love flowers, and Peeps make an exceptionally sweet way to bring vibrant colors to your Easter table. See p. 169.

Lemon Curd Tartlets (p. 163)
Crunchy Chocolate Eggs (p. 160)
Jelly Bean Bark (p. 164)

NO-BAKE **EASTER DESSERTS**

Crunchy Chocolate Eggs

PICTURED ON PAGE 158

I've been making these chocolate candies since my children were young, and we never tire of the taste. You can also shape them into footballs for a tailgating treat.
—**JANIS PLOURDE** SMOOTH ROCK FALLS, ON

PREP: 40 MIN. + STANDING • **MAKES:** ABOUT 4½ DOZEN

1 cup packed brown sugar
1 cup light corn syrup
1 cup peanut butter
2 cups cornflakes
2 cups crisp rice cereal
½ cup finely chopped peanuts
3¾ cups semisweet chocolate chips
1½ teaspoons shortening
  Candy sprinkles

1. In a heavy saucepan, combine brown sugar, corn syrup and peanut butter. Cook and stir over medium heat until smooth. Remove from the heat; stir in cereals and peanuts.

2. When cool enough to handle, drop by tablespoonfuls onto waxed paper-lined baking sheets. Form into egg shapes. Refrigerate until firm.

3. In a microwave, melt chocolate chips and shortening; stir until smooth. Dip eggs in chocolate; allow excess to drip off. Place on waxed paper-lined baking sheets. Decorate with sprinkles. Let stand until set.

NOTE *Reduced-fat peanut butter is not recommended for this recipe.*

Lime Angel Food Cake

For my husband's family reunion, I took a store-bought angel food cake and turned it into this special dessert with a lovely lime cream frosting topped with toasted coconut. It went over big!
—**NANCY FOUST** STONEBORO, PA

PREP: 20 MIN. + CHILLING • **COOK:** 15 MIN. + CHILLING • **MAKES:** 12 SERVINGS

2 eggs
2 egg yolks
½ cup plus 3 tablespoons sugar, divided
6 tablespoons lime juice
2 teaspoons grated lime peel
½ cup cold butter, cubed
1 cup heavy whipping cream
½ teaspoon vanilla extract
1 prepared angel food cake (8 to 10 ounces)
1 cup flaked coconut, toasted

1. In the top of a double boiler, beat eggs and yolks. Stir in ½ cup sugar, lime juice and peel. Cook over simmering water while gradually whisking in butter. Cook and stir until mixture is thickened and reaches 160°. Strain; refrigerate until completely cool.

2. In a small bowl, beat cream and vanilla until stiff peaks form; gradually beat in remaining sugar. Gently fold into lime mixture.

3. Split cake horizontally into three layers. Place bottom layer on a serving plate. Spread with ⅔ cup lime mixture. Repeat. Place top layer on cake. Frost top and sides with remaining lime mixture. Sprinkle with coconut. Refrigerate for at least 30 minutes before slicing.

Blueberry Cloud Pie

I always make two of these pies at a time because my family devours them! The filling is light and fluffy, and the Rice Krispie treat crust puts an extra-playful spin on cloud pie.

—DENISE HEATWOLE
WAYNESBORO, GA

PREP: 15 MIN. + CHILLING
MAKES: 8 SERVINGS

- 1¼ cups miniature marshmallows
- 3 tablespoons butter, cubed
- 2½ cups crisp rice cereal
- 1 package (3 ounces) berry blue gelatin
- ½ cup boiling water
- ½ cup cold water
- 2 cups heavy whipping cream
- 5 tablespoons confectioners' sugar
- 1⅔ cups fresh blueberries
  Additional fresh blueberries

1. In a large saucepan, combine marshmallows and butter. Cook and stir over medium heat until marshmallows are melted. Stir in cereal. With greased hands, press onto the bottom and up the sides of a greased 9-in. pie plate; set aside.

2. In a large bowl, dissolve gelatin in boiling water; stir in cold water. Refrigerate until partially set, about 1 hour.

3. In a small bowl, beat cream until it begins to thicken. Add confectioners' sugar; beat until soft peaks form.

4. Fold berries and 3 cups whipped cream into gelatin mixture. Pour into crust. Refrigerate pie and remaining whipped cream for up to 4 hours. Garnish with reserved cream and additional blueberries.

Breezy Lemon-Berry Dessert

Because I love the combination of berries and lemon, I wanted to come up with a light, refreshing and tasty dessert that used them both.
—ANNA GINSBERG AUSTIN, TX

PREP: 30 MIN. + CHILLING
MAKES: 12 SERVINGS

- 2 **envelopes unflavored gelatin**
- ½ **cup cold water**
- 1 **package (3 ounces) ladyfingers, split**
- 1½ **cups fat-free milk**
- ½ **cup refrigerated French vanilla nondairy creamer**
- 1 **package (3.4 ounces) instant lemon pudding mix**
- 1 **carton (12 ounces) frozen reduced-fat whipped topping, thawed, divided**
- 3 **cups mixed fresh berries**
- 2 **cups sliced fresh strawberries**

1. In a small saucepan, sprinkle gelatin over cold water; let stand for 1 minute. Cook over low heat, stirring until gelatin is completely dissolved. Remove from the heat and set aside.

2. Cut ladyfingers in half widthwise; arrange cut side down around the sides of an ungreased 9-in. springform pan. Place remaining ladyfingers in the bottom of the pan (bottom will not be completely covered).

3. In a large bowl, whisk the milk, creamer and pudding mix for 2 minutes. Let stand for 2 minutes or until soft-set. Stir in gelatin mixture. Fold in 3 cups whipped topping.

4. Spread 2 cups of filling evenly into prepared pan; top with mixed berries. Spread with remaining filling (filling will be higher than ladyfinger border). Cover and refrigerate for 5 hours or until set. Garnish with remaining whipped topping and the strawberries.

Coconut Pistachio Pie

This two-ingredient crust consisting of coconut and butter is a must-try!
To toast the coconut, spread it in a 15-inch x 10-inch x 1-inch baking pan.
Bake at 350° for 5-10 minutes or until lightly browned, stirring occasionally.
—TASTE OF HOME TEST KITCHEN

PREP: 20 MIN. + CHILLING • **MAKES:** 8 SERVINGS

2½ cups flaked coconut, lightly toasted
⅓ cup butter, melted
2 cups cold 2% milk
2 packages (3.4 ounces each) instant pistachio pudding mix
1 cup whipped topping
2 tablespoons chopped pistachios, optional

1. In a small bowl, combine the coconut and butter. Press onto the bottom and up the sides of a greased 9-in. pie plate. Refrigerate for at least 30 minutes or until firm.

2. In a small bowl, whisk milk and pudding mixes for 2 minutes. Let stand for 2 minutes or until soft-set. Spread 1½ cups over the crust.

3. Fold whipped topping into remaining pudding; spread over pie. Sprinkle with pistachios if desired. Cover and refrigerate for at least 2 hours.

Lemon Curd Tartlets

PICTURED ON PAGE 158

The lemon curd in these adorable little tarts is reminiscent of lemon meringue pie and is so simple to make. I like to top them with any kind of fresh berries and a dab of whipped cream.
—JESSICA FEIST BROOKFIELD, WI

PREP: 35 MIN. + CHILLING • **MAKES:** 15 TARTLETS

3 eggs
1 cup sugar
½ cup lemon juice
1 tablespoon grated lemon peel
¼ cup butter, cubed
1 package (1.9 ounces) frozen miniature phyllo tart shells, thawed
Fresh raspberries, mint leaves and/or sweetened whipped cream, optional

1. In a small heavy saucepan over medium heat, whisk the eggs, sugar, lemon juice and peel until blended. Add butter; cook, whisking constantly, until mixture is thickened and coats the back of a metal spoon. Transfer to a small bowl; cool for 10 minutes. Cover and refrigerate until chilled.

2. Just before serving, spoon lemon curd into tart shells. Garnish with raspberries, mint and/or whipped cream if desired. Refrigerate leftovers.

A SWEET-TART CONDIMENT

This simple recipe for lemon curd is good for more than just filling tart shells. Also try spreading it on English muffins, stirring it into plain yogurt, using it as a crepe filling, serving it with pancakes and French toast or folding it into whipped cream.

Orange Cream Cheesecake

I love serving this impressive-looking cheesecake with its pretty layers and silky-smooth texture. The combination of orange, cream cheese and whipped topping is simply irresistible.
—MADONNA FAUNCE BOISE, ID

PREP: 25 MIN. + CHILLING • **MAKES:** 10-12 SERVINGS

- 2 cups graham cracker crumbs
- 1 teaspoon ground cinnamon
- 1 teaspoon grated orange peel
- ½ cup butter, melted

FILLING

- 1 package (3 ounces) orange gelatin
- 3 packages (8 ounces each) cream cheese, softened
- 1¼ cups sugar
- 1 can (5 ounces) evaporated milk
- ⅓ cup thawed orange juice concentrate
- 1 teaspoon lemon juice
- 1 teaspoon vanilla extract
- 1 envelope unflavored gelatin
- 2 tablespoons cold water
- 2 tablespoons boiling water
- 1 carton (8 ounces) frozen whipped topping, thawed

TOPPING

- 2 cups whipped topping
- ¼ cup sugar
  Citrus fruits and lemon balm, optional

1. In a large bowl, combine the cracker crumbs, cinnamon, orange peel and butter. Press onto the bottom of a greased 10-in. springform pan. Refrigerate for at least 30 minutes.

2. Prepare orange gelatin according to package directions. Set aside ½ cup at room temperature. Chill remaining gelatin until slightly thickened, 40-60 minutes.

3. In a large bowl, beat cream cheese and sugar until smooth. Beat in the milk, orange juice concentrate, lemon juice and vanilla. Beat on medium-high speed 2 minutes longer.

4. In a small bowl, sprinkle unflavored gelatin over cold water; let stand for 2 minutes. Stir in boiling water until gelatin is completely dissolved. Stir into the room-temperature orange gelatin. Stir into cream cheese mixture, then fold in whipped topping. Pour into crust.

5. For topping, in a large bowl, beat whipped topping and sugar. Beat in refrigerated orange gelatin (mixture will be thin). Chill for 30 minutes. Gently spoon over filling (pan will be full). Refrigerate for 8 hours or overnight. Remove sides of pan. Garnish with fruit and lemon balm if desired.

Jelly Bean Bark

PICTURED ON PAGE 159

Here's a fun and super-simple candy to make with or for kids at Eastertime. Only three ingredients—that's it! And every piece has a different flavor combination.
—MAVIS DEMENT MARCUS, IA

START TO FINISH: 15 MIN. • **MAKES:** 2 POUNDS

- 1 tablespoon melted butter
- 1¼ pounds white candy coating, chopped
- 2 cups miniature jelly beans

1. Line a 15-in. x 10-in. x 1-in. pan with foil. Brush with butter; set aside. In a microwave, melt candy coating; stir until smooth.

2. Spread into prepared pan. Sprinkle with jelly beans. Let stand until set before breaking into pieces.

Pineapple Orange Trifle

Dreamsicle meets tropical is the only way to describe this citrus-infused trifle. Make sure you get a big scoop; you'll be glad you did!

—RENEE SCHWEBACH
DUMONT, MN

PREP: 20 MIN. + CHILLING
MAKES: 12 SERVINGS

- 1 can (14 ounces) pineapple tidbits
- 2 cups cold 2% milk
- 2 packages (3.4 ounces each) instant vanilla pudding mix
- 1 cup (8 ounces) sour cream
- 1 can (11 ounces) mandarin oranges, drained
- 1 prepared angel food cake (8 to 10 ounces), cut into 1-inch cubes
- 1 carton (8 ounces) frozen whipped topping, thawed
- ½ teaspoon orange extract
- ⅓ cup flaked coconut, toasted

1. Drain pineapple, reserving ⅔ cup juice; set pineapple aside. In a large bowl, whisk the milk, pineapple juice and pudding mixes for 2 minutes. Let stand for 2 minutes or until soft-set. Whisk in sour cream; fold in oranges and pineapple.

2. Place a third of the cake cubes in a 3-qt. trifle bowl; top with a third of the pudding mixture. Repeat layers twice. Cover and refrigerate for 3 hours. Combine whipped topping and extract; spread over the top. Sprinkle with the coconut.

Sherbet Cream Cake

For an Easter ice cream social, it doesn't get any more showstopping than this dessert. Although it takes a little time to prepare, it's easy and it turns out beautiful and delicious! In my family, this is how we celebrate special occasions and birthdays.
—PAULA WIPF ARLINGTON, VA

PREP: 30 MIN. + FREEZING
MAKES: 14-16 SERVINGS

- 3 **cups each raspberry, orange and lime sherbet**
- 3 **quarts vanilla ice cream, softened, divided**
- 2 **cups chopped pecans, divided**
- 2 **cups miniature semisweet chocolate chips, divided**
- 3 **cups heavy whipping cream, whipped**
  Raspberries and orange and lime slices, optional

1. Using a ¼-cup ice cream scoop, shape sherbet into balls. Place on a waxed paper-lined baking sheet. Freeze for 1 hour or until firm.

2. In a large bowl, combine 1 qt. vanilla ice cream, 1 cup pecans and 1 cup chocolate chips. Spread into a 10-in. tube pan.

3. Alternately arrange 12 sherbet balls, four of each color, against the center tube and outer edge of pan. Freeze for 30 minutes.

4. Spread with 1 qt. ice cream; freeze for 30 minutes. Top with remaining sherbet balls. Combine remaining ice cream, pecans and chips; spread over sherbet balls. Cover and freeze overnight.

5. Run a knife around edge of pan; dip pan in lukewarm water until loosened. Invert cake onto a serving plate. Frost with whipped cream. Return to freezer. Remove from the freezer 10 minutes before serving. Garnish with raspberries and orange and lime slices if desired.

Strawberry Sorbet Sensation

This is my figure-friendly dessert for a warm spring or summer day. I love the taste of strawberries and vanilla, but this two-toned treat can be done in a variety of flavor combinations, and with just five ingredients.

—KENDRA DOSS COLORADO SPRINGS, CO

PREP: 20 MIN. + FREEZING • **MAKES:** 8 SERVINGS

- **2 cups strawberry sorbet, softened**
- **1 cup cold fat-free milk**
- **1 package (1 ounce) sugar-free instant vanilla pudding mix**
- **1 carton (8 ounces) frozen reduced-fat whipped topping, thawed, divided**
- **1 cup sliced fresh strawberries**

1. Line an 8-in. x 4-in. loaf pan with heavy-duty foil. Spoon sorbet into pan; freeze for 15 minutes.

2. In a small bowl, whisk milk and pudding mix for 2 minutes. Let stand for 2 minutes or until soft-set. Set aside ½ cup whipped topping for garnish; refrigerate until serving. Fold remaining whipped topping into pudding; spoon over sorbet. Cover and freeze for 4 hours or overnight.

3. Remove from the freezer 10-15 minutes before serving; unmold onto a serving plate and remove foil. Serve with strawberries and reserved whipped topping.

Cream Cheese Clouds

The easiest way to impress guests with a fun, seasonal dessert is to make these sweet, meringue-like clouds the night before and pop them into the freezer. Just before serving, top them with fresh strawberries or pie filling.

—MARY ANN MARINO WEST PITTSBURGH, PA

PREP: 10 MIN. + FREEZING • **MAKES:** 10 SERVINGS

- **1 package (8 ounces) cream cheese, softened**
- **¾ cup confectioners' sugar**
- **½ teaspoon vanilla extract**
- **1 cup heavy whipping cream**
- **2 quarts fresh strawberries, sliced**
- **1 carton (8 ounces) frozen whipped topping, thawed**

1. In a large bowl, beat the cream cheese, confectioners' sugar and vanilla until smooth. Gradually add cream, beating until thickened.

2. Spoon mixture into 10 mounds on a waxed paper-lined baking sheet. Using the back of a spoon, shape into 3-in. cups. Freeze for 2 hours or overnight.

3. To serve, fill with strawberries and garnish with whipped topping.

FROZEN DOLLOPS

If you have leftover heavy whipping cream, don't let it go bad. Whip it up, drop rounded spoonfuls on a cookie sheet and freeze 'em. Then drop the frozen dollops in a freezer bag and return to the freezer. The next time you have hot chocolate or iced coffee, add a dollop.

Frozen Lemonade Squares

When I was growing up, this was a special warm-weather treat. Whenever I see the temperature start to climb, I make sure I put a batch in the freezer.
—KARA O'REILLY TIGARD, OR

PREP: 15 MIN. + FREEZING • **MAKES:** 24 SERVINGS

1⅓ cups graham cracker crumbs
⅔ cup crushed vanilla wafers (about 18 wafers)
½ cup sugar
½ cup butter, melted
2 quarts vanilla ice cream, softened
¾ cup thawed pink lemonade concentrate

1. In a small bowl, mix cracker crumbs, wafer crumbs and sugar; stir in butter. Reserve ¼ cup for topping. Press remaining crumb mixture onto bottom of a greased 13x9-in. baking pan.

2. In a large bowl, mix ice cream and lemonade concentrate. Spread over crust; top with reserved crumb mixture. Freeze overnight or until firm.

Strawberries & Cream Pie

For a lighter no-bake dessert to serve a crowd, turn to these cool strawberry pies. They take just minutes to prepare, so they're an excellent make-ahead option if you're expecting company.
—KATIE HOUSEMAN BYRON CENTER, MI

PREP: 15 MIN. + CHILLING • **MAKES:** 2 PIES (8 SERVINGS EACH)

1 envelope unflavored gelatin
¼ cup cold water
1 cup boiling water
⅔ cup sugar
1 teaspoon vanilla extract
1 cup (8 ounces) fat-free plain yogurt
1 cup (8 ounces) fat-free sour cream

1 carton (8 ounces) frozen whipped topping, thawed
3 cups sliced fresh strawberries, divided
2 graham cracker crusts (9 inches each)

1. In a large bowl, sprinkle gelatin over cold water. Add boiling water and stir until dissolved. Stir in sugar and vanilla; cool.

2. Whisk in yogurt and sour cream. Fold in whipped topping. Stir in 2 cups strawberries. Pour into crusts. Refrigerate until set. Top with remaining strawberries.

NO-BAKE GRAHAM CRACKER PIE CRUST

If you want to make a graham cracker pie crust, begin by crushing 24 graham cracker squares to yield 1½ cups crumbs. In a mixing bowl, combine the crumbs with ¼ cup sugar. Melt ⅓ cup butter; add to crumb mixture and blend well. Press mixture onto the bottom and up the sides of an ungreased 9-inch pie plate. Refrigerate for 30 minutes before filling.

Peeps Stick Together

Easter candy rises to the occasion in this cheery topiary.

Bring vibrant marshmallow Peeps out of the Easter basket and make them the life of the party!

We used floral pins for stability, so our version is strictly for decorating. Want yours to be edible? Use toothpicks instead of pins, and assemble shortly before serving—Peeps harden quickly.

MATERIALS

Several packages of colored Peeps (we used chicks)
Acrylic craft paint, green and blue
Clear acrylic sealer (optional)
Flat paintbrush
½- x 18-inch wooden dowel rod
4- to 5-inch-tall terra cotta pot
5-inch-wide white Styrofoam ball
Small piece of floral foam to fit pot
Metal floral pins
Permanent glue
Green paper grass
½- to 1-inch-wide patterned ribbon

DIRECTIONS

1. Paint the dowel rod green and the pot's exterior blue. Use as many coats as needed for full coverage, allowing to dry fully between coats. Apply sealer to rod and pot if desired and let dry.

2. Glue floral foam in bottom of pot. Put a small amount of glue on end of rod and insert in foam.

3. Fill pot top with green paper grass. Tie a bow around rod slightly above grass.

4. Use rod to poke a hole, 1½ to 2 in. deep, in the Styrofoam ball.

Beginning at the hole, draw a line around ball's center.

5. Leaving hole open, use floral pins to attach a row of pink Peeps, sides touching, along the drawn line. (We pinned through the tails to hide pins.) Next, attach a row of blue Peeps, followed by rows of yellow and pink, ending with a blue one in the center. Repeat rows on ball's opposite side.

6. Put a small amount of glue on the top of the rod. Insert rod into hole in Styrofoam ball; let glue dry.

specialcelebrations

Let your creative spirit shine in the kitchen with any of the exciting recipes and party themes found here. Throw a swinging '60s cocktail soiree, root for the home team with crowd favorites and let honey be the golden ingredient in your next holiday affair. You can count on these ideas to help you make any occasion one to remember.

Because sometimes you just want to throw a good old-fashioned cocktail party: Who wouldn't cheer to that? The classics you know and love, from gimlets to Manhattans, make a stylish appearance. But it simply wouldn't be right without the company of a few time-honored finger foods. You know the ones—little sausages, meatballs, shrimp cocktail, deviled eggs.

Call it a Mad Men Affair or a '60s Social; either way you get to don a swanky vintage dress while the fellas compete to be the most dapper gentleman in the room.

COASTER FLAIR

We know it's hard to part with your drink, but when it's time to grab a nibble, rest your cocktail in style on a custom '60s-style coaster. See p. 181.

’60s **COCKTAIL PARTY**

Party Puffs

PICTURED ON PAGE 173

Ham salad makes a comeback on the appetizer tray, and egg salad can tag along.
I like to tuck both salads into homemade cream puffs.

—KAREN OWEN RISING SUN, IN

PREP: 25 MIN. • **BAKE:** 20 MIN. + COOLING • **MAKES:** 7½ DOZEN

1 cup water
½ cup butter
1 cup all-purpose flour
4 eggs

EGG SALAD FILLING
6 hard-cooked eggs, chopped
⅓ cup mayonnaise
3 tablespoons chutney, finely chopped
2 green onions, finely chopped
1 teaspoon salt
½ teaspoon curry powder

HAM SALAD FILLING
1 can (4¼ ounces) deviled ham
1 package (3 ounces) cream cheese, softened

2 tablespoons finely chopped green pepper
1½ teaspoons prepared horseradish
1 teaspoon lemon juice

1. In a saucepan over medium heat, bring water and butter to a boil. Add flour all at once and stir until a smooth ball forms. Remove from the heat; let stand for 5 minutes.

2. Add eggs, one at a time, beating well after each addition. Continue beating until mixture is smooth and shiny. Drop by teaspoonfuls 2 in. apart onto greased baking sheets.

3. Bake at 400° for 20-25 minutes or until lightly browned. Remove to wire racks. Immediately cut a slit in each puff to allow steam to escape; cool completely.

4. In separate bowls, combine the ingredients for egg salad filling and ham salad filling. Split puffs and remove soft dough from inside. Just before serving, spoon fillings into cream puffs; replace tops. Refrigerate leftovers.

Martini

PICTURED ON PAGE 172

You can't have a cocktail party without a martini on the menu, and this queen-of-the-cocktail-hour drink comes shaken, not stirred.

—TASTE OF HOME TEST KITCHEN

START TO FINISH: 5 MIN.
MAKES: 1 SERVING

Ice cubes
3 ounces gin or vodka
½ ounce dry vermouth
Pimiento-stuffed olives

Fill a shaker three-fourths full with ice. Add gin and vermouth; cover and shake until condensation forms on outside of shaker. Strain into a chilled cocktail glass. Garnish with olives.

Manhattan

Straight up or over ice, this is the classic New York drink for the ages.

—TASTE OF HOME TEST KITCHEN

START TO FINISH: 5 MIN.
MAKES: 1 SERVING

Ice cubes
2 ounces whiskey
½ ounce sweet vermouth
2 to 3 dashes bitters, optional
Maraschino cherry

Fill a shaker three-fourths full with ice. Add the whiskey, vermouth and bitters if desired; cover and shake until condensation forms on outside of shaker. Strain into an ice-filled glass. Garnish with a cherry.

Gimlet

PICTURED AT RIGHT

A touch of confectioners' sugar sweetens the deal in this lime-infused concoction.

—TASTE OF HOME TEST KITCHEN

START TO FINISH: 5 MIN.
MAKES: 1 SERVING

Ice cubes
2 ounces gin
1 ounce lime juice
1 teaspoon confectioners' sugar
Lime slices

Fill a shaker three-fourths full with ice. Add the gin, lime juice and confectioners' sugar; cover and shake for 10-15 seconds or until condensation forms on outside of shaker. Strain into an ice-filled glass. Garnish with lime.

Brandy Old-Fashioned Sweet

Here in Wisconsin, we make this old-fashioned favorite using brandy in place of whiskey, and soda instead of water, for a milder, sweet cocktail.

—TASTE OF HOME TEST KITCHEN

START TO FINISH: 10 MIN.
MAKES: 1 SERVING

- 1 orange slice
- 1 maraschino cherry
- 1½ ounces maraschino cherry juice
- 1 teaspoon bitters
- ¼ to ⅓ cup ice cubes
- 1½ ounces brandy
- 2 teaspoons water
- 1 teaspoon orange juice
- 3 ounces lemon-lime soda

In a rocks glass, muddle orange slice, cherry, cherry juice and bitters. Add ice. Pour in the brandy, water, orange juice and soda.

UP, OR ON THE ROCKS

Both martinis and Manhattans can be ordered "up," without ice, or "on the rocks," with ice. A rocks glass is used with ice, whereas a funnel-shaped glass, known as a martini glass, is used if your drink is served "up."

Rumaki Appetizers

Polynesian food was all the rage in the '60s, and recipes like this remind us why. My Rumaki Appetizers with pineapple have come to be an annual tradition in our home.

—JANICE THOMAS MILFORD, NE

PREP: 30 MIN. • **BROIL:** 10 MIN.
MAKES: 14 APPETIZERS

- ½ cup packed brown sugar
- ¼ cup mayonnaise
- ¼ cup chili sauce
- 14 whole water chestnuts, drained
- 1 can (8 ounces) pineapple chunks, drained
- 7 bacon strips, halved

1. In a small saucepan, combine the brown sugar, mayonnaise and chili sauce. Cook and stir over medium heat until mixture comes to a boil; set aside.

2. Place a water chestnut and a pineapple chunk on each piece of bacon; roll up bacon and secure with a toothpick. Place on a broiler pan. Broil 4-5 in. from the heat 4-5 minutes on each side or until bacon is crisp. Serve with sauce.

Shrimp Cocktail

During the '60s, shrimp cocktail was one of the most popular party foods around. Even today, it's the one appetizer that I serve for every special occasion.
—**PEGGY ALLEN** PASADENA, CA

PREP: 30 MIN. + CHILLING • **MAKES:** ABOUT 6 DOZEN (1¼ CUPS SAUCE)

3 quarts water
1 small onion, sliced
½ medium lemon, sliced
2 sprigs fresh parsley
1 tablespoon salt
5 whole peppercorns
1 bay leaf
¼ teaspoon dried thyme
3 pounds uncooked large shrimp, peeled and deveined (tails on)

SAUCE
1 cup chili sauce
2 tablespoons lemon juice
2 tablespoons prepared horseradish
4 teaspoons Worcestershire sauce
½ teaspoon salt
Dash cayenne pepper

1. In a Dutch oven, combine the first eight ingredients; bring to a boil. Add shrimp. Reduce heat; simmer, uncovered, for 4-5 minutes or until shrimp turn pink.
2. Drain shrimp and immediately rinse in cold water. Refrigerate for 2-3 hours or until cold. In a small bowl, combine the sauce ingredients. Refrigerate until serving.
3. Arrange shrimp on a serving platter; serve with sauce.

Waldorf Celery Sticks
PICTURED ON PAGE 173

This is my play on the traditional Waldorf salad. I added a strong, tangy cheese to give it a slightly sharper taste. I think it works well with the sweetness of the apples.
—**STACIE HULL** SENECA, SC

START TO FINISH: 15 MIN. • **MAKES:** 1 DOZEN

½ cup finely chopped apple
¼ cup finely chopped walnuts
3 tablespoons mayonnaise
2 tablespoons crumbled blue cheese
12 celery ribs

In a small bowl, combine the apple, walnuts, mayonnaise and blue cheese. Cut celery ribs into smaller serving sizes if desired. Fill celery with apple mixture. Chill until serving.

Sweet Sausage Rolls

Pigs in a blanket are among those appetizers that are hard to stop eating. I've made these several times, and everyone who tastes them thinks they're addicting!

—LORI CABUNO CANFIELD, OH

PREP: 25 MIN. • **BAKE:** 15 MIN.
MAKES: 2 DOZEN

- 1 **tube (8 ounces) refrigerated crescent rolls**
- 24 **miniature smoked sausage links**
- ½ **cup butter, melted**
- ½ **cup chopped nuts**
- 3 **tablespoons honey**
- 3 **tablespoons brown sugar**

1. Unroll crescent dough and separate into triangles; cut each lengthwise into three triangles. Place sausages on wide end of triangles; roll up tightly.

2. Combine the remaining ingredients in an 11-in. x 7-in. baking dish. Arrange sausage rolls, seam side down, in the butter mixture. Bake, uncovered, at 400° for 15-20 minutes or until golden brown.

Best Deviled Eggs

No old-fashioned cocktail party would be complete without deviled eggs. Don't bother with the fancy mix-ins and fillings; this tried-and-true recipe delivers on the flavors people expect—and love.

—**JESSE & ANNE FOUST** BLUEFIELD, WV

START TO FINISH: 15 MIN. • **MAKES:** 2 DOZEN

½ cup mayonnaise
2 tablespoons 2% milk
1 teaspoon dried parsley flakes
½ teaspoon dill weed
½ teaspoon minced chives
½ teaspoon ground mustard
¼ teaspoon salt
¼ teaspoon paprika
⅛ teaspoon garlic powder
⅛ teaspoon pepper
12 hard-cooked eggs
  Minced fresh parsley and additional paprika

In a small bowl, combine the first 10 ingredients. Slice eggs in half lengthwise; remove yolks and set whites aside. In another bowl, mash yolks; add to mayonnaise mixture, mixing well. Stuff or pipe filling into egg whites. Sprinkle with parsley and additional paprika. Refrigerate until serving.

MAKING THE CUT

To make deviled eggs to take to a party, I cut them the short way instead of the long way. After washing Styrofoam egg cartons, I line them with mini muffin liners, then set in my deviled egg halves. At the party, I cut off the top of each carton ... and folks help themselves.

—**JEAN STREHLOW**
WEST ALLIS, WI

Asparagus Appetizer Roll-Ups

In a nod to the iconic Wonder Bread, fresh asparagus is wrapped up in crustless slices of soft, white bread slathered with a bacon and onion cream cheese and sprinkled with Parmesan. I like to serve them right from the oven.

—**HOWARD LANSINGER** PINEOLA, NC

START TO FINISH: 25 MIN. • **MAKES:** 1 DOZEN

1 container (8 ounces) spreadable cream cheese
8 bacon strips, cooked and crumbled
2 tablespoons chopped green onion
12 slices white bread, crusts removed
24 fresh asparagus spears, trimmed
¼ cup butter, melted
3 tablespoons grated Parmesan cheese

1. In a small bowl, combine the cream cheese, bacon and green onion. Flatten bread slices with a rolling pin; spread tops with cream cheese mixture. Trim asparagus 2 in. longer than bread. Place two spears on each slice; roll up bread and place seam side down on a greased baking sheet. Brush with butter; sprinkle with Parmesan cheese.

2. Bake at 400° for 10-12 minutes or until lightly browned. Serve immediately.

Barbecued Meatballs

PICTURED ON PAGE 173

The secret's out. Grape jelly and chili sauce are what make the sauce on these meatballs so fantastic. But what I love even more about this recipe is how easy it is to prepare in advance.

—**IRMA SCHNUELLE** MANITOWOC, WI

PREP: 20 MIN. • **COOK:** 15 MIN. • **MAKES:** ABOUT 3 DOZEN

- ½ cup dry bread crumbs
- ⅓ cup finely chopped onion
- ¼ cup milk
- 1 egg, lightly beaten
- 1 tablespoon minced fresh parsley
- 1 teaspoon salt
- 1 teaspoon Worcestershire sauce
- ½ teaspoon pepper
- 1 pound lean ground beef (90% lean)
- ¼ cup canola oil
- 1 bottle (12 ounces) chili sauce
- 1 jar (10 ounces) grape jelly

1. In a large bowl, combine the first eight ingredients. Crumble beef over mixture and mix well. Shape into 1-in. balls. In a large skillet, brown meatballs in oil on all sides.

2. Remove meatballs and drain. In the same skillet, combine chili sauce and jelly; cook and stir over medium heat until jelly has melted. Return meatballs to pan; heat through.

White Chocolate Brandy Alexander

A Brandy Alexander combines brandy and creme de cacao into a delicious, creamy drink that was increasingly popular in the '60s. My husband and I love to entertain in winter, so this warm version of the recipe is a keeper.

—**SHARON DELANEY-CHRONIS** SOUTH MILWAUKEE, WI

START TO FINISH: 15 MIN. • **MAKES:** 6 SERVINGS

- 3½ cups milk
- ⅛ teaspoon salt
- 6 ounces white baking chocolate, finely chopped
- ⅓ cup brandy
- ¼ cup creme de cacao
- ½ teaspoon vanilla extract
  Whipped topping and white chocolate shavings, optional

1. In a large saucepan, heat the milk and salt over medium heat just until mixture comes to a simmer. Remove from the heat. Add chocolate; whisk until mixture is smooth. Stir in brandy, creme de cacao and vanilla.

2. Fill mugs or cups three-fourths full. Top with whipped topping and chocolate shavings if desired.

THE ORIGINAL ALEXANDER

Brandy Alexanders are traditionally made with brandy, creme de cacao and sweet cream. Replace the brandy with gin, and you've got yourself a cocktail that goes simply by the name Alexander.

Decoupage Coasters

Or, as we like to call them, custom cocktail place mats. Make one for each guest as a party favor so they'll always remember your stylish '60s soiree.

MATERIALS (FOR A SET OF 8)

Two 12-inch-square sheets of chipboard in choice of color
Several 4½-inch-square or larger scraps of patterned card stock
Compass, ruler and pencil
Matte decoupage glue
Polyurethane or waterproof clear sealer
Sponge brush

DIRECTIONS

1. Using the compass, ruler and pencil, trace four 4-in. circles spaced evenly onto each chipboard sheet. Cut out all eight circles.

2. Using sponge brush, coat one side of each circle with a thin layer of decoupage glue. Adhere each circle to the back of a card stock scrap. Let glue dry. Trim card stock to the edge of each circle.

3. Coat the top (patterned) side of each coaster with a couple of layers of decoupage glue. Let glue dry to the touch between each layer.

4. Finally, coat the top side of each coaster with a thick layer of clear sealer. Let coasters dry 24 hours before using. To clean, wipe with a damp cloth. Do not submerge in water.

Did somebody say waffles? You bet! Only this time, hold the whip and berries and get ready to try something a little more adventurous.

Inspired by an eclectic roundup of ingredients, from jalapeno jelly to instant coffee, every recipe in this sweet and savory collection of whimsical batters is as surprising as it is delicious.

For birthdays, dinner parties or National Waffle Week (the first week in September), let the waffle iron out of captivity and enjoy some wildly tasty creations—for breakfast, dinner or dessert.

Tex-Mex Chicken and Waffles (p. 187)

I'M MAKING **WAFFLES!**

Bacon Potato Waffles with Applesauce

My mother used to add bacon to a lot of recipes for extra flavor. So I modified this potato waffle by doing just that. It's a smart recipe for using up leftover mashed potatoes, and it goes so well with applesauce.
—LAURA FALL-SUTTON BUHL, ID

PREP: 15 MIN. • **BAKE:** 5 MIN./BATCH • **MAKES:** 12 WAFFLES

- 1 cup all-purpose flour
- 2 tablespoons sugar
- 2 teaspoons baking powder
- 1 teaspoon salt
- 2 eggs
- 1½ cups mashed potatoes
- 1 cup 2% milk
- 5 tablespoons bacon drippings or canola oil
- 4 bacon strips, cooked and crumbled
- ¼ cup finely chopped onion
  Chunky applesauce

1. In a large bowl, combine the flour, sugar, baking powder and salt. In another bowl, whisk the eggs, mashed potatoes, milk and bacon drippings. Stir into dry ingredients just until moistened. Fold in bacon and onion.

2. Bake in a preheated waffle iron according to manufacturer's directions until golden brown. Serve with applesauce.

Oatmeal Waffles with Orange Ricotta Topping

I like how the oatmeal lends a natural sweetness and nutty flavor to these waffles. Instead of serving them with maple syrup, try them with an orange ricotta spread.
—PAULINE AUFRECHT BEAVERTON, OR

PREP: 20 MIN. • **BAKE:** 5 MIN./BATCH • **MAKES:** 12 WAFFLES (1¼ CUPS TOPPING)

- 1 cup boiling water
- ¾ cup old-fashioned oats
- 1¼ cups all-purpose flour
- 3 tablespoons sugar
- 1½ teaspoons baking powder
- 1½ teaspoons baking soda
- ½ teaspoon salt
- 1¼ cups buttermilk
- 3 tablespoons canola oil
- 1 egg
- 1 egg white

TOPPING
- 1 cup ricotta cheese
- 2 tablespoons orange juice
- 2 tablespoons honey
- 1 teaspoon grated orange peel

1. In a small bowl, combine boiling water and oats; let stand for 3 minutes. Meanwhile, in a large bowl, combine the flour, sugar, baking powder, baking soda and salt. In another bowl, whisk the buttermilk, oil, egg and egg white; stir in oatmeal mixture. Add to dry ingredients; stir just until combined.

2. Bake in a preheated waffle iron according to manufacturer's directions until golden brown. Combine topping ingredients; serve with waffles.

Corn Fritter Waffles with Spicy Maple Syrup

My family used to vacation at a resort in Vermont that served corn fritters with maple syrup. These waffles remind me of our trips together.
—**JENNIFER BECKMAN** FALLS CHURCH, VA

PREP: 15 MIN.
BAKE: 5 MIN./BATCH
MAKES: 6 ROUND WAFFLES
(1 CUP SYRUP)

- 2 **cups all-purpose flour**
- 2 **tablespoons sugar**
- 3 **teaspoons baking powder**
- ½ **teaspoon salt**
- 2 **eggs**
- 2 **cups 2% milk**
- ½ **cup canola oil**
- 1½ **cups fresh whole kernel corn or frozen corn**
- 1 **cup maple syrup**
- ¼ **teaspoon cayenne pepper**
   Cooked whole kernel corn, optional

1. In a large bowl, combine the flour, sugar, baking powder and salt. In another bowl, whisk the egg, milk and oil. Stir into dry ingredients just until moistened. Stir in corn.

2. Bake in a preheated round Belgian waffle iron according to manufacturer's directions until golden brown. Meanwhile, combine syrup and cayenne. Serve with waffles and, if desired, cooked corn.

Waffled Pizza Bites

The whole family will love this playful twist on waffles. Mozzarella and Parmesan cheeses are sandwiched between two layers of dough and cooked up in the waffle iron. It's like a pizza grilled cheese waffle!

—DEIRDRE COX KANSAS CITY, KS

START TO FINISH: 20 MIN.
MAKES: 8 APPETIZERS
(1¾ CUPS SAUCE)

- 1¼ **cups shredded part-skim mozzarella cheese**
- ¼ **cup shredded Parmesan cheese**
- ½ **teaspoon dried basil**
- ½ **teaspoon dried oregano**
- 2 **tubes (8 ounces each) refrigerated crescent rolls**
- 32 **slices pepperoni (about 2 ounces)**
- 1 **jar (14 ounces) pizza sauce, warmed**
  Optional toppings: sliced pepperoni, shredded mozzarella cheese and basil

1. In a small bowl, combine the cheeses, basil and oregano. Separate each roll of crescent dough into two 7-in. x 6-in. rectangles; seal perforations.

2. Place one rectangle on a preheated greased 8-in. square waffle iron (dough will not cover entire surface). Layer with half the cheese mixture and half the pepperoni to ½ in. of edges; top with another rectangle. Bake for 4-5 minutes or until golden brown. Repeat.

3. Remove to a cutting board and cool slightly. Cut into triangles; serve warm with pizza sauce and, if desired, toppings.

Tex-Mex Chicken and Waffles

PICTURED ON PAGE 183

While visiting Texas I bought a small bottle of jalapeno pepper jelly, which inspired me to try this recipe. It's like a kicked-up Southern classic, and the syrup can be used as a dipping sauce.

—**DEBRA GOFORTH** NEWPORT, TN

PREP: 30 MIN. + MARINATING • **COOK:** 20 MIN. • **MAKES:** 4 SERVINGS

- 4 **boneless skinless chicken breast halves (4 ounces each)**
- ½ **cup buttermilk**
- ¼ **teaspoon hot pepper sauce**

JALAPENO SYRUP
- 1 **cup sugar**
- ½ **cup coarsely chopped green pepper**
- 2 **jalapeno peppers, seeded and quartered**
- 3 **tablespoons cider vinegar**

COATING
- ⅓ **cup all-purpose flour**
- ⅓ **cup yellow cornmeal**
- 2 **teaspoons salt**
- ½ **teaspoon pepper**
- ¼ **teaspoon cayenne pepper**
- ¼ **teaspoon ground cumin**
- 1 **teaspoon paprika**
- ¼ **cup canola oil**

WAFFLES
- ¾ **cup all-purpose flour**
- ¼ **cup cornstarch**
- ¼ **cup yellow cornmeal**

- ½ **teaspoon baking powder**
- ¼ **teaspoon baking soda**
- ¼ **teaspoon salt**
- ¾ **cup buttermilk**
- ¼ **cup canola oil**
- 1 **egg**
- ¼ **cup shredded pepper jack cheese**
  Optional toppings: salsa, sliced avocadoes and fresh cilantro

1. Flatten each chicken breast to ¼-in. thickness. Place in a large resealable plastic bag. Add buttermilk and hot pepper sauce; seal bag and turn to coat. Refrigerate 2 hours or overnight.

2. In a small saucepan, combine all syrup ingredients; bring to a boil, stirring to dissolve sugar. Reduce heat; simmer for 5 minutes, stirring occasionally. Remove from the heat; steep for 1 hour. Strain and discard peppers. Cover and refrigerate syrup until serving.

3. In a large resealable plastic bag, mix the flour, cornmeal and seasonings. Drain chicken, discarding marinade. Add chicken to flour mixture, one piece at a time, and shake to coat. In a large skillet, heat oil over medium heat. Add chicken; cook for 3-4 minutes on each side or until no longer pink. Drain on paper towels; keep warm.

4. In a large bowl, combine the first six waffle ingredients. In another bowl, whisk buttermilk, oil and egg until blended. Add to flour mixture; stir just until moistened. Stir in cheese.

5. Bake in a preheated waffle iron according to manufacturer's directions until golden brown. Serve with chicken, warmed syrup and, if desired, toppings.

Asiago Cheese Waffles

I make these cheesy waffles to go with sausage and apples for brunch. They're loaded with Asiago flavor and come out crisp and golden every time.

—**SUZANNE BANFIELD** BASKING RIDGE, NJ

PREP: 15 MIN. • **BAKE:** 5 MIN./BATCH • **MAKES:** 14 WAFFLES

- 2¼ **cups pancake mix**
- 1 **teaspoon dried sage leaves**
- ½ **teaspoon salt**
- 2 **eggs, separated**
- 1 **cup 2% milk**
- ¼ **cup canola oil**
- 1½ **cups shredded Asiago cheese**
- ¼ **teaspoon lemon juice**
  Maple syrup, optional

1. In a large bowl, combine the pancake mix, sage and salt. In a small bowl, whisk the egg yolks, milk and oil. Stir into dry ingredients just until moistened. Stir in cheese.

2. In a large bowl, beat egg whites and lemon juice until stiff peaks form. Fold into batter. Bake in a preheated waffle iron according to manufacturer's directions until golden brown. Serve with maple syrup if desired.

Herbed Mushroom & Bacon Waffles

All my family's favorites—crispy bacon, sauteed mushrooms and fresh parsley—are combined into one delicious buttermilk waffle. It's the absolute best brunch, and they're even good for sandwiches.
—**JENNIFER WHITE** COLUMBUS, OH

PREP: 25 MIN. • **COOK:** 5 MIN./BATCH • **MAKES:** 10 WAFFLES

- ½ **pound sliced baby portobello mushrooms, chopped**
- 2 **teaspoons olive oil**
- ½ **cup crumbled cooked bacon**
- 2 **tablespoons minced fresh parsley**
- 2 **cups all-purpose flour**
- 1½ **teaspoons baking soda**
- 1 **teaspoon sugar**
- ½ **teaspoon salt**
- ¼ **teaspoon pepper**
- 2 **eggs**
- 1¾ **cups buttermilk**
- ¼ **cup butter, melted**
   Sour cream and tomato slices, optional

1. In a large skillet, saute mushrooms in oil until tender. Remove from the heat; stir in bacon and parsley.

2. In a large bowl, combine the flour, baking soda, sugar, salt and pepper. In another bowl, whisk the eggs, buttermilk and butter. Add to dry ingredients; stir just until combined. Stir in mushroom mixture.

3. Bake in a preheated waffle iron according to manufacturer's directions until golden brown. If desired, serve with sour cream and tomato slices.

Overnight Crisp Yeast Waffles

I had a baby shower brunch for my niece many years ago and these waffles were a hit. One friend told me recently that she still remembers the waffles from that day.
—**JOAN HALLFORD** NORTH RICHLAND HILLS, TX

PREP: 10 MIN. + CHILLING • **BAKE:** 5 MIN./BATCH • **MAKES:** 20 WAFFLES

- 1 **package (¼ ounce) active dry yeast**
- ½ **cup warm water (110° to 115°)**
- 2 **cups 2% warm milk, (110° to 115°)**
- ⅓ **cup butter, melted**
- 3 **cups all-purpose flour**
- 1 **teaspoon salt**
- 2 **eggs, lightly beaten**
- 1½ **teaspoons baking soda**
   Fresh strawberries and sweetened whipped cream, optional

1. In a large bowl, dissolve yeast in warm water. Let stand for 5 minutes. Add milk and butter; mix well. Combine flour and salt; stir into milk mixture. Cover loosely and refrigerate overnight.

2. Add eggs and baking soda; mix well. Bake in a preheated waffle iron according to manufacturer's directions until golden brown. Serve warm, with strawberries and whipped cream if desired.

PREVENT WAFFLES FROM STICKING

The amount of oil or butter in your batter will affect whether or not waffles stick to the waffle iron. If you notice that your waffles consistently stick, try increasing the oil or butter.

Chocolate Brownie Waffle Sundaes

One of my best friends loves chocolate as much as I do, so I like to make this over-the-top treat when we're together playing board games or cards in the winter.

—VICKI DUBOIS MILLTOWN, IN

START TO FINISH: 30 MIN. • **MAKES:** 8 WAFFLES

- 2 **ounces unsweetened chocolate, chopped**
- 1¼ **cups all-purpose flour**
- 1 **cup packed brown sugar**
- ½ **teaspoon salt**
- ½ **teaspoon baking soda**
- ¼ **teaspoon ground cinnamon**
- 2 **eggs**
- ½ **cup 2% milk**
- ¼ **cup canola oil**
- 1 **teaspoon vanilla extract**
- ¼ **cup chopped pecans**

- 4 **scoops vanilla ice cream**
- ¼ **cup chopped pecans, toasted**
  Hot caramel and/or fudge ice cream toppings

1. In a microwave, melt chocolate; stir until smooth. Cool slightly.

2. In a large bowl, combine the flour, brown sugar, salt, baking soda and cinnamon. In another bowl, whisk the eggs, milk, oil and vanilla; stir into dry ingredients until smooth. Stir in pecans and melted chocolate (batter will be thick).

3. Bake in a preheated waffle iron according to manufacturer's directions until golden brown. Serve with ice cream, toasted pecans and ice cream toppings.

Red Velvet Waffles with Coconut Syrup

My daughter loves red velvet cake and I'm always looking for ways to use pecans, so this recipe makes both of us happy.
—**CHERYL PERRY** HERTFORD, NC

PREP: 25 MIN.
BAKE: 5 MIN./BATCH
MAKES: 7 ROUND WAFFLES
(1 CUP TOPPING AND 2 CUPS SYRUP)

- 2 **cups all-purpose flour**
- ¾ **cup sugar**
- ¼ **cup baking cocoa**
- 1 **teaspoon baking soda**
- ¼ **teaspoon salt**
- 2 **eggs**
- 2 **cups buttermilk**
- ¼ **cup butter, melted**
- 3 **tablespoons red food coloring**
- 1 **teaspoon vanilla extract**

TOPPING
- ¾ **cup butter, softened**
- 4 **ounces cream cheese, softened**
- ½ **teaspoon ground cinnamon**
- ½ **cup finely chopped pecans**

SYRUP
- 2 **cups light corn syrup**
- ½ **cup flaked coconut, toasted**
- 1 **teaspoon coconut extract**

1. In a large bowl, combine the flour, sugar, cocoa, baking soda and salt. In a large bowl, whisk the eggs, buttermilk, butter, food coloring and vanilla. Stir into dry ingredients just until moistened.

2. Bake in a preheated round Belgian waffle iron according to manufacturer's directions until golden brown.

3. Meanwhile, in a small bowl, beat the butter, cream cheese and cinnamon until smooth; stir in pecans. In another bowl, combine the corn syrup, coconut and extract. Serve topping and syrup with waffles.

Mocha Waffles with Syrup

Coffee-infused waffles—is there any better way to start the day?
I think these are perfect for serving a brunch bunch.
—**TAMMY LOVE** DALLAS, NC

PREP: 15 MIN. • **BAKE:** 5 MIN./BATCH • **MAKES:** 12 WAFFLES (1 CUP SYRUP)

- 4 teaspoons instant coffee granules
- ¼ cup boiling water
- 2 cups self-rising flour
- ¼ cup baking cocoa
- 2 tablespoons sugar
- 2 eggs
- 1 cup 2% milk
- ¼ cup butter, melted
- 2 teaspoons vanilla extract

MOCHA SYRUP
- 1 cup maple syrup
- 1 teaspoon instant coffee granules
- 1 tablespoon boiling water

1. Dissolve coffee granules in boiling water. Meanwhile, in a large bowl, combine the flour, cocoa and sugar. In a small bowl, whisk the eggs, milk, butter, vanilla and coffee mixture. Add to dry ingredients; stir just until combined.

2. Bake in a preheated waffle iron according to manufacturer's directions until crisp. Meanwhile, in a small saucepan, heat maple syrup. Dissolve coffee granules in boiling water; stir into syrup. Serve warm with waffles.

NOTE *As a substitute for 1 cup of self-rising flour, place 1½ teaspoons baking powder and ½ teaspoon salt in a measuring cup. Add all-purpose flour to measure 1 cup.*

Gingerbread Belgian Waffles

I like to combine the sweet and spicy taste of gingerbread with the cool and dreamy
taste of cream cheese frosting. It's a heavenly breakfast to wake up to!
—**JANNINE FISK** MALDEN, MA

PREP: 25 MIN. • **COOK:** 5 MIN./BATCH • **MAKES:** 6 WAFFLES (1½ CUPS ICING)

- 2 cups all-purpose flour
- ¼ cup packed brown sugar
- 3 teaspoons baking powder
- 1½ teaspoons ground ginger
- 1 teaspoon baking soda
- 1 teaspoon ground cinnamon
- ½ teaspoon salt
- ¼ teaspoon ground nutmeg
- 4 eggs, separated
- 2 cups buttermilk
- ½ cup butter, melted
- ½ cup molasses
- 2 teaspoons vanilla extract

CREAM CHEESE ICING
- ½ cup butter, softened
- ¼ cup cream cheese, softened
- ½ teaspoon vanilla extract
- ⅛ teaspoon salt
- 1½ cups confectioners' sugar
- 2 tablespoons 2% milk

1. In a large bowl, combine the first eight ingredients. In another bowl, whisk the egg yolks, buttermilk, butter, molasses and vanilla. Add to dry ingredients; stir just until combined.

2. In a small bowl, beat egg whites until stiff. Gently fold into batter.

3. Bake in a preheated waffle iron according to manufacturer's directions until golden brown. Meanwhile, combine the icing ingredients until smooth. Serve with waffles.

omeone's expecting a bundle of joy. This calls for a celebration! Show the mother-to-be just how much she's loved: Surround her with friends and family, shower her with gifts, and—most important—let her enjoy a few baby-free moments to eat! (Is that Strawberry Popcorn? Yes!)

With inspiring recipes for the perfect cutesy finger foods, recruiting helping hands to prepare a garden-fresh buffet will be a piece of cake. Here's to motherhood, and all the special moments to follow.

PEAS IN A POD

From the baby shower to the bubble bath, Sweet Peas party favors are a simple and adorable way to say thanks. See p. 203.

LI'L BITES &
A BABY SHOWER

Colorful Papaya Panzanella

PICTURED ON PAGE 193

I like to combine fruits and vegetables with homemade croutons to create pizzazzy (my new favorite word) side dishes. This one is as pretty as it is delicious!
—**KATHLEEN GILL** PAHRUMP, NV

PREP: 35 MIN. • **MAKES:** 16 SERVINGS (1 CUP EACH)

1 **loaf whole wheat boule or sourdough bread (1 pound), cut into 1-in. cubes**
1 **cup balsamic vinaigrette, divided**
4 **cups torn mixed salad greens**
2 **medium zucchini, cubed**
2 **medium yellow zucchini, cubed**
2 **cups cubed peeled ripe papaya**
2 **cups grape tomatoes**
8 **thin slices sweet onion, quartered**

1. In a large bowl, toss bread cubes with ⅔ cup vinaigrette. Transfer to baking sheets. Bake at 375° for 14-16 minutes or until lightly browned, stirring occasionally. Cool to room temperature.

2. In a large bowl, combine the salad greens, zucchini, papaya, tomatoes, onion and bread. Drizzle with remaining dressing. Serve immediately.

Mini BLT Appetizers

Five simple ingredients are all it takes to wow friends and family with a tasty appetizer. I love to make these as much as I love to share them.
—**NICK BERG** MILWAUKEE, WI

START TO FINISH: 30 MIN. • **MAKES:** ABOUT 2½ DOZEN

30 **cherry tomatoes**
¾ **cup reduced-fat mayonnaise**
2 **Bibb or Boston lettuce leaves, torn into 1-inch pieces**
¼ **cup salad croutons, broken into pieces**
3 **bacon strips, cooked and crumbled**
Coarsely ground pepper

1. Cut a thin slice off the top of each tomato. Scoop out and discard pulp; invert tomatoes on paper towels to drain. Pipe mayonnaise into tomatoes.
2. Top each with a piece of rolled-up lettuce, croutons and bacon. Sprinkle with pepper. Cover and refrigerate up to 1 hour.

THE MAIN SQUEEZE

A quick and easy way to pipe mayonnaise into cherry tomatoes is to transfer the mayo to a clean squeeze bottle. Or, place the mayo in a plastic sandwich bag, cut a small opening at the bag's bottom corner and gently press the mayonnaise through the opening.

Fresh Fruit Salsa with Cinnamon Chips

Lime and basil really brighten the flavors in this colorful salsa.
It's best when scooped up on a homemade cinnamon chip.
—**NAVALEE HYLTON** LAUDERHILL, FL

PREP: 30 MIN. • **COOK:** 10 MIN.
MAKES: 4½ CUPS SALSA (64 CHIPS)

SALSA

- 1 **medium pear, peeled and finely chopped**
- 1 **medium apple, peeled and finely chopped**
- 1 **medium kiwifruit, peeled and finely chopped**
- 1 **small peach, peeled and finely chopped**
- ½ **cup fresh blueberries**
- ½ **cup finely chopped fresh pineapple**
- ½ **cup finely chopped fresh strawberries**
- 2 **tablespoons honey**
- 1 **tablespoon lime juice**
- ¾ **teaspoon grated lime peel**
- 3 **small fresh basil leaves, thinly sliced**
- 3 **fresh mint leaves, thinly sliced**

CINNAMON CHIPS

- 8 **flour tortillas (8 inches)**
  Cooking spray
- ½ **cup sugar**
- 1 **teaspoon ground cinnamon**

1. In a large bowl, combine the salsa ingredients; mix lightly. Refrigerate until serving.

2. Lightly spritz both sides of tortillas with cooking spray; cut each into eight wedges. In a large bowl, combine sugar and cinnamon. Add tortillas; toss to coat.

3. Arrange in a single layer on ungreased baking sheets. Bake at 350° for 10-12 minutes or until golden brown. Serve with salsa.

Layered Mediterranean Dip with Pita Chips

Not your ordinary layer dip, the bold combination of hummus and Greek yogurt will be a new most-requested recipe at your next baby shower or gathering.

—ELIZABETH DUMONT
BOULDER, CO

PREP: 15 MIN. + CHILLING
BAKE: 10 MIN.
MAKES: 5 CUPS (120 CHIPS)

- 1 **cup (8 ounces) plain Greek yogurt**
- 1 **medium seedless cucumber, chopped**
- 1 **teaspoon white wine vinegar**
- 2 **teaspoons minced fresh mint or 1 teaspoon dried mint**
- 1 **carton (10 ounces) hummus**
- 1 **medium red onion, chopped**
- 1 **cup chopped roasted sweet red peppers, drained**
- 2 **packages (4 ounces each) crumbled feta cheese**
- ½ **cup pitted Greek olives, sliced**
- 2 **plum tomatoes, chopped**
  Minced fresh parsley and additional minced fresh mint, optional

PITA CHIPS
- 20 **pita pocket halves**
- ¼ **cup olive oil**
- ½ **teaspoon salt**
- ¼ **teaspoon pepper**

1. Line a strainer with four layers of cheesecloth or one coffee filter and place over a bowl. Place yogurt in prepared strainer and cover with edges of cheesecloth. Refrigerate for 8 hours or overnight. In a small bowl, combine the strained yogurt, cucumber, vinegar and mint.

2. Spread hummus in the bottom of a 9-in. deep-dish pie plate. Layer with onion, peppers, feta cheese, olives, tomatoes and yogurt mixture. Top with parsley and additional mint if desired. Chill until serving.

3. Cut each pita half into three wedges; separate each wedge into two pieces. Place in a single layer on ungreased baking sheets. Brush both sides with olive oil; sprinkle with salt and pepper.

4. Bake at 400° for 8-10 minutes or until crisp, turning once. Serve with dip.

Artichoke Phyllo Cups

One of my favorite appetizers (which I find addicting!) is spinach and artichoke dip. I wanted to create a bite-size version that captures the savory richness in a baked phyllo cup.

—NEEL PATEL CHAMPAIGN, IL

START TO FINISH: 30 MIN. • **MAKES:** ABOUT 3½ DOZEN

- 3 packages (1.9 ounces each) frozen miniature phyllo tart shells
- 1 can (14 ounces) water-packed artichoke hearts, rinsed, drained and finely chopped
- ½ cup shredded part-skim mozzarella cheese
- 3 green onions, chopped
- ¼ cup whipped cream cheese
- 2 tablespoons minced fresh parsley
- 2 tablespoons grated Parmesan cheese
- 2 tablespoons sour cream
- 1 tablespoon mayonnaise
- 2 garlic cloves, minced
- ½ teaspoon salt
- ¼ teaspoon pepper

1. Place tart shells on a baking sheet. In a small bowl, combine the remaining ingredients; spoon into tart shells.

2. Bake at 350° for 10-15 minutes or until lightly browned. Serve warm. Refrigerate leftovers.

HOT OR COLD

The beauty of this simple recipe is that it can be served unbaked and chilled, or hot from the oven. Either way, the filling can be made ahead and stored in the fridge until ready to serve or bake.

Twice-Baked Mini Potatoes

PICTURED ON PAGE 193

I love to take tried-and-true recipes like twice-baked potatoes and add new twists. I consider these to be the ultimate party appetizer.

—LYNDSAY WELLS LADYSMITH, BC

PREP: 25 MIN. • **BAKE:** 15 MIN. • **MAKES:** 30 APPETIZERS

- 15 small Yukon Gold potatoes
- 2 tablespoons butter
- ¼ cup 2% milk
- 2 tablespoons spreadable garlic and herb cream cheese
- 1½ teaspoons prepared horseradish
- ¼ teaspoon salt
- ¼ teaspoon pepper
- 3 slices bacon strips, cooked and crumbled
- ½ green onion, thinly sliced
- ⅔ cup shredded cheddar cheese, divided
- 2 teaspoons minced chives

1. Place potatoes in a Dutch oven; cover with water. Bring to a boil. Reduce heat; cover and simmer for 10-12 minutes or until just tender. Drain. Cool slightly and cut each potato in half lengthwise. Gently scoop out the pulp, leaving thin shells.

2. In a large bowl, mash pulp with butter, milk, cream cheese, horseradish, salt and pepper. Stir in the bacon, onion and half of the cheese. Spoon mixture into potato shells; sprinkle with remaining cheese.

3. Transfer to a greased 15-in. x 10-in. x 1-in. baking pan. Bake at 350° for 15-20 minutes or until heated through. Top with chives.

Ham & Cheese Rolls

PICTURED ON PAGE 200

For parties, this is my favorite thing to prepare. The sandwiches marinate overnight and are baked just before serving.

—LEAH FORTH FLORA, IL

PREP: 15 MIN. + CHILLING • **BAKE:** 20 MIN. • **MAKES:** 12 SERVINGS

---

8 **ounces thinly sliced deli ham**

6 **slices Swiss cheese (¾ ounce each), cut in half**

1 **package (12 ounces) Hawaiian sweet rolls, split**

½ **cup spreadable chive and onion cream cheese**

¼ **cup butter, melted**

4 **teaspoons Dijon mustard**

3 **teaspoons dried minced onion**

1½ **teaspoons poppy seeds**

½ **teaspoon Worcestershire sauce**

1. Place ham and cheese on each roll bottom. Spread cream cheese over tops. Replace tops. Arrange in a single layer in a greased 13-in. x 9-in. baking pan.

2. In a small bowl, combine the remaining ingredients; brush over rolls. Cover with foil. Refrigerate for several hours or overnight.

3. Bake, covered, at 350° for 20-23 minutes or until heated through.

Broccoli-Cauliflower Salad

Not sure whether to make bean salad or broccoli salad for the occasion? I like to serve this refreshing combination as a side dish or as a vegetarian entree.

—BRENDA HUFF HOTCHKISS, CO

PREP: 20 MIN. + CHILLING • **MAKES:** 12 SERVINGS (¾ CUP EACH)

---

1 **cup mayonnaise**

¼ **cup sugar**

¼ **cup cider vinegar**

1 **small head cauliflower, broken into florets**

1 **bunch broccoli, cut into florets**

1 **small red onion, chopped**

1 **celery rib, chopped**

1 **can (16 ounces) kidney beans, rinsed and drained**

1 **jar (2 ounces) diced pimientos, drained**

1. In a small bowl, whisk the mayonnaise, sugar and vinegar; set aside.

2. In a large bowl, toss the cauliflower, broccoli, onion and celery. Stir in kidney beans and pimientos. Pour over salad; toss to coat. Refrigerate for 4 hours before serving.

Italian Chicken Salad

Everyone loves chicken salad, but this mayo-free version always stands out. Cooking the chicken in the slow cooker gives it so much more flavor! For parties and showers, you can serve it on croissants or in lettuce cups.

—ANDRIA LINT
FLOWERY BRANCH, GA

PREP: 25 MIN. + CHILLING
MAKES: 16 SERVINGS (9 CUPS)

¼ cup red wine vinegar
2 tablespoons lemon juice
1 teaspoon honey
½ teaspoon salt
½ teaspoon freshly ground pepper
½ cup olive oil
5 cups shredded cooked chicken
1 medium sweet red pepper, coarsely chopped
1 medium sweet yellow pepper, coarsely chopped
½ cup thinly sliced red onion
½ cup slivered almonds, toasted
¼ cup drained capers
Salt and pepper to taste
16 Bibb lettuce leaves
½ cup shredded Parmesan cheese

1. Place the first five ingredients in a blender. While processing, gradually add oil in a steady stream. Set aside.
2. In a large bowl, combine the chicken, sweet peppers, onion, almonds and capers; stir in vinaigrette. Season with salt and pepper. Refrigerate for at least 1 hour. Serve on lettuce; sprinkle with cheese.

Strawberry Popcorn

I love to make this slightly sweet snack because there's really nothing like it.
The dehydrated strawberries processed with sugar make a pretty-in-pink
coating that's perfect for wedding or baby showers.
—**EDEN DRANGER** LOS ANGELES, CA

START TO FINISH: 20 MIN.
MAKES: 4 QUARTS

- ½ **cup freeze-dried strawberries**
- ⅓ **cup sugar**
- ¾ **teaspoon salt**
- ½ **cup popcorn kernels**
- 3 **tablespoons canola oil**
  Butter-flavored cooking spray

1. Place strawberries and sugar in a food processor; cover and process until finely ground. Transfer to a small bowl; add salt and set aside.

2. In a Dutch oven over medium heat, cook popcorn kernels and oil until oil begins to sizzle. Cover and shake for 2-3 minutes or until popcorn stops popping.

3. Transfer to a large bowl; spritz with butter-flavored spray. Add strawberry mixture and toss to coat. Continue spritzing and tossing until popcorn is coated.

Turtle Brownie Bites

PICTURED AT LEFT

A dear friend of mine who loves chocolate was having a party, so I whipped these brownie bites up for her event. They were a hit, and she has asked for them ever since.
—**SALETA LAWRENCE** BENBROOK, TX

PREP: 40 MIN. • **BAKE:** 40 MIN. + STANDING • **MAKES:** 4 DOZEN

1 package fudge brownie mix (13-inch x 9-inch pan size)
1 package fudge brownie mix (8-inch-square pan size)
½ cup plus ⅓ cup canola oil
3 eggs
6 tablespoons water
TOPPINGS
1½ cups dark chocolate chips
1 cup plus 1½ teaspoons heavy whipping cream, divided
3 tablespoons unsalted butter
¾ cup Kraft caramel bits
1½ teaspoons water
48 pecan halves, toasted

1. In a large bowl, combine the brownie mixes, oil, eggs and water. Transfer to a greased, parchment paper-lined 13x9-in. baking pan.
2. Bake at 350° for 38-42 minutes or until a toothpick inserted near the center comes out clean. Cool. Cut brownies into 1½-in. squares.
3. Place a wire rack over a baking sheet lined with waxed paper. Transfer brownie squares to the wire rack.

4. Place chocolate chips in a small bowl. In a small saucepan, bring 1 cup cream and butter just to a boil. Pour over chocolate; whisk until smooth. Spoon chocolate over each brownie, covering top and sides. Let stand for 30 minutes.
5. In a microwave, melt the caramel bits, water and remaining cream; stir until smooth. Drizzle over chocolate. Top each with a pecan half.

Lemon Bark

PICTURED AT LEFT

I wasn't a fan of white chocolate until I made this two-ingredient candy. It's tangy, sweet and creamy all at the same time.
—**DIANA WING** CENTERVILLE, UTAH

PREP: 10 MIN. + CHILLING • **MAKES:** 1¾ POUNDS

2 packages (10 to 12 ounces each) white baking chips
1 cup crushed hard lemon candies, divided

1. Line a 15-in. x 10-in. x 1-in. pan with foil; set aside. In top of a double boiler or a metal bowl over barely simmering water, melt baking chips; stir until smooth. Stir in ⅔ cup crushed candies; spread into prepared pan. Sprinkle with remaining candies. Cool. Refrigerate for 1 hour or until set.
2. Break into pieces. Store in an airtight container.

Ginger Ale Mock Champagne

This is delightful for baby showers. If you know the baby is a girl, use pink lemonade concentrate, add a few drops of red food coloring and garnish with strawberries.

—MONA DARROCH LETHBRIDGE, AB

PREP: 10 MIN. + FREEZING • **MAKES:** 16 SERVINGS

3 cups apple cider or juice
3 cups unsweetened pineapple juice
¾ cup frozen lemonade concentrate, thawed
¼ cup sugar
2 liters ginger ale, chilled

1. In a 2½-qt. freezer container, combine the apple cider, pineapple juice, lemonade concentrate and sugar. Cover and freeze overnight. Remove from freezer and let stand at room temperature for 2 hours before serving.

2. Just before serving, break up mixture with a wooden spoon; transfer to a punch bowl. Stir in ginger ale.

Smooth Sweet Tea

PICTURED ON PAGE 193

You don't have to be in the South to appreciate the sweeter things in life. We think this recipe has the perfect amount of sugar.

—KELSEYLOUISE TASTE OF HOME ONLINE COMMUNITY

PREP: 15 MIN. + CHILLING • **MAKES:** 7 SERVINGS

2 cups water
6 individual black tea bags
⅛ teaspoon baking soda
⅔ cup sugar
6 cups cold water

1. In a small saucepan, bring 2 cups of water to a boil. Remove from the heat; add tea bags. Cover and steep for 10 minutes. Discard tea bags.

2. Sprinkle baking soda into a 2-qt. pitcher. Transfer tea to pitcher; stir in sugar. Add cold water. Refrigerate until chilled.

THE BAKING SODA TRICK

Adding a pinch of baking soda to your sweet tea makes a world of difference. The baking soda reduces any bitterness, leaving you with a refreshingly smooth-tasting beverage.

Sweet Peas

Invite the girls over to make a batch or two of these adorable bubble bath party favors. Guests will be forever grateful.

MATERIALS (FOR ONE)

Three 1-inch round bath balls
4- x 8-inch piece of cloth
Twine
Choice of tag (optional)
Pinking shears (optional)

DIRECTIONS

1. If desired, trim the edges of your cloth with pinking shears to reduce fraying.

2. Cut 2 lengths of twine each about 6 in. long.

3. Gather one short side of the cloth about 1 in. from the end. Wrap a length of twine around it and tie a knot to secure in place.

4. Put the bath balls in a row beginning at the tied end. Once the bath balls are in place, gather the other short side of the cloth, wrap with twine and tie a knot to secure all the bath balls in place. Be sure the bath balls fit tightly side by side.

5. If desired, add a tag to one tied end. Then trim the twine to desired length.

Come spring, when the MLB Opening Day countdown clock strikes zero, it's time to round up your buds, fire up the grill and root, root, root for the home team. Even non-ticket-holders will have a reason to cheer with tailgate munchies like this.

Crowds go wild for Grilled Italian Sandwiches, Cantina Beer-Cheese Dip and Smokin' Spiced Corn. But what would a game-day celebration be without peanuts and hot dogs? Better yet, Sweet and Spicy Peanuts and Bacon-Wrapped Stuffed Hot Dogs.

A new fan favorite this year will be the Refreshing Beer Margaritas. And competing for the No. 1 salty-sweet treat: Chocolate-Peanut Butter Crunch Bars vs. Buttery Potato Chip Cookies. May the best dessert win.

Cantina Beer-Cheese Dip (p. 206)
Sweet and Spicy Peanuts (p. 213)
Grilled Italian Sandwiches (p. 210)
Smokin' Spiced Corn (p. 210)
Baja Bean Salad (p. 209)

OPENING DAY **TAILGATE**

Cantina Beer-Cheese Dip

PICTURED ON PAGE 204

Ever since I found a recipe for beer-cheese dip, which my husband loves, I've made it many times. Being adventurous, I wanted to make a Mexican-style version for variety. It's perfect for tailgating, even in your living room.

—PATRICIA HARMON BADEN, PA

START TO FINISH: 20 MIN. • **MAKES:** ABOUT 3 CUPS

- 2 cups (8 ounces) shredded cheddar cheese
- ½ cup sour cream
- ¼ cup butter, softened
- ¼ cup beer
- 1 envelope onion soup mix
- 1 garlic clove, minced
- 1 teaspoon ground mustard
- 1 teaspoon Worcestershire sauce
- ¾ cup chunky salsa
- 2 tablespoons apricot preserves
- 4 bacon strips, cooked and crumbled
  Blue corn tortilla chips

1. In a food processor, combine cheese, sour cream, butter, beer, onion soup mix, garlic, mustard and Worcestershire sauce. Cover and process until smooth. Spread onto a serving plate.

2. Combine salsa and apricot preserves. Spoon over cheese mixture. Sprinkle with bacon. Serve with tortilla chips.

Caesar Coleslaw

PICTURED AT RIGHT

If you're in the mood to take something a little different to the cookout, here's a reliable slaw I make whenever we're grilling or roasting for a crowd. It lasts in the fridge for days, and leftovers would be terrific burger or sandwich toppers.

—SARAH DE RUITER EAST LANSING, MI

START TO FINISH: 20 MIN. • **MAKES:** 12 SERVINGS

- 1 Chinese or napa cabbage, thinly sliced
- 3 bunches green onions, thinly sliced
- 1 cup mayonnaise
- ⅓ cup lemon juice
- 3 garlic cloves, minced
- ½ teaspoon salt
- ½ teaspoon pepper
- 1 can (2 ounces) anchovy fillets, drained and finely chopped, optional
- ½ cup grated Parmesan cheese

In large bowl, combine cabbage and green onions. In a small bowl, whisk mayonnaise, lemon juice, garlic, salt and pepper. Stir in anchovies if desired. Pour over cabbage mixture; toss. Chill until serving. Toss with cheese to serve.

Bacon-Wrapped Stuffed Hot Dogs

It sounds like the ultimate dude food, but the whole family loves this one. We find it outstanding for picnics and tailgating because the hot dogs can be wrapped in foil to be transported to the party.

—PETER HALFERTY
CORPUS CHRISTI, TX

PREP: 25 MIN. • **GRILL:** 10 MIN.
MAKES: 8 SERVINGS

- 12 bacon strips
- 8 cheese beef hot dogs
- 8 bakery hot dog buns, split and toasted
- ¼ cup chopped red onion
- 2 cups sauerkraut, rinsed and well drained
  Optional condiments: mayonnaise, ketchup or Dijon mustard

1. In a large skillet, cook bacon over medium heat until partially cooked but not crisp. Remove to paper towels to drain; cool slightly. Wrap 1½ strips of bacon around each hot dog, securing with toothpicks as needed (do not wrap tightly or bacon may tear during grilling).

2. Grill, covered, over medium heat or broil 4 in. from the heat 6-8 minutes or until bacon is crisp and hot dogs are heated through, turning frequently. Discard toothpicks. Serve hot dogs in buns with onion and sauerkraut; top with condiments of your choice.

Favorite Chili Cheeseburgers

I like to change things up when making burgers. This cheese-stuffed patty packs in flavor without messing up the grill. Sometimes I use a combination of ground beef and ground turkey.

—DEB WILLIAMS PEORIA, AZ

START TO FINISH: 20 MIN. • **MAKES:** 4 SERVINGS

1 pound ground beef
2 tablespoons chili sauce
1 tablespoon chili powder
½ cup shredded cheddar cheese
4 hamburger-size pretzel buns or hamburger buns, split
½ cup nacho cheese sauce, warmed

1. In a large bowl, combine beef, chili sauce and chili powder, mixing lightly but thoroughly. Shape into eight ¼-in.-thick patties. Place 2 tablespoons cheese onto the center of each of four patties. Top with the remaining patties; press edges firmly to seal.

2. Grill burgers, covered, over medium heat or broil 4 in. from heat 4-6 minutes on each side or until a thermometer reads 160°. Serve on buns with cheese sauce.

Buffalo Chicken Pasta Salad

Full of Buffalo wing flavors, this is one of my favorite side dishes at potlucks and tailgate parties, but you could also serve it as a main. It can be eaten warm or cold so it's convenient to make ahead of time. Sometimes I even use precooked small shrimp instead of the chicken, or leave out the meat if I need a vegetarian dish.
—**LISA HUFF** WILTON, CT

START TO FINISH: 30 MIN. • **MAKES:** 10 SERVINGS

2½ cups uncooked penne pasta
2 cups chopped cooked chicken
3 medium carrots, shredded
2 celery ribs, thinly sliced
½ cup Louisiana-style hot sauce
⅓ cup olive oil
1 tablespoon lemon juice
¼ teaspoon onion powder
¼ teaspoon garlic powder
¼ teaspoon celery salt
1½ cups (6 ounces) crumbled blue cheese

1. Cook penne according to package directions. Meanwhile, in a large bowl, combine the chicken, carrots and celery. In a small bowl, whisk the hot sauce, oil, lemon juice, onion and garlic powders and celery salt.

2. Drain pasta and rinse in cold water. Add to chicken mixture. Pour dressing over salad; toss to coat. Stir in blue cheese. Cover and refrigerate until serving.

Baja Bean Salad

PICTURED ON PAGE 205

My mayo-free Baja Bean Salad uses the bright, fresh flavors of lime, jalapeno and cilantro to really make this colorful bean medley come to life.
—**JEANNE HOLT** MENDOTA HEIGHTS, MN

PREP: 30 MIN. + CHILLING • **MAKES:** 12 SERVINGS (¾ CUP EACH)

1 pound cut fresh green beans
1 can (15 ounces) black beans, rinsed and drained
1 can (15 ounces) garbanzo beans or chickpeas, rinsed and drained
1 can (14½ ounces) cut wax beans, drained
1 cup julienned peeled jicama
1 medium sweet red pepper, finely chopped
4 green onions, thinly sliced
2 tablespoons finely chopped seeded jalapeno pepper
⅓ cup sugar

⅓ cup cider vinegar
¼ cup canola oil
2 tablespoons lime juice
2 tablespoons minced fresh cilantro
½ teaspoon salt
¼ teaspoon pepper

1. In a large saucepan, bring 5 cups water to a boil. Add green beans; cover and cook for 4-6 minutes or until crisp-tender. Drain and immediately place beans in ice water. Drain and pat dry.

2. In a large bowl, combine the black beans, garbanzo beans, wax beans, jicama, red pepper, onions, jalapeno and green beans.
3. In a small bowl, whisk the sugar, vinegar, oil, lime juice, cilantro, salt and pepper. Pour over salad; toss to coat. Cover and refrigerate for at least 1 hour before serving. Serve with a slotted spoon.
NOTE *Wear disposable gloves when cutting hot peppers; the oils can burn skin. Avoid touching your face.*

Grilled Italian Sandwiches

PICTURED ON PAGE 204

I made this for a family gathering and everyone raved about it. It's a fun recipe to grill for a crowd and can be adjusted for other favorite sandwich fillings.

—**TAMMY KRIZ** MARSHALL, MN

PREP: 30 MIN. • **GRILL:** 10 MIN. • **MAKES:** 12 SERVINGS

- 1 small sweet yellow pepper, julienned
- 1 small sweet red pepper, julienned
- 1 small green pepper, julienned
- 1 tablespoon olive oil
- ⅛ teaspoon salt
  Dash pepper
- ½ cup butter, softened
- 1 tablespoon prepared mustard
- 2 teaspoons minced chives
- 1 garlic clove, minced
- ¼ teaspoon crushed red pepper flakes
- 1 loaf (18 ounces) unsliced Italian bread
- 6 ounces sliced provolone cheese
- ⅓ pound thinly sliced hard salami
- 6 ounces sliced cheddar cheese
- ⅓ pound sliced deli roast beef

1. In a large skillet, saute peppers in oil just until tender. Sprinkle with salt and pepper. Meanwhile, in a small bowl, combine the butter, mustard, chives, garlic and pepper flakes.

2. Cut bread into ½-in. slices, leaving slices attached at the bottom. Cut loaf through the two center slices, separating loaf into two halves. Cut off and discard end slices. Place each loaf on heavy-duty foil coated with cooking spray. Spread butter mixture between every other slice. Alongside buttered slices, insert cheese, meat and peppers, using provolone cheese and salami in one loaf and cheddar cheese and roast beef in the other.

3. Wrap each loaf tightly in foil; place on grill rack. Grill, covered, over indirect medium heat for 8-10 minutes or until cheese is melted. Using a serrated knife, separate sandwiches.

TO BAKE SANDWICHES *Bake foil-wrapped loaves at 350° for 20-25 minutes or until cheese is melted.*

Smokin' Spiced Corn

PICTURED ON PAGE 205

My dad, the family gardener, grew corn in abundance, so it graced our table A LOT. This is one of the ways my grandmother spiced it up on the grill.

—**SHIRLEY HODGE** BANGOR, PA

START TO FINISH: 25 MIN. • **MAKES:** 6 SERVINGS

- 3 tablespoons butter
- ½ cup honey
- 1 to 2 tablespoons hot pepper sauce
- 2 garlic cloves, minced
- ½ teaspoon salt
- ¼ teaspoon smoked paprika
- ¼ teaspoon ground cumin
- ¼ teaspoon pepper
- 6 medium ears sweet corn, husks removed

1. In a small saucepan, melt butter. Stir in the honey, pepper sauce, garlic and seasonings until blended; heat through. Brush some over corn.

2. Moisten a paper towel with cooking oil; using long-handled tongs, lightly coat the grill rack. Grill corn, covered, over medium heat for 10-15 minutes or until corn is tender, turning and basting occasionally with the remaining sauce.

Refreshing Beer Margaritas

I'm always surprised when people say they didn't know this drink existed. It's an ideal summertime cocktail, and it's easy to double or triple the recipe.
—ARIANNE BARNETT
KANSAS CITY, MO

START TO FINISH: 5 MIN.
MAKES: 6 SERVINGS

Lime slices and kosher salt, optional
2 bottles (12 ounces each) beer
1 can (12 ounces) frozen limeade concentrate, thawed
¾ cup tequila
¼ cup sweet and sour mix
Ice cubes
GARNISH
Lime slices

1. If desired, use lime slices to moisten the rims of six margarita or cocktail glasses. Sprinkle salt on a plate; hold each glass upside down and dip rims into salt. Discard remaining salt on plate.
2. In a pitcher, combine the beer, concentrate, tequila and sweet and sour mix. Serve in prepared glasses over ice. Garnish with lime slices.

Chocolate-Peanut Butter Crunch Bars

My twist on rice cereal bars layers on a peanut butter coating underneath a rich, chocolate topping garnished with crunchy peanuts and pretzels. Guys will love these bars!

—SHERRI MELOTIK OAK CREEK, WI

PREP: 20 MIN. + CHILLING • **MAKES:** 3 DOZEN

- **3 cups miniature pretzels, coarsely chopped**
- **10 tablespoons butter, divided**
- **1 package (10½ ounces) miniature marshmallows**
- **3 cups Rice Krispies**
- **½ cup light corn syrup, divided**
- **¾ cup peanut butter chips**
- **1 cup (6 ounces) semisweet chocolate chips**
- **¼ cup dry roasted peanuts, chopped**

1. Reserve ⅓ cup chopped pretzels. In a large microwave-safe bowl, microwave 6 tablespoons butter on high for 45-60 seconds or until melted. Stir in the marshmallows; cook 1 to 1½ minutes or until marshmallows are melted, stirring every 30 seconds. Stir in Rice Krispies and remaining chopped pretzels. Immediately press into a greased 13x9-in. baking pan.

2. In another microwave-safe bowl, combine 2 tablespoons butter and ¼ cup corn syrup. Microwave, uncovered, on high for 45-60 seconds or until butter is melted, stirring once. Add peanut butter chips; cook 30-40 seconds or until chips are melted, stirring once. Spread over cereal layer.

3. In a microwave-safe bowl, combine remaining corn syrup and remaining butter. Cook on high for 45-60 seconds or until butter is melted, stirring once. Add chocolate chips; cook 30-40 seconds longer or until chips are melted, stirring once. Spread over top.

4. Sprinkle with peanuts and reserved pretzels; press down gently. Cover and refrigerate 30 minutes or until set. Cut into bars. Store in airtight containers.

NOTE *This recipe was tested in a 1,100-watt microwave.*

Sweet and Spicy Peanuts

PICTURED ON PAGE 204

If watching baseball makes you crave peanuts, try this spiced-up snack. I love how quick and easy it is to put together. And it's always rewarding to see your guests reaching for more.
—**BRENDA L. CAUGHELL** DURHAM, NC

START TO FINISH: 15 MIN. • **MAKES:** 2 CUPS

¼ cup sugar
4½ teaspoons water
½ teaspoon Cajun seasoning
⅛ teaspoon salt
⅛ teaspoon cayenne pepper
⅛ teaspoon pepper
2 cups dry roasted peanuts

1. In a small saucepan, combine the first six ingredients. Cook and stir over medium heat until mixture comes to a boil. Cook and stir for 2 minutes. Remove from the heat.

2. Gradually stir peanuts into mixture. Stir for 1 minute. Pour onto waxed paper; cool. Store in an airtight container.

Buttery Potato Chip Cookies

PICTURED AT LEFT

Can't decide whether to take chips or cookies to the tailgate? These crisp and buttery cookies make plenty for the crowd and will keep people guessing about the secret ingredient.
—**RACHEL ROBERTS** LEMOORE, CA

PREP: 15 MIN. • **BAKE:** 10 MIN./BATCH • **MAKES:** 4½ DOZEN

2 cups butter, softened
1 cup sugar
1 teaspoon vanilla extract
3½ cups all-purpose flour
2 cups crushed potato chips
¾ cup chopped walnuts

1. In a large bowl, cream butter and sugar until light and fluffy. Beat in vanilla. Gradually add flour to creamed mixture and mix well. Stir in potato chips and walnuts.

2. Drop by rounded tablespoonfuls 2 in. apart onto ungreased baking sheets. Bake at 350° for 10-12 minutes or until lightly browned. Cool for 2 minutes before removing from pans to wire racks.

BETTER WITH BUTTER

When making drop cookies such as the Buttery Potato Chip Cookies above, be sure to use real butter. Whipped, tub, soft, liquid or reduced-fat products contain air and water and will produce flat, tough, underbrowned cookies.

So you're taking the family out to the parade? Before you turn your kids loose to catch candy and cheer on the fire engines, fuel up with friends and family by hosting a casual summer brunch.

Even those who may have hit snooze for just a little too long will enjoy these grab-and-go eats. From fruit salad cones and muffins to bite-size stratas and granola bars, you'll be ready to join fellow parade-goers for a morning of merriment.

PRE-PARADE **BRUNCH**

Ham and Cheese Stratas

Almost too cute to eat, these mini egg bakes make a handy portable meal. Even with a creamy texture, they hold their shape and have the perfect amount of mix-ins.

—SHIRLEY WARREN
THIENSVILLE, WI

PREP: 20 MIN. • **BAKE:** 25 MIN.
MAKES: 1 DOZEN

- 1 small onion, chopped
- 1 teaspoon canola oil
- 5 eggs
- 1½ cups 2% milk
- 1 cup (4 ounces) shredded cheddar cheese
- 2 teaspoons Dijon mustard
- ¼ teaspoon salt
- ⅛ teaspoon pepper
- 3 cups cubed day-old Italian bread (½-inch cubes)
- 1 cup cubed fully cooked ham
- 1 plum tomato, seeded and chopped

1. In small skillet, saute onion in oil until tender. In large bowl, whisk eggs, milk, cheese, mustard, salt and pepper. Stir in bread cubes, ham, tomato and onion.

2. Spoon into greased or foil-lined muffin cups. Bake, uncovered, at 350° for 22-26 minutes or until a knife inserted near the center comes out clean.

Bacon and Egg Breakfast Pizza

PICTURED ON PAGE 215

My husband has been trying to get the pizza place down the street to serve breakfast pizza.
When he told me his idea, I came up with this bacon and egg version,
but I put sausage on his half. The spicy salsa gives this pizza a flavorful zing!
—**DARLENE BRENDEN** SALEM, OR

PREP: 10 MIN. + RISING • **BAKE:** 20 MIN. • **MAKES:** 8 SERVINGS

1 envelope (¼ ounce) quick-rise yeast
1 teaspoon sugar
½ teaspoon salt
1⅓ to 1⅔ cups all-purpose flour
½ cup water
1 tablespoon vegetable oil
1 tablespoon cornmeal
TOPPINGS
1 tablespoon butter
4 eggs
¼ teaspoon salt
Dash pepper
¾ cup salsa
⅓ pound Canadian bacon, chopped
4 bacon strips, cooked and crumbled
1¼ cups (5 ounces) shredded part-skim mozzarella cheese

1. In a large bowl, combine the yeast, sugar, salt and ¾ cup flour; set aside. In a small saucepan, heat water and oil to 120°-130°; stir into dry ingredients. Stir in enough remaining flour to form a soft dough (dough will be sticky).

2. Turn onto a floured surface; knead until smooth and elastic, about 6-8 minutes. Place in a greased bowl, turning once to grease the top. Cover with plastic wrap and let rest for 10 minutes.

3. Grease a 14-in. pizza pan; sprinkle with cornmeal. Roll out and transfer dough to prepared pan; build up edges slightly. Bake at 400° for 13-15 minutes or until edges are lightly browned.

4. Meanwhile, in a small skillet, melt butter over medium heat. Whisk eggs, salt and pepper; add to skillet. Cook and stir until just set.

5. Spread salsa over pizza crust; layer with meats, egg mixture and cheese. Bake 5-6 minutes longer or until cheese is melted.

Blueberry Cream Cheese Danish

I love cream cheese and blueberries, so I tweaked one of my grandmother's recipes to come up
with this Danish. It's a quick and easy crowd-pleaser, especially for breakfast or brunch.
—**NICOLE WHEELER** MILLEN, GA

PREP: 20 MIN. • **BAKE:** 30 MIN. + CHILLING • **MAKES:** 16 SERVINGS

1 package (8 ounces) cream cheese, softened
½ cup sugar
1 egg, separated
2 tubes (8 ounces each) refrigerated crescent rolls
4 cups fresh blueberries
2 tablespoons coarse sugar

1. In a small bowl, beat the cream cheese, sugar and egg yolk until smooth.

2. Unroll one tube of crescent dough; seal the seams and perforations. Press onto the bottom and up the sides of an ungreased 13-in. x 9-in. baking pan. Spread cream cheese mixture into crust. Sprinkle with berries.

3. Unroll remaining crescent dough; place over filling, sealing seams. Whisk egg white and brush over top. Sprinkle with coarse sugar.

4. Bake at 350° for 30-35 minutes or until golden brown. Cool completely. Cover and refrigerate for at least 3 hours before serving.

Baked Scrambled Egg Wraps

PICTURED ON PAGE 214

I love breakfast scrambles, but when you're entertaining, it is just too time-consuming. So I came up with this baked egg dish. Now I can enjoy the scramble without scrambling around the kitchen when company's here.

—DARLYN PFEIFFER REESEVILLE, WI

PREP: 20 MIN. • **BAKE:** 40 MIN. • **MAKES:** 12 SERVINGS

- 1 **pound small red potatoes, cooked and cubed**
- 3 **ounces cream cheese, cubed**
- ½ **pound bacon strips, cooked and crumbled**
- 2 **plum tomatoes, seeded and chopped**
- 2 **cups (8 ounces) shredded mozzarella and provolone cheese blend, divided**
- 12 **eggs**
- ¼ **cup half-and-half cream**
- ¾ **teaspoon salt**
- ¼ **teaspoon pepper**
- 12 **flour tortillas (8 inches)**
- 3 **medium ripe avocados, peeled and cubed**
  Optional toppings: sour cream, salsa and/or fresh basil

1. In a greased 13-in. x 9-in. baking dish, layer the potatoes, cream cheese, bacon and tomatoes. Sprinkle with 1 cup cheese. In a large bowl, whisk the eggs, cream, salt and pepper until well blended. Pour over top.

2. Bake at 350° for 30 minutes; sprinkle with remaining cheese. Bake 10-15 minutes longer or until set. Serve warm in tortillas with avocados. If desired, serve with toppings.

Savory Sausage Scones

Some say these are like a breakfast casserole in a scone. Everyone loves the unusual combination of lemon and dill, and the scones taste marvelous with scrambled eggs.

—MARY MARLOWE LEVERETTE COLUMBIA, SC

PREP: 20 MIN. • **BAKE:** 30 MIN. • **MAKES:** 8 SCONES

- 2 **cups all-purpose flour**
- ¼ **cup grated Parmesan cheese**
- 3 **tablespoons sugar**
- 2 **tablespoons minced fresh chives**
- 2 **tablespoons snipped fresh dill**
- 2 **tablespoons minced fresh parsley**
- 2 **teaspoons grated lemon peel**
- 2 **teaspoons baking powder**
- ½ **teaspoon baking soda**
- ¼ **teaspoon salt**
- ¼ **cup cold butter**
- ⅔ **cup 2% milk**
- 1 **egg**
- 1 **pound bulk pork sausage, cooked and drained**

1. In a large bowl, combine the first 10 ingredients. Cut in butter until mixture resembles coarse crumbs. Whisk milk and egg; stir into crumb mixture just until moistened. Stir in sausage.

2. Turn onto a floured surface; knead 10 times. Transfer to a greased baking sheet. Pat into a 9-in. circle. Cut into eight wedges, but do not separate. Bake at 350° for 28-32 minutes or until lightly browned. Serve warm.

STASHING SCONES

Store muffins, biscuits and scones in an airtight container at room temperature. (If they're made with cream cheese, store in the refrigerator.) While muffins stay fresh for up to 3 days, biscuits and scones should be eaten within 1 to 2 days. You can freeze muffins for up to 1 month and biscuits and scones for up to 3 months.

Chocolate-Peanut Granola Bars

Nutella and peanut butter meet to make some amazing granola bars. People always think they're eating something naughty when I serve these, but the bars are full of oats and healthy fats.
—**BRENDA L. CAUGHELL** DURHAM, NC

START TO FINISH: 30 MIN. • **MAKES:** 2 DOZEN

2½ **cups old-fashioned oats**
¾ **cup lightly salted dry roasted peanuts, coarsely chopped**
¾ **cup wheat germ**
¾ **cup sunflower kernels**
½ **cup honey**
¼ **cup packed brown sugar**
3 **tablespoons butter**
⅓ **cup creamy peanut butter**
⅓ **cup Nutella**

1. In an ungreased 15-in. x 10-in. x 1-in. baking pan, combine the oats, peanuts, wheat germ and sunflower kernels. Bake at 400° for 8-12 minutes or until toasted, stirring occasionally. Cool on a wire rack.

2. In a small saucepan, combine the honey, brown sugar and butter. Cook and stir over medium heat until mixture comes to a boil; cook 2 minutes longer. Remove from the heat; stir in peanut butter and Nutella until blended.

3. Transfer oat mixture to a large bowl; add honey mixture and toss to coat. Press into a greased 13-in. x 9-in. pan. Cool. Cut into bars.

French Toast with Crushed Apple Sauce

Heading out to a morning parade or festival? My handy French toast sticks make surprisingly good on-the-go breakfasts—complete with an apple dipping sauce. Leftovers freeze well, too.

—CINDY KERSCHNER SCHNECKSVILLE, PA

PREP: 10 MIN. • **COOK:** 25 MIN.
MAKES: 8 SERVINGS (1 CUP SAUCE)

- 1 **cup unsweetened apple juice**
- 1 **medium apple, peeled and chopped**
- ½ **cup packed brown sugar**
- 2 **teaspoons butter**

FRENCH TOAST

- 3 **eggs**
- ½ **cup 2% milk**
- 1 **teaspoon vanilla extract**
- 2 **tablespoons butter, divided**
- ½ **loaf (1 pound) country bread, cut into 1-inch slices**
  Ground cinnamon

1. In a small saucepan, combine the juice, apple, brown sugar and butter; bring to a boil. Reduce heat; simmer for 12-15 minutes or until apple is tender, stirring occasionally. Mash apple to desired consistency; keep warm.

2. Meanwhile, in a shallow bowl, whisk the eggs, milk and vanilla. In a large skillet, melt 1 tablespoon butter over medium heat. Dip both sides of bread slice in egg mixture, allowing each side to soak for 30 seconds.

3. Place in skillet; lightly sprinkle with cinnamon. Toast each side until golden brown. Repeat with remaining butter and bread.

4. Cut French toast into 1-in. strips; serve with sauce.

Fruit Salad Cups

PICTURED ON PAGE 215

I've been serving this fruit salad for breakfast and brunch for years. The peach pie filling makes it irresistible to eat, and serving it in waffle cones adds to the fun. Kids just love it.

—JUDY HORTON FORT WORTH, TX

PREP: 20 MIN. + CHILLING • **MAKES:** 12 SERVINGS

- 1 **can (21 ounces) peach pie filling**
- 2 **cups fresh strawberries, halved**
- 2 **cups green grapes, halved**
- 2 **cups cubed fresh pineapple**
- 3 **medium kiwifruit, peeled, halved and sliced**
- 2 **medium bananas, sliced**
- 1 **can (15 ounces) mandarin oranges, drained**
- 1 **jar (6 ounces) maraschino cherries, drained and halved**
- 12 **ice cream waffle bowls or cones**
- ¼ **cup chopped walnuts, toasted Mint sprigs, optional**

1. In a large bowl, combine the first eight ingredients. Refrigerate until serving.

2. Just before serving, spoon salad into waffle bowls and sprinkle with walnuts. Garnish with mint sprigs if desired.

WAFFLE CONE SURPRISE

When serving ice cream, fruit salad or yogurt parfaits in waffle or sugar cones, place a marshmallow or jelly bean at the bottom of the cone. Not only is it a tasty surprise, but it helps prevent dripping.

Blueberry-Filled Muffins

PICTURED ON PAGE 215

I consider this recipe a blank canvas for different combinations of preserves and zest. The blueberry-lemon version is a tried-and-true favorite, but apricot preserves with orange zest or blackberry preserves and lime zest would be fun to try.

—MARIA REGAKIS SOMERVILLE, MA

PREP: 15 MIN. • **BAKE:** 20 MIN. • **MAKES:** 16 MUFFINS

- 2¾ **cups all-purpose flour**
- 1 **cup sugar**
- 1 **tablespoon baking powder**
- ¾ **teaspoon baking soda**
- ¾ **teaspoon salt**
- 2 **eggs**
- 1 **cup buttermilk**
- ½ **cup butter, melted**
- 2 **teaspoons grated lemon peel**
- ⅓ **cup blueberry preserves**

TOPPING
- ¼ **cup packed brown sugar**
- 3 **tablespoons all-purpose flour**
- 2 **tablespoons cold butter**
- ¼ **cup chopped walnuts**

1. In a large bowl, combine flour, sugar, baking powder, baking soda and salt. In another bowl, whisk the eggs, buttermilk and butter. Stir into dry ingredients just until moistened. Stir in lemon peel.

2. Fill greased or paper-lined muffin cups one-third full. Drop preserves by teaspoonfuls into the center of each muffin. Top with remaining batter. For topping, in a small bowl, combine brown sugar and flour; cut in butter until crumbly. Stir in walnuts. Sprinkle over tops.

3. Bake at 375° for 18-20 minutes or until a toothpick inserted in muffin comes out clean. Cool for 5 minutes before removing from pans to wire racks. Serve warm.

Cinnamon Bagel Bread Pudding

My son works at a bagel shop and always brings home leftover cinnamon bagels. As a family with five kids, we hate to waste food, so I came up with this incredible-tasting bread pudding that we all love.
—**REBECCA MORELAND** BRISTOL, TN

PREP: 20 MIN. + STANDING • **BAKE:** 45 MIN. + STANDING • **MAKES:** 15 SERVINGS

- 4 **eggs**
- 3½ **cups 2% milk**
- 2½ **teaspoons vanilla extract**
- 4 **cinnamon crunch bagels, cut into 1-inch pieces (about 10 cups)**
- ¼ **cup butter, cubed**
- ½ **cup packed brown sugar**

1. In a large bowl, combine the eggs, milk and vanilla. Gently stir in bagels. Transfer to a greased 13-in. x 9-in. baking dish; let stand for 15 minutes or until bagels are softened. Meanwhile, place butter and brown sugar in a small saucepan; cook and stir over medium-low heat until sugar is melted. Pour over baking dish.

2. Bake, uncovered, at 350° for 45-50 minutes or until the top is puffed and center is almost set. Let stand for 15 minutes. Serve warm.

WHEN LIFE GIVES YOU BAGELS...

Besides Cinnamon Bagel Bread Pudding, you could also make bagel chips with leftover bagels. Refrigerate 2 bagels for 1 hour and cut into ¼-inch slices. Place on an ungreased baking sheet. Melt 2 tablespoons butter and brush over bagel slices. Bake at 325° for 15 to 20 minutes. Cool on a wire rack.

Overnight Berry-Crunch Coffee Cake

I had some extra blueberries and raspberries after a company dinner, and I was looking for a recipe to use them up. I made some alterations to a coffee cake recipe and came up with this delicious overnight bake.
—**LISA VARNER** EL PASO, TX

PREP: 30 MIN. + CHILLING • **BAKE:** 30 MIN. • **MAKES:** 16 SERVINGS

- ⅔ **cup butter, softened**
- 1 **cup sugar**
- 1 **cup packed brown sugar, divided**
- 2 **eggs**
- 2 **teaspoons vanilla extract**
- 2 **cups all-purpose flour**
- 1 **teaspoon baking powder**
- 1 **teaspoon baking soda**
- ½ **teaspoon salt**
- 1½ **teaspoons ground cinnamon, divided**
- 1 **cup sour cream**
- ½ **cup chopped pecans**
- 1 **cup fresh blueberries**
- 1 **cup fresh raspberries**

1. In a large bowl, cream the butter, sugar and ½ cup brown sugar until light and fluffy. Add eggs, one at a time, beating well after each addition. Beat in vanilla.

2. Combine flour, baking powder, baking soda, salt and 1 teaspoon cinnamon; add to creamed mixture alternately with sour cream, beating well after each addition. Spoon half of batter into a greased 13-in. x 9-in. baking dish.

3. Combine the pecans and remaining brown sugar and cinnamon. Sprinkle half of the mixture over batter; layer with berries. Top with remaining batter and sprinkle with remaining pecan mixture. Cover and refrigerate overnight.

4. Remove from the refrigerator 30 minutes before baking. Bake at 325° for 30-35 minutes or until golden brown. Serve warm.

Potluck Cinnamon Roll Twists

When I'm craving a good sweet bread with a twist, this is the recipe I reach for. The twists turn out soft and tender with swirls of cinnamon throughout.
—**REBEKAH BEYER** SABETHA, KS

PREP: 45 MIN. + RISING
BAKE: 25 MIN.
MAKES: 2 DOZEN

- 1 **tablespoon active dry yeast**
- 1 **cup warm water (110° to 115°)**
- 1 **egg, beaten**
- ¼ **cup butter, melted**
- ¼ **cup sugar**
- ½ **teaspoon salt**
- 3¼ to 3¾ **cups all-purpose flour**
- 1 **cup packed brown sugar**
- 3 **teaspoons ground cinnamon**
- ½ **cup butter, softened**

GLAZE
- 2 **cups confectioners' sugar**
- 4 to 5 **tablespoons heavy whipping cream**
- 1 **teaspoon vanilla extract**

1. In a small bowl, dissolve yeast in warm water. In a large bowl, combine the egg, melted butter, sugar, salt, yeast mixture and 1½ cups flour; beat on medium speed for 3 minutes or until smooth. Stir in enough remaining flour to form a soft dough.

2. Turn onto a floured surface; knead until smooth and elastic, about 6-8 minutes. Place in a greased bowl, turning once to grease the top. Cover with plastic wrap and let rise in a warm place until doubled, about 1 hour. Meanwhile, combine brown sugar and cinnamon.

3. Punch dough down. Divide in half. Roll each portion into a 12-in. square. Spread each with softened butter; sprinkle with brown sugar mixture. Fold each square into thirds. Cut widthwise into 1-in.-wide strips. Twist each strip 2-3 times and place in two greased 13-in. x 9-in. baking dishes. Cover and let rise until almost doubled.

4. Bake at 350° for 25-30 minutes or until golden brown. Cool. Whisk glaze ingredients until smooth; drizzle over twists.

H as anyone ever told you your cooking is the bee's knees? Pure and simple, there's a single ingredient that can sweeten most any dish with a promise that the food to follow will have diners buzzing with joy. You guessed it: honey. Whatever this nectarous topping touches turns to gold.

So don't let that syrupy goodness sit ignored in your pantry. There are hams to be glazed, lentils to be baked and cheesecakes to be made. From caramelized sauces to honey and herb-spiked lemonade, you'll find all the recipes you need to celebrate nature's candy. Isn't that right, Pooh Bear?

OFF THE BEE-TIN PATH

Make your own beeswax lip balm case and let your creativity take flight. See p. 233.

Smoked Honey-Peppercorn Salmon (p. 230)
Glazed Parmesan Potatoes (p. 228)
Grilled Lemon & Thyme Lemonade (p. 227)

HONEY-LICIOUS

Pancetta-Wrapped Shrimp with Honey-Lime Glaze

Requested every year by my dinner guests during the holidays, these honey-coated bites are my family's version of bacon-wrapped shrimp.
—JENN TIDWELL FAIR OAKS, CA

START TO FINISH: 25 MIN.
MAKES: 1½ DOZEN

- **6** thin slices pancetta
- **18** uncooked large shrimp, peeled and deveined
- **¼** cup honey
- **2** tablespoons lime juice
- **1** teaspoon hot water
- **1** tablespoon minced fresh cilantro

1. Cut each slice of pancetta into three strips. Wrap one strip around each shrimp; secure with a toothpick. Place in a foil-lined 15-in. x 10-in. x 1-in. baking pan. In a small bowl, whisk the honey, lime juice and water until blended; reserve 2 tablespoons for brushing cooked shrimp.

2. Brush half of the remaining honey mixture over shrimp. Bake at 375° for 5 minutes. Turn shrimp; brush with remaining half of the honey mixture. Bake 4-6 minutes longer or until pancetta is crisp and shrimp turn pink.

3. Remove from oven; brush with the reserved 2 tablespoons honey mixture. Sprinkle with cilantro.

Grilled Lemon & Thyme Lemonade

PICTURED ON PAGE 225

We use our grill for most summer dinners, so we thought, *why not grill the lemonade?* The flavor is surprisingly smooth, with just the right amount of honey and herbs. We call it "Thyme for Lemonade."

—**SUSAN JORDAN** DENVER, CO

PREP: 25 MIN. + STANDING • **COOK:** 5 MIN. • **MAKES:** 9 SERVINGS (1 CUP EACH)

- 15 **fresh thyme sprigs**
- 2 **cups water, divided**
- 1 **cup sugar, divided**
- 9 **medium lemons, halved**
- ¼ **cup honey**
- ¼ **teaspoon almond extract**
- 5 **cups cold water**

1. In a small bowl, soak thyme sprigs in 1 cup water while preparing lemons. Place ¼ cup sugar on a plate; dip cut sides of lemons in sugar.

2. Cover and grill lemons, cut side down, over medium-high heat for 1-2 minutes or until golden brown. Cool slightly. Drain thyme; grill for 1-2 minutes or until lightly browned, turning once.

3. In a small saucepan, combine 1 cup water, honey and remaining sugar; bring to a boil, stirring constantly to dissolve the sugar. Remove from the heat. Add grilled thyme sprigs and extract; let stand for 1 hour to steep. Discard thyme.

4. Meanwhile, squeeze lemons to obtain 1½ cups juice; strain. In a large pitcher, combine 5 cups cold water, thyme syrup and lemon juice. Serve over ice.

Baked Brie with Peaches and Honey

I consider this the perfect sweet and savory peach-season appetizer—especially when served with almond cookie crackers.

—**BRIANNE BOYER** IRVINE, CA

START TO FINISH: 25 MIN. • **MAKES:** 8 SERVINGS

- 1 **round (8 ounces) Brie cheese**
- 3 **small peaches, chopped**
- 3 **tablespoons honey, divided**
  Thinly sliced fresh basil leaves, optional
  Assorted crackers

1. Place Brie in a greased 9-in.-square baking pan. Top and surround Brie with peaches. Bake at 350° for 10 minutes. Drizzle with 2 tablespoons honey. Broil 3-4 in. from the heat for 4-6 minutes or until edges of Brie are lightly browned.

2. Transfer Brie to a serving plate and spoon peaches over top. Drizzle with remaining honey and sprinkle with basil if desired. Serve with crackers.

A SPOONFUL OF HONEY

When I need to measure honey for baking, I first oil the measuring cup or spoon. The honey comes off easily, and I get the full measure without the messy process of scraping the utensils.

—**BARBARA R.**
PORTLAND, OR

Glazed Parmesan Potatoes

PICTURED ON PAGE 225

Potatoes are the ultimate comfort food to me. If you haven't eaten them with a touch of honey, you really should try this sure-to-satisfy, savory-sweet combination.

—**STEPHANIE SHAY** ORWIGSBURG, PA

PREP: 10 MIN. • **BAKE:** 40 MIN. • **MAKES:** 6 SERVINGS

1¾ pounds red potatoes, cut into 1-inch cubes
5 tablespoons butter, melted
3 tablespoons honey
¾ teaspoon salt
½ teaspoon garlic powder
¼ teaspoon pepper
¼ cup grated Parmesan cheese

1. Place potatoes in a greased 13-in. x 9-in. baking dish. In a small bowl, combine the butter, honey, salt, garlic powder and pepper; drizzle over potatoes.

2. Bake at 375° for 35-40 minutes or until potatoes are tender. Stir potatoes and sprinkle with cheese. Bake 5-10 minutes longer or until cheese is lightly browned.

CRYSTALS BE GONE

Honey should be stored at room temperature. Storing it in the refrigerator will accelerate the crystallization process. But this doesn't mean the honey is spoiled. To get rid of the crystals, place the honey container in warm water, stirring gently until the crystals dissolve.

Honey-Wheat Cinnamon Swirl Bread

I have been making this bread for our bed-and-breakfast guests for years. When I serve it as toast, I butter it and top it with a sprinkling of cinnamon and sugar. It's also good with a powdered sugar frosting.

—**ALICE SHAFFER** GREGORY, SD

PREP: 25 MIN. + RISING • **BAKE:** 40 MIN. + COOLING • **MAKES:** 2 LOAVES (16 SLICES EACH)

2 packages (¼ ounce each) active dry yeast
1 cup warm water (110° to 115°)
2½ cups whole wheat flour
1 cup warm whole milk (110° to 115°)
½ cup honey
2 eggs
3 tablespoons butter, melted
2 teaspoons salt
2¾ to 3¼ cups all-purpose flour
½ cup sugar
2 tablespoons ground cinnamon

1. In a large bowl, dissolve yeast in warm water. Add the whole wheat flour, milk, honey, eggs, butter, salt and 2 cups all-purpose flour. Beat until smooth. Stir in enough remaining flour to form a firm dough.

2. Turn onto a floured surface; knead until smooth and elastic, about 6-8 minutes. Place in a greased bowl, turning once to grease the top. Cover and let rise in a warm place until doubled, about 1 hour.

3. Punch dough down; divide in half. Roll each portion into an 18-in. x 9-in. rectangle. Combine the sugar and cinnamon; sprinkle over dough. Roll up jelly-roll style, starting with a short side; pinch seams to seal and tuck ends under. Place in two greased 9-in. x 5-in. loaf pans. Cover and let rise in a warm place until doubled, about 35 minutes.

4. Bake at 350° for 35-40 minutes or until bread sounds hollow when tapped. Remove from pans to a wire rack to cool.

Strawberry, Cucumber & Honeydew Salad

Strawberries and cucumbers together—I just love this combination! Growing up in upstate New York, we used to eat a lot of cucumbers. We'd get them, along with strawberries and melons, from fruit and veggie stands to make this sweet and tangy salad.
—**MELISSA MCCABE** LONG BEACH, CA

START TO FINISH: 20 MIN. • **MAKES:** 8 SERVINGS

1 **container (16 ounces) fresh strawberries, halved**

1 **English cucumber, halved lengthwise and cut into ¼-inch slices**

1 **cup cubed honeydew (½-inch cubes)**

3 **tablespoons honey**

2 **tablespoons lime juice**

1 **teaspoon grated lime peel**

1. In a large bowl, combine strawberries, cucumber and honeydew. Chill until serving.

2. In a small bowl, whisk the remaining ingredients. Just before serving, drizzle over strawberry mixture; toss gently to coat.

Honey-Maple Glazed Ham

PICTURED ON THE COVER

My graham cracker-crusted ham gets a double coating of a simple honey-maple glaze. The first half melts into the ham while the second half forms a sweet, caramelized topping.

—ALAN SPROLES KNOXVILLE, TN

PREP: 15 MIN. • **BAKE:** 2 HOURS • **MAKES:** 15 SERVINGS

- 1 spiral-sliced fully cooked bone-in ham (7 to 9 pounds)
- ½ cup maple syrup
- ½ cup butter, softened
- ½ cup packed brown sugar
- ½ cup graham cracker crumbs
- ½ cup honey

1. Line a roasting pan with heavy-duty foil. Place ham on a rack in prepared pan. Pour maple syrup over ham, separating slices. In a small bowl, beat the remaining ingredients until blended; spread ¾ cup over ham.

2. Bake, uncovered, at 325° for 1½ hours. Spread remaining butter mixture over ham; bake 30-45 minutes longer or until a thermometer reads 140°, basting occasionally with pan drippings.

GRAHAM CRACKER CRUMBS

Graham cracker crumbs taste noticeably fresher when you process them from crackers, rather than buying the crumbs. For this recipe, process 8 graham crackers (4 sheets) to equal ½ cup of crumbs.

Smoked Honey-Peppercorn Salmon

PICTURED ON PAGE 225

I found this recipe in an Alaska fishing guide. Now it's the only way we do salmon. The hickory wood chips give it a distinct smoky flavor.

—JUDY ASHBY JAMESTOWN, TN

PREP: 20 MIN. + MARINATING • **GRILL:** 45 MIN. • **MAKES:** 4 SERVINGS

- 1 cup packed brown sugar
- 1 cup water
- ⅓ cup salt
- 1 tablespoon minced fresh gingerroot
- 2 bay leaves
- 1 teaspoon ground allspice
- ½ cup cold water
- 1 salmon fillet (1 pound)
- ¼ cup honey
- 1 tablespoon whole peppercorns, crushed
- 2 cups soaked hickory wood chips

1. In a small saucepan, combine the first six ingredients. Bring to a boil. Cook and stir until brown sugar and salt are dissolved. Remove from the heat. Add the cold water to cool the brine to room temperature.

2. Place salmon in a large resealable plastic bag; carefully pour cooled brine into bag. Squeeze out as much air as possible; seal bag and turn to coat. Refrigerate for 4 hours, turning occasionally.

3. Drain and discard brine; rinse salmon and pat dry. Spread honey over fillet; sprinkle with peppercorns.

4. Add wood chips to grill according to manufacturer's directions. Moisten a paper towel with cooking oil; using long-handled tongs, lightly coat the grill rack.

5. Place salmon on grill rack, skin side down. Grill, covered, over indirect medium heat for 45-50 minutes or until fish flakes easily with a fork.

Lavender Honey Cheesecake

I love the scent of lavender, and the edible flowers make this cheesecake truly unique.
You can use lavender honey in this recipe for extra flavor,
but even without it, the lavender is very distinct.

—JULIE PALMER LAFAYETTE HILL, PA

PREP: 25 MIN. + CHILLING
MAKES: 16 SERVINGS

- 4 **tablespoons dried lavender flowers, divided**
- ¼ **cup boiling water**
- 1½ **cups crushed shortbread cookies (about 21 cookies)**
- 3 **tablespoons butter, melted**
- 2 **packages (8 ounces each) cream cheese, softened**
- ¾ **cup honey**
- 1¼ **cups heavy whipping cream**
  Lavender sugar and fresh mint leaves, optional

1. In a small bowl, combine 3 tablespoons lavender and water. Cover and steep for 15 minutes. Strain water, discarding lavender. Set lavender water aside.

2. Crush remaining lavender flowers. In a small bowl, combine the cookie crumbs, butter and crushed lavender. Press onto the bottom of a greased 9-in. springform pan. Cover and refrigerate for at least 30 minutes.

3. For filling, in a large bowl, beat cream cheese and honey until smooth. Gradually beat in lavender water. In another bowl, beat cream until stiff peaks form. Fold into filling. Spoon over crust.

4. Refrigerate overnight. Run a knife around edge of pan to loosen; remove sides of pan. Sprinkle with lavender sugar and mint leaves if desired.

NOTE *Look for dried lavender flowers in spice shops. If you're using lavender from the garden, make sure it hasn't been treated with chemicals.*

Honey and Spice
New England Apple Pie

If they're in season, use Honeycrisp apples. With the brown sugar and spices,
they make the juiciest, most flavorful apple pie you have ever tasted!
—**JANNINE FISK** MALDEN, MA

PREP: 55 MIN. • **BAKE:** 65 MIN. + COOLING • **MAKES:** 8 SERVINGS

- 2½ cups all-purpose flour
- ½ teaspoon sugar
- ½ teaspoon salt
- 1 cup cold butter, cubed
- ½ cup ice water
- 1 egg
- 1 teaspoon water

FILLING

- 8 large Honeycrisp apples, peeled and sliced
- 1 tablespoon lemon juice
- ⅓ cup honey
- ⅓ cup sugar
- ¼ cup all-purpose flour
- 2 tablespoons brown sugar
- 1½ teaspoons ground cinnamon
- ¼ teaspoon ground ginger
- ¼ teaspoon ground nutmeg
- ⅛ teaspoon ground allspice
- 2 tablespoons butter, cubed

- 1 tablespoon half-and-half cream
- 2 teaspoons coarse sugar

1. In a large bowl, combine the flour, sugar and salt; cut in the butter until crumbly. Gradually add ice water, tossing with a fork until dough forms a ball.

2. Divide dough in half so that one portion is slightly larger than the other; wrap each in plastic wrap. Refrigerate for 40 minutes or until easy to handle.

3. On a lightly floured surface, roll out larger portion of dough to fit a 9-in. pie plate. Transfer pastry to pie plate. Trim pastry even with edge. Whisk egg and water; brush over pastry.

4. In a large bowl, sprinkle apples with lemon juice; toss to coat. Drizzle with honey and toss to coat. Combine the sugar, flour, brown sugar, cinnamon, ginger, nutmeg and allspice; toss with apple mixture. Transfer to crust and dot with butter.

5. Roll out remaining pastry to fit top of pie. Place over filling. Trim, seal and flute edges. Cut slits in pastry. Brush with cream and sprinkle with coarse sugar. Place on a baking sheet.

6. Bake at 400° for 15 minutes. Reduce heat to 350°; bake 50-60 minutes longer or until crust is golden brown and filling is bubbly. Cover edges with foil during the last 15 minutes to prevent overbrowning if necessary.

Olive Oil Cookies

One of my favorite combinations is honey, olive oil and sea salt—not only in these cookies, but in savory recipes as well. Add notes of lemon and rosemary and you've got yourself a one-of-a-kind treat.
—**BRYAN KENNEDY** KANEOHE, HI

PREP: 15 MIN. • **BAKE:** 10 MIN./BATCH • **MAKES:** ABOUT 2 DOZEN

- ¾ cup sugar
- ½ cup olive oil
- 1 egg
- ¼ cup honey
- ¼ teaspoon lemon extract
- 1 cup all-purpose flour
- 1 cup whole wheat flour
- 2 tablespoons minced fresh rosemary
- 2 teaspoons grated lemon peel

- 1½ teaspoons baking soda
- ¼ teaspoon plus 2 teaspoons sea salt, divided

1. In a large bowl, beat sugar and oil until blended. Beat in the egg, then honey and lemon extract. Combine the flours, rosemary, lemon peel, baking soda and ¼ teaspoon salt. Gradually add to sugar mixture; mix just until combined.

2. Drop by tablespoonfuls 2 in. apart onto parchment paper-lined baking sheets. Sprinkle tops with remaining sea salt. Bake at 350° for 9-12 minutes or until lightly browned. Remove to wire racks. Store in an airtight container.

Off the Bee-Tin Path

Design your own beeswax lip balm case.

MATERIALS (FOR ONE)

Choice of small, lidded food-safe container(s)
Stovetop
Cooking pot and glass measuring cup for double boiler
Stirring spoon
Toothpick
Scraps of patterned card stock or other decoration for lid(s)
Scrapbook adhesive

INGREDIENTS

2 **tablespoons grated or finely chopped beeswax**
1 **tablespoon coconut oil**
3 **small vitamin E capsules**
1 **to 2 drops essential oil (optional)**

DIRECTIONS
(MAKES ABOUT 2 OZ.)

1. Combine beeswax, coconut oil and vitamin E oil in glass measuring cup. Use toothpick to puncture vitamin E capsules, squeezing out contents into cup. Discard capsule shells.

2. Using the double-boiler heating method, slowly heat measuring cup with ingredients on stovetop in a cooking pot with shallow boiling water. Use spoon to stir constantly as ingredients melt together. Once ingredients are completely melted and combine into a light yellow liquid, remove from stovetop.

3. If desired, add 1-2 drops of essential oil of your choice of fragrance into mixture and stir. Be careful not to add very much essential oil as it can hurt the skin if too concentrated.

4. Carefully pour mixture into container(s) and let sit for at least an hour to cool and harden.

5. Cut a piece of patterned card stock to fit front surface size of each lid. Use scrapbook adhesive to adhere card stock and other embellishments to lid. Then place lid on container once lip balm has completely hardened.

NOTE *We bought our cute tin containers at Elements Bath and Body (elementsbathandbody.com). They can also be found online at both Etsy and Amazon.*

Celebrated Nov. 1-2 in Mexico, *Dia de los Muertos* (Day of the Dead) may sound like a spooky ritual, but in fact it's quite the opposite—it's a vibrant and spirited celebration of life.

At home, people create altars to display portraits, favorite foods and special mementos to honor family members who have passed away. Wildly decorated sugar skulls are crafted to represent an individual's vitality of life, and a preferred alcoholic beverage is used to make a toast.

Put together an offering of Spanish-inspired favorites—from quesadillas to cumin rice to Tres Leches Cupcakes—and raise a glass to recognize the ones you love.

GET CRAFTY

Handmade crafts and tissue-paper designs are common Day of the Dead decorations. Make your own custom creations using the tips on page 245.

Mock Champagne (p. 241)
Tres Leches Cupcakes (p. 244)
Day of the Dead Cookies (p. 242)

DAY OF THE **DEAD**

Chicken Tamales

I have been cooking and baking since I got my first Easy-Bake Oven.
I now cook for my husband and four children, and I enjoy making tamales from scratch.
It's a little time-consuming, but I promise it's worth it.

—CINDY PRUITT GROVE, OK

PREP: 2½ HOURS + SOAKING • **COOK:** 45 MIN. • **MAKES:** 20 TAMALES

- 20 **dried corn husks**
- 1 **broiler/fryer chicken (3 to 4 pounds), cut up**
- 3 **quarts water**
- 1 **medium onion, quartered**
- 2 **teaspoons salt**
- 1 **garlic clove, crushed**

DOUGH
- 1 **cup shortening**
- 3 **cups masa harina**

CHICKEN CHILI FILLING
- 6 **tablespoons canola oil**
- 6 **tablespoons all-purpose flour**
- ¾ **cup chili powder**
- ½ **teaspoon salt**
- ¼ **teaspoon garlic powder**
- ¼ **teaspoon pepper**
- 2 **cans (2¼ ounces each) sliced ripe olives, drained**

1. Place corn husks in a large bowl; cover with cold water and soak for at least 2 hours.

2. Meanwhile, in a Dutch oven, combine the chicken, water, onion, salt and garlic. Bring to a boil. Reduce heat; cover and simmer for 45-60 minutes or until meat is tender. Remove chicken from broth; set aside until cool enough to handle. Strain broth; skim fat. Finely chop or shred chicken.

3. For dough, in a large bowl, beat the shortening until light and fluffy, about 1 minute. Add small amounts of masa harina alternately with 2 cups reserved broth, beating until well blended.

4. Drop a small amount of dough into a cup of cold water; dough should float to the top. If dough does not float, continue beating until dough is light enough to float.

5. In a Dutch oven, heat oil over medium heat; stir in flour until blended. Cook and stir for 7-9 minutes or until lightly browned. Stir in the spices, chicken and 4 cups reserved broth. Bring to a boil. Reduce heat; simmer, uncovered, for 45 minutes or until filling is thickened, stirring occasionally.

6. Drain corn husks and pat dry. Place a corn husk on a work surface with the small end pointing away from you. On large end, spread 3 tablespoons dough to within 1 in. of edges. Top with 2 tablespoons chicken mixture and 2 teaspoons olives. Fold long sides of husk over filling, overlapping slightly. Fold over ends of husk; tie with string to secure. Repeat.

7. In a large steamer basket, position tamales upright. Place basket in a Dutch oven over 1 in. of water. Bring to a boil; cover and steam for 45-50 minutes or until dough peels away from husk, adding additional hot water to pan as needed.

Smoky Corn Salad

I love to try new dishes for my husband and myself, and also for when we entertain.
My recipes come from all over the world, and I appreciate the bold Southwestern flavors
that shine through in this five-ingredient salad. It's a keeper in my book.

—SHARON DELANEY-CHRONIS SOUTH MILWAUKEE, WI

START TO FINISH: 20 MIN. • **MAKES:** 6 SERVINGS

- 4 **cups fresh or frozen corn, thawed**
- 2 **tablespoons lime juice**
- ½ **teaspoon salt**
- ¼ **teaspoon ground chipotle pepper**
- 2 **large sweet red peppers, chopped**
- ½ **cup minced fresh cilantro**

1. In a large heavy skillet coated with cooking spray, saute corn until lightly browned. Transfer to a serving bowl.

2. Stir in the lime juice, salt and chipotle pepper. Cool for 5 minutes. Stir in red peppers and cilantro.

Black Bean Quesadillas

Back when our youngsters were in grade school, I copied this recipe from an old Mexican cookbook to serve at a Mexican festival in the classroom. Since then, we've made it many times. It's an easy appetizer or dinner.

—**DIXIE TERRY** GOREVILLE, IL

START TO FINISH: 25 MIN.
MAKES: 4 SERVINGS

- 1 **cup canned black beans, rinsed and drained**
- 1 **green onion, chopped**
- 2 **tablespoons chopped red onion**
- 2 **tablespoons finely chopped roasted sweet red pepper**
- 1 **tablespoon minced fresh cilantro**
- 1 **tablespoon lime juice**
- 1 **garlic clove, minced**
- 4 **flour tortillas (10 inches)**
- 1 **cup (4 ounces) shredded Muenster or Monterey Jack cheese**

1. In a small bowl, mash beans with a fork; stir in the green onion, red onion, pepper, cilantro, lime juice and garlic. Spread ¼ cup bean mixture over half of each tortilla; top with ¼ cup cheese. Fold over.

2. Cook on a griddle coated with cooking spray over low heat for 1-2 minutes on each side or until cheese is melted. Cut into wedges.

Mini Chicken Empanadas

When I was still teaching, a friend of mine gave me this recipe.
I used it for multiple school luncheons and events because everyone liked these cheesy pastries.
—BETTY FULKS ONIA, AR

PREP: 30 MIN.
BAKE: 15 MIN./BATCH
MAKES: ABOUT 2½ DOZEN

- 1   **cup finely chopped cooked chicken**
- ⅔   **cup shredded Colby-Monterey Jack cheese**
- 3   **tablespoons cream cheese, softened**
- 4   **teaspoons chopped sweet red pepper**
- 2   **teaspoons chopped seeded jalapeno pepper**
- 1   **teaspoon ground cumin**
- ½   **teaspoon salt**
- ⅛   **teaspoon pepper**
- 1   **package (14.1 ounces) refrigerated pie pastry**

1. In a small bowl, combine the first eight ingredients. On a lightly floured surface, roll each pastry sheet into a 15-in. circle. Cut with a floured 3-in. round biscuit cutter.

2. Place about 1 teaspoon filling on one half of each circle. Moisten pastry edges with water. Fold pastry over filling. Press edges with a fork to seal.

3. Transfer to greased baking sheets. Bake at 400° for 12-15 minutes or until golden brown. Remove to wire racks. Serve warm.

NOTE *Wear disposable gloves when cutting hot peppers; the oils can burn skin. Avoid touching your face.*

Salsa Roja

With the help of my food processor, I can have fresh, homemade salsa ready in 15 minutes. The lime juice works wonders bringing out all the flavors, and you can really taste the cilantro.
—**AMBER MASSEY** ARGYLE, TX

START TO FINISH: 15 MIN. • **MAKES:** 7 CUPS

1 can (28 ounces) whole tomatoes, drained
1 can (14½ ounces) diced tomatoes with garlic and onion, drained
1 can (14½ ounces) Mexican stewed tomatoes, drained
1 can (10 ounces) diced tomatoes and green chilies, drained
1 medium onion, quartered
2 banana peppers, seeded and coarsely chopped
2 jalapeno peppers, seeded and coarsely chopped
3 garlic cloves, minced
2 teaspoons salt
¼ teaspoon ground cumin
½ cup minced fresh cilantro
¼ cup lime juice
2 medium ripe avocados, peeled and cubed
Tortilla chips

1. Place the first 10 ingredients in a food processor; cover and process until chopped. Add cilantro and lime juice; cover and pulse until combined.

2. Transfer to a bowl; stir in avocados. Serve with tortilla chips.

NOTE *Wear disposable gloves when cutting hot peppers; the oils can burn skin. Avoid touching your face.*

Enchilada Casser-Ole!

We love Mexican foods, but my husband especially enjoys this casserole. Since I'm a lazy cook, I'm happy this combines everything in one dish.
—**MARSHA WILLS** HOMOSASSA, FL

PREP: 25 MIN. • **BAKE:** 30 MIN. • **MAKES:** 8 SERVINGS

1 pound lean ground beef (90% lean)
1 large onion, chopped
2 cups salsa
1 can (15 ounces) black beans, rinsed and drained
¼ cup reduced-fat Italian salad dressing
2 tablespoons reduced-sodium taco seasoning
¼ teaspoon ground cumin
6 flour tortillas (8 inches)
¾ cup reduced-fat sour cream
1 cup (4 ounces) shredded reduced-fat Mexican cheese blend
1 cup shredded lettuce
1 medium tomato, chopped
¼ cup minced fresh cilantro

1. In a large skillet, cook beef and onion over medium heat until meat is no longer pink; drain. Stir in the salsa, beans, dressing, taco seasoning and cumin. Place three tortillas in an 11-in. x 7-in. baking dish coated with cooking spray. Layer with half of the meat mixture, sour cream and cheese. Repeat layers.

2. Cover and bake at 400° for 25 minutes. Uncover; bake 5-10 minutes longer or until heated through. Let stand for 5 minutes; top with lettuce, tomato and cilantro.

Cumin Rice with Avocado

Add some excitement to your rice with picante sauce and creamy avocado. In this imaginative combination, cumin and chicken bouillon do the rest of the seasoning, making this a suitable side for a south-of-the border fiesta.

—MARGARET ALLEN ABINGDON, VA

PREP: 10 MIN. • **COOK:** 25 MIN. • **MAKES:** 6 SERVINGS

- 2¼ cups water
- 1 tablespoon butter
- 2 teaspoons reduced-sodium chicken bouillon granules
- ¾ teaspoon ground cumin
- 1 cup uncooked long grain rice
- ⅓ cup picante sauce

- 1 medium ripe avocado, peeled and cubed
- 2 green onions, sliced

1. In a large saucepan, combine the water, butter, bouillon and cumin; bring to a boil. Stir in rice; return to a boil. Reduce heat; cover and simmer for 20-25 minutes or until rice is tender.

2. Stir in picante sauce; heat through. Stir in avocado and green onions.

Home-Style Refried Beans

This is much better than opening a can of refried beans and is just as easy. It's fun to top or garnish them with shredded cheese and salsa, but I think they're tasty just as they are.

—MYRA INNES AUBURN, KS

START TO FINISH: 15 MIN. • **MAKES:** 2⅔ CUPS

- ⅔ cup finely chopped onion
- 4 teaspoons canola oil
- 4 garlic cloves, minced
- 1 teaspoon ground cumin
- ½ teaspoon salt
- ¼ teaspoon cayenne pepper
- 2 cans (15 ounces each) pinto beans, rinsed and drained
- ½ cup water
- 4 teaspoons lime juice

In a large saucepan, saute onion in oil until tender. Stir in the garlic, cumin, salt and cayenne; cook and stir for 1 minute. Add beans and mash. Add water; cook and stir until heated through and water is absorbed. Remove from the heat; stir in lime juice.

PAINTED BEANS

The pinto bean is named for its speckled skin—*frijol pinto* literally means "painted bean." It's most commonly eaten mashed and refried and is one of the official state vegetables of New Mexico (the other is the chili pepper).

Mock Champagne

As the parents of two college girls, my husband, Chris, and I have tried to be good role models over the years. But you don't have to sacrifice everything for good taste. This is a wonderfully refreshing nonalcoholic champagne.
—**PAM ION** GAITHERSBURG, MD

PREP: 10 MIN. + FREEZING
MAKES: 8 SERVINGS

- 3 cups white grape juice, divided
- 2 cans (12 ounces each) ginger ale, chilled
- ½ cup chilled club soda
  Orange slices and sliced fresh strawberries

1. Pour 2 cups juice into ice cube trays; freeze until set.

2. Transfer ice cubes to a pitcher; add remaining juice. Slowly stir in ginger ale and club soda. Garnish with oranges and strawberries. Serve immediately.

Blue Lagoon Margaritas

A special toast to anyone who mixes up a mysterious batch of lagoon margaritas for a Halloween soiree. Guests will swoon over the citrusy sweet tang and electrifying shade of blue.
—**WILLIE DEWAARD** CORALVILLE, IA

START TO FINISH: 15 MIN. • **MAKES:** 4 SERVINGS

- 4 lime slices
- 3 tablespoons coarse sugar
- ½ cup chilled lemon-lime soda
- ½ cup tequila
- ½ cup blue curacao
- ⅓ cup partially thawed frozen limeade concentrate
- 2 cups ice cubes

1. Using lime slices, moisten the rims of four margarita or cocktail glasses. Set aside lime slices for garnish. Sprinkle sugar on a plate; hold each glass upside down and dip rim into sugar. Set aside. Discard remaining sugar on plate.

2. In a blender, combine the remaining ingredients; cover and process until blended. Pour into prepared glasses. Garnish with reserved lime slices. Serve immediately.

Day of the Dead Cookies

I make these almond butter cookies for all occasions. In the spring, I cut them in flower shapes and insert a lollipop stick in them to make a bouquet. Using candies, food coloring and a wild imagination, try your hand at this Day of the Dead-inspired version.

—KRISTINE FOSSMEYER HUNTLEY, IL

PREP: 2 HOURS + CHILLING
BAKE: 10 MIN./BATCH + COOLING
MAKES: 1 DOZEN

1¼ cups butter, softened
1¾ cups confectioners' sugar
2 ounces almond paste
1 egg
¼ cup 2% milk
1 teaspoon vanilla extract
4 cups all-purpose flour
½ teaspoon salt
2 packages (12 ounces each) white Wilton candy melts
Red Wilton candy melts, melted
Decorations of your choice: jumbo sprinkles, peppermint candies, candy-coated sunflower kernels, Skittles, Twizzlers Rainbow Twists and Good & Plenty candies
Black paste food coloring

1. In a large bowl, cream butter and confectioners' sugar until light and fluffy; add almond paste. Beat in the egg, milk and vanilla. Combine flour and salt; gradually add to creamed mixture and mix well. Cover and refrigerate for 1 hour.

2. On a lightly floured surface, roll out dough to ¼-in. thickness. Cut out with a floured 5-in. skull-shaped cookie cutter. Place 1 in. apart on ungreased baking sheets.

3. Bake at 375° for 7-9 minutes or until firm. Let stand for 2 minutes before removing to wire racks to cool completely.

4. In a large, shallow microwave-safe dish, melt white candy melts according to package directions. Dip top side of each cookie into coating, allowing excess to drip off; place on waxed paper. Immediately place a few drops of melted red candy melts on cheeks of skull; swirl with a toothpick.

5. Add decorations as desired. Tint remaining white coating black; pipe on eyes and mouth. Let stand until set.

Savory Corn Bread Pops

Not all cake was created sweet, but it's all delicious in our book. These handheld cake pops make festive appetizers, too.
—TASTE OF HOME TEST KITCHEN

PREP: 1 HOUR • **BAKE:** 25 MIN. + FREEZING • **MAKES:** 2½ DOZEN

1 package (8½ ounces) corn bread/muffin mix
2 packages (3 ounces each) cream cheese, softened
2 tablespoons Louisiana-style hot sauce
1 to 3 tablespoons finely chopped pickled jalapeno slices
30 lollipop sticks
¼ cup butter, melted
Crushed corn chips

1. Prepare and bake corn bread according to package directions, using a greased 8-in. baking pan. Cool completely on a wire rack.

2. In a small bowl, beat the cream cheese, hot sauce and pickled jalapenos until blended. Crumble corn bread over cream cheese mixture and mix well. Shape into 1-in. balls. Place on baking sheets; insert sticks. Freeze for at least 2 hours or until firm.

3. Dip in melted butter and roll in corn chips. Refrigerate until serving.

CORN POP BOUQUET

Once your Corn Bread Pops are finished, arrange an edible bouquet. Start by gluing floral foam (available in craft stores) to the bottom of a decorative container or clay pot. Insert pops into the foam and cover the top of the foam with crushed corn chips or shredded lettuce.

Mexican Fried Ice Cream

Fried ice cream is one of my favorite desserts to order from Mexican restaurants, so when my sister and I found this recipe, we knew we had to try it. It's a fun way to end a meal.
—MANDY WRIGHT SPRINGVILLE, UT

PREP: 25 MIN. + FREEZING • **COOK:** 5 MIN. • **MAKES:** 9 SERVINGS

½ gallon French vanilla ice cream, softened
3 cups crushed cornflakes
4 teaspoons ground cinnamon
Oil for deep-fat frying
Honey and whipped topping, optional

1. Place nine 3-in. scoops of ice cream on a baking sheet. Freeze for 1 hour or until firm.

2. In a shallow bowl, combine cornflake crumbs and cinnamon. Roll ice cream balls in crumb mixture. Place on baking sheet; freeze overnight. Wrap each scoop separately in plastic wrap; transfer to a freezer bag. May be frozen for up to 2 months.

3. In an electric skillet or deep-fat fryer, heat oil to 375°. Unwrap ice cream; fry one scoop at a time for 8-10 seconds. Place in chilled bowls; serve immediately. Top with honey and whipped topping if desired.

Tres Leches Cupcakes

Infused with a sweet silky mixture using a trio of milks, these little cakes are three times as good. Because they soak overnight, they're an ideal make-ahead dessert for an upcoming fiesta.

—TASTE OF HOME TEST KITCHEN

PREP: 45 MIN. + CHILLING
BAKE: 20 MIN. + COOLING
MAKES: 2 DOZEN

1 **package yellow cake mix (regular size)**
1¼ **cups water**
4 **eggs**
1 **can (14 ounces) sweetened condensed milk**
1 **cup coconut milk**
1 **can (5 ounces) evaporated milk**
   Dash salt
   Whipped cream and assorted fresh fruit

1. In a large bowl, combine the cake mix, water and eggs; beat on low speed for 30 seconds. Beat on medium for 2 minutes. Fill paper-lined muffin cups two-thirds full.

2. Bake at 350° for 18-22 minutes or until a toothpick inserted near center comes out clean. Cool for 10 minutes before removing from pans to wire racks to cool.

3. Combine sweetened condensed milk, coconut milk, evaporated milk and salt. Using the end of a wooden spoon handle, poke a hole into the center of each cupcake. Transfer milk mixture to a heavy-duty resealable plastic bag; cut a small hole in a corner of bag.

4. Gently squeeze filling into the cavity of each cupcake until you feel a slight resistance. Brush any remaining milk mixture over tops of cupcakes. Cover and refrigerate for 4 hours or overnight. Serve with whipped cream and fruit.

Get Crafty!

Making colorful tissue-paper flowers, painted masks and decorated coffins is a common tradition on Day of the Dead. Create your own decorations for your Mexican-themed event with a few simple instructions.

MASKS & COFFINS

Pick up paper masks, skulls and coffin boxes from a craft store. Spray-paint them white, then use bright paints to embellish with your own playful folk art designs.

FLOWERS

For each flower, cut seven layers of brightly colored tissue paper into 5-in. to 9-in. squares, then fold the stack of tissue accordion style. (Each stack should consist of seven pieces of the same size squares.) Cinch at the center with wire or a pipe cleaner, then carefully separate and fluff each piece of tissue to form a pompom shape. For streamers, attach pompoms to fishing line or string. For tabletop floral displays, use pipe cleaners for flower stems.

GENERAL RECIPE INDEX

This index lists every recipe by food category and major ingredient.

CHEESE (continued)

Marinated Cheese with Peppers and Olives, 22
Pizza Fondue, 84
Smoked Gouda and Ham Appetizer Tarts, 64
Spinach Artichoke-Stuffed Tomatoes, 139
Three-Cheese Fondue, 87
Tomato Cheddar Fondue, 83

BREADS

Blueberry Cream Cheese Danish, 217
Cheddar-Bacon Swirled Rolls, 30
Parmesan-Oat Pull Aparts, 31
Parmesan-Sage Beer Bread, 37
Sausage and Cheddar Scones, 30

DESSERTS

Cream Cheese Clouds, 167
Gingerbread Cheesecake, 53
Ham & Cheese Rolls, 198
Lavender Honey Cheesecake, 231
Marbled Cappuccino Fudge Cheesecake, 15
Orange Cream Cheesecake, 164
Orange Ricotta Cake Roll, 26
Pumpkin Pie Cannoli, 122

MAIN DISHES

Baked Scrambled Egg Wraps, 218
Black Bean Quesadillas, 237
Ham and Cheese Stratas, 216
Oatmeal Waffles with Orange Ricotta Topping, 184

SALADS & SIDES

Blue Cheese Pear Salad, 131
Decadent Broccoli Souffle, 149
Glazed Parmesan Potatoes, 228
Parmesan-Romano Mashed Potatoes, 107
Parsnips & Turnips Au Gratin, 43
Pear & Blue Cheese Salad, 110
Spinach Orzo Salad, 140
Parsnips & Turnips Au Gratin, 43

SOUPS

Golden Gouda Mushroom Soup, 9
Parmesan Artichoke Soup, 138

CHICKEN
APPETIZERS

Mini Chicken Empanadas, 238

MAIN DISHES

Chicken Tamales, 236
Chicken with Potato Stuffing, 42
Mahogany-Glazed Cornish Hens, 128
Tex-Mex Chicken and Waffles, 187

SALADS

Buffalo Chicken Pasta Salad, 209
Italian Chicken Salad, 199

CHOCOLATE
BEVERAGES

Hazelnut Mocha Coffee, 25
White Chocolate Brandy Alexander, 180

CAKE & CUPCAKES

Chocolate Gingerbread Toffee Cake, 56
Gingerbread Cheesecake, 53
Marbled Cappuccino Fudge Cheesecake, 15

CANDY & TRUFFLES

Crunchy Chocolate Eggs, 160
Eggnog Truffle Cups, 16
Gingerbread Truffles, 59

COOKIES & BROWNIES

Chocolate Brownie Waffle Sundaes, 189
No-Bake Cookie Balls, 76
Turtle Brownie Bites, 201

DESSERTS

Chocolate Almond Fondue, 86
Chocolate Caramel Fondue, 89
German Chocolate Fondue, 82
Kiwi Tiki Torches, 89
Mocha Waffles with Syrup, 191
Red Velvet Waffles with Coconut Syrup, 190

SNACKS

Chocolate-Peanut Butter Crunch Bars, 212
Chocolate-Peanut Granola Bars, 219

CINNAMON

Cinnamon Cranberry Bagels, 62
Cranberry Cinnamon Applesauce, 66
Fresh Fruit Salsa with Cinnamon Chips, 195
Gingerbread Ice Cream Sandwiches, 54
Gingerbread Meringue Bars, 57
Honey-Wheat Cinnamon Swirl Bread, 228
Mexican Fried Ice Cream, 243
Pecan-Coconut Sweet Potatoes, 143
Potluck Cinnamon Roll Twists, 223
Spiced Pudding Cake, 47

COCONUT

Ambrosia Fruit Salad, 44
Coconut Almond Bombs, 79
Coconut Pistachio Pie, 163
Cranberry Coconut Cake with Marshmallow Cream Frosting, 68
Kiwi Tiki Torches, 89
Lime Angel Food Cake, 160
Macaroon Kisses, 72
Pineapple Orange Trifle, 165
Red Velvet Waffles with Coconut Syrup, 190

COFFEE

Hazelnut Mocha Coffee, 25
Mocha Waffles with Syrup, 191

COFFEE CAKES

Overnight Berry-Crunch Coffee Cake, 222
Pear-Cranberry Gingerbread Cake, 58

COOKIES & BARS

Browned–Butter Sandwich Spritz, 76
Buttery Potato Chip Cookies, 213
Chocolate-Peanut Butter Crunch Bars, 212
Coconut Almond Bombs, 79
Cran-Orange Icebox Cookies, 73
Day of the Dead Cookies, 242
Gingerbread Ice Cream Sandwiches, 54
Gingerbread Kisses, 52
Gingerbread Macaroons, 52
Gingerbread Meringue Bars, 57
Good Fortune & Cheer Cookies, 74
Holiday Shortbread Cookies, 79
Lemon Snowflakes, 75

Linzer Cookies, 72
Little Italy Pignoli Cookies, 25
Macaroon Kisses, 72
Meringue Candy Canes, 78
No-Bake Cookie Balls, 76
Olive Oil Cookies, 232
Roly-Poly Santas, 77
Vanilla Walnut Crescents, 75

CORN
Corn Fritter Waffles with Spicy
  Maple Syrup, 185
Smokin' Spiced Corn, 210
Smoky Corn Salad, 236

CORN BREAD & CORNMEAL
Make-Ahead Corn Bread Dressing, 104
Mushroom Corn Muffins with
  Chive Butter, 32
Savory Corn Bread Pops, 243

CRANBERRIES
Apricot-Apple Cranberry Sauce, 113
Beef Tenderloins with Cranberry
  Sauce, 67
Cinnamon Cranberry Bagels, 62
Cran-Orange Icebox Cookies, 73
Cranberry-Apple Lattice Pie, 120
Cranberry Chevre Lollipops, 65
Cranberry Cinnamon Applesauce, 66
Cranberry Coconut Cake with
  Marshmallow Cream Frosting, 68
Cranberry Endive Appetizers, 11
Cranberry Ginger Mojito, 62
Cranberry Ginger Tart, 118
Cranberry-Glazed Lamb Skewers, 65
Cranberry-Lime Semifreddo with
  Pound Cake, 69
Cranberry-Orange Sangria, 63
Cranberry-Sesame Vinaigrette, 66
Pear-Cranberry Gingerbread Cake, 58
Roasted Turkey with Maple
  Cranberry Glaze, 96
Smoked Gouda and Ham
  Appetizer Tarts, 64
Wild Rice & Cranberry Loaves, 35

DESSERTS *(also see Cakes & Cupcakes; Candy; Chocolate; Cookies & Bars; Fondue; Ice Cream, Sherbet & Sorbet; Pies & Tarts)*

Breezy Lemon-Berry Dessert, 162
Cinnamon Bagel Bread Pudding, 222
Holiday Gingerbread Trifle, 55
Lemon Curd Tartlets, 163
Pineapple Orange Trifle, 165
Pumpkin Pie Cannoli, 122
Sticky Toffee Rice Pudding with
  Caramel Cream, 121
Swedish Rice Ring, 48

DIPS *(also see Fondue)*
Cantina Beer-Cheese Dip, 206
Chili con Queso Dip, 85
Creamy Hot Beef Dip, 41
Fresh Fruit Salsa with Cinnamon
  Chips, 195
Layered Mediterranean Dip with
  Pita Chips, 196
Salsa Roja, 239
Super Sausage Dip, 82

EGGS
Bacon and Egg Breakfast Pizza, 217
Baked Scrambled Egg Wraps, 218
Best Deviled Eggs, 179
Ham and Cheese Stratas, 216
Party Puffs, 174

FENNEL
Fennel Salad with Orange-Balsamic
  Vinaigrette, 23

FISH *(see Seafood)*

FONDUE
Chili con Queso Dip, 85
Chocolate Almond Fondue, 86
Chocolate Caramel Fondue, 89
German Chocolate Fondue, 82
Kiwi Tiki Torches, 89
Marinated Beef Fondue, 85
Pizza Fondue, 84
Raspberry Fondue Dip, 86
Super Sausage Dip, 82
Three-Cheese Fondue, 87
Tomato Cheddar Fondue, 83

FRENCH TOAST
French Toast with Crushed Apple
  Sauce, 220

FRUIT *(also see specific kinds)*
Ambrosia Fruit Salad, 44
Fresh Fruit Salsa with Cinnamon
  Chips, 195
Fruit with Honey-Ginger Dressing, 144
Strawberry, Cucumber & Honeydew
  Salad, 229

GARLIC
Garlic Lemon Butter, 16
Herbed Garlic Mashed Potatoes, 105
Lemon Garlic Turkey, 97
Mashed Potatoes with Garlic-Olive
  Oil, 108

GINGER
Chocolate Gingerbread Toffee
  Cake, 56
Cranberry Ginger Mojito, 62
Cranberry Ginger Tart, 118
Fruit with Honey-Ginger Dressing, 144
Gingerbread Belgian Waffles, 191
Gingerbread Cheesecake, 53
Gingerbread Ice Cream
  Sandwiches, 54
Gingerbread Kisses, 52
Gingerbread Macaroons, 52
Gingerbread Meringue Bars, 57
Gingerbread Truffles, 59
Gingerbread with Fig-Walnut
  Sauce, 59
Holiday Gingerbread Trifle, 55
Pear-Cranberry Gingerbread Cake, 58
Spiced Pudding Cake, 47

GRAVY
Apple Butter & Onion Gravy, 100
Foolproof Gravy, 101
Mushroom Sour Cream Gravy, 100
Roast Turkey with Cider Gravy, 99
Turkey Giblet Gravy, 99

HAM & PROSCIUTTO
Ham & Cheese Rolls, 198
Ham and Cheese Stratas, 216
Honey-Maple Glazed Ham, 230
Party Puffs, 174
Smoked Gouda and Ham
  Appetizer Tarts, 64
Stuffed Sweet Onions, 154

HONEY

Baked Brie with Peaches and
    Honey, 227
Fruit with Honey-Ginger Dressing, 144
Glazed Parmesan Potatoes, 228
Grilled Lemon & Thyme
    Lemonade, 227
Honey and Spice New England
    Apple Pie, 232
Honey-Maple Glazed Ham, 230
Honey Mustard Green Beans, 127
Honey-Wheat Cinnamon Swirl
    Bread, 228
Lavender Honey Cheesecake, 231
Olive Oil Cookies, 232
Pancetta-Wrapped Shrimp with
    Honey-Lime Glaze, 226
Smoked Honey-Peppercorn
    Salmon, 230
Smokin' Spiced Corn, 210
Strawberry, Cucumber &
    Honeydew Salad, 229

ICE CREAM,
SHERBET & SORBET

Chocolate Brownie Waffle
    Sundaes, 189
Frozen Lemonade Squares, 168
Gingerbread Ice Cream
    Sandwiches, 54
Mexican Fried Ice Cream, 243
Rhubarb Ice Cream, 145
Sherbet Cream Cake, 166
Strawberry Sorbet Sensation, 167

LAMB

Cranberry-Glazed Lamb Skewers, 65

LEMON

Breezy Lemon-Berry Dessert, 162
Frozen Lemonade Squares, 168
Garlic Lemon Butter, 16
Grilled Lemon & Thyme
    Lemonade, 227
Lemon Bark, 201
Lemon Chess Pie with Berry
    Sauce, 117
Lemon Curd Tartlets, 163
Lemon Garlic Turkey, 97
Lemon Meringue Angel Cake, 144
Lemon Snowflakes, 75
Lemony Cooler, 138
Olive Oil Cookies, 232

LIME

Cranberry-Lime Semifreddo with
    Pound Cake, 69
Lime Angel Food Cake, 160

MARSHMALLOWS

Blueberry Cloud Pie, 161
Cranberry Coconut Cake with
    Marshmallow Cream Frosting, 68

MERINGUE

Banana Cream Meringue Pie, 49
Gingerbread Meringue Bars, 57
Lemon Meringue Angel Cake, 144
Meringue Candy Canes, 78

MINT

Meringue Candy Canes, 78
Minted Orzo, 156
Pinwheel Mints, 49

MUFFINS *(see Biscuits, Muffins &*
Scones)

MUSHROOMS

Golden Gouda Mushroom Soup, 9
Herbed Mushroom & Bacon
    Waffles, 188
Mushroom Corn Muffins with
    Chive Butter, 32
Mushroom Sour Cream Gravy, 100
Portobello Bruschetta with
    Rosemary Aoli, 20
Smashed Potatoes Portobello, 108

NUTS & PEANUT BUTTER

(also see Seeds)

Chocolate Almond Fondue, 86
Chocolate-Peanut Butter
    Crunch Bars, 212
Chocolate-Peanut Granola Bars, 219
Christmas Special Fruitcake, 46
Coconut Almond Bombs, 79
Coconut Pistachio Pie, 163
Crunchy Chocolate Eggs, 160
Gingerbread with Fig-Walnut
    Sauce, 59
Li'l Pecan Pies, 133
Linzer Cookies, 72
Little Italy Pignoli Cookies, 25
No-Bake Cookie Balls, 76
Pecan-Coconut Sweet Potatoes, 143

Roasted Butternut Squash Salad with
    Caramelized Pumpkin Seeds, 110
Sherbet Cream Cake, 166
Sweet and Spicy Peanuts, 213
Vanilla Walnut Crescents, 75
Whiskey-Glazed Pecans, 132

OATS & GRANOLA

Chocolate-Peanut Granola Bars, 219
Oatmeal Waffles with Orange
    Ricotta Topping, 184
Parmesan-Oat Pull Aparts, 31

OLIVES

Marinated Cheese with Peppers
    and Olives, 22

ONIONS

Apple Butter & Onion Gravy, 100
Onion Crescents, 33
Peas a la Francaise, 140
Stuffed Sweet Onions, 154

ORANGE

Ambrosia Fruit Salad, 44
Cran-Orange Icebox Cookies, 73
Cranberry-Orange Sangria, 63
Fennel Salad with Orange-Balsamic
    Vinaigrette, 23
Layered Spinach & Orange Salad, 139
Oatmeal Waffles with Orange Ricotta
    Topping, 184
Orange Cream Cheesecake, 164
Orange Ricotta Cake Roll, 26
Pineapple Orange Trifle, 165
Roasted Orange Turkey, 95
Sweet Potato Patties with Orange
    Relish, 116

PANCAKES & WAFFLES

Asiago Cheese Waffles, 187
Bacon Potato Waffles with
    Applesauce, 184
Chocolate Brownie Waffle
    Sundaes, 189
Corn Fritter Waffles with Spicy
    Maple Syrup, 185
Gingerbread Belgian Waffles, 191
Herbed Mushroom & Bacon
    Waffles, 188
Mocha Waffles with Syrup, 191
Oatmeal Waffles with Orange
    Ricotta Topping, 184

ALPHABETICAL RECIPE INDEX

Refer to this index for a complete alphabetical listing of all recipes in this book.

SHARE YOUR **MOST-LOVED RECIPES**

Do you have a special recipe that has become part of your family's holiday tradition? Are homemade gifts and crafts included in your celebrations? We want to hear from you. To submit a recipe or craft for editorial consideration, visit **tasteofhome.com/submit.**

PAGE 79

PAGE 123

PAGE 203

PAGE 214